100 THINGS
CARDINALS FANS
SHOULD KNOW & DO
BEFORE THEY DIE

100 THINGS CARDINALS FANS SHOULD KNOW & DO BEFORE THEY DIE

Kent Somers

TRIUMPH
BOOKS

Copyright © 2016 by Kent Somers

No part of this publication may be reproduced, stored in a retrieval system, or transmitted in any form by any means, electronic, mechanical, photocopying, or otherwise, without the prior written permission of the publisher, Triumph Books LLC, 814 North Franklin Street, Chicago, Illinois 60610.

Library of Congress Cataloging-in-Publication Data

Names: Somers, Kent, author.
Title: 100 things Cardinals fans should know & do before they die / Kent Somers.
Other titles: One hundred things Cardinals fans should know and do before they die
Description: Chicago, Illinois : Triumph Books LLC, [2016]
Identifiers: LCCN 2016008275 | ISBN 9781629371832
Subjects: LCSH: Arizona Cardinals (Football team)—History. | Arizona Cardinals (Football team)—Miscellanea.
Classification: LCC GV956.A75 S66 2016 | DDC 796.332/640977866—dc23 LC record available at http://lccn.loc.gov/2016008275

This book is available in quantity at special discounts for your group or organization. For further information, contact:
Triumph Books LLC
814 North Franklin Street
Chicago, Illinois 60610
(312) 337-0747
www.triumphbooks.com

Printed in U.S.A.
ISBN: 978-1-62937-183-2
Design by Patricia Frey
Photos courtesy of AP Images unless otherwise indicated

To my parents, Frank and Jean Somers, who still like nothing better than putting their stadium seats in the car and going to games.

Contents

teams. But what a change I've witnessed in Arizona. In 2015 we went to Chicago, and Cardinals fans were probably 6,000 deep at that game against the Bears. They were loud, passionate, and took over Soldier Field.

Today, we play in one of the NFL's best stadiums, and players are anxious to come here.

Seriously, more than ever the past few years, an opponent has come up to me during a game and said, "Hey, Fitz, my contract is up after this season. Put in a good word for me." Believe me, that

Larry Fitzgerald has been a Cardinal since Bill Bidwell (left) and Dennis Green (right) drafted him in the first round of the 2004 NFL Draft.

never used to happen. How we're perceived around the league has taken a drastic turn.

A lot of the credit goes to team president Michael Bidwill, who was his dad's successor in running the team. The changes under his watch have been stunning. We have a new indoor practice bubble, a renovated training facility, and a state-of-the-art stadium. Along with a lot of other guys, I feel like I've been a part of the change, too. Even though we struggled early in my career, we had players who shared their wisdom with youngsters such as myself. When I was a rookie, running back Emmitt Smith taught me how to be professional. He taught me how to practice, how to study, and how to take care of my body, so I could make it through a season.

He taught me how to look like a pro, and to this day, I still bring two suits on road trips—one to wear to the plane in Phoenix and one to wear home. Emmitt taught me that. Another Hall of Fame-level player, Kurt Warner, taught me lessons about unselfishness and attention to detail. "Do it this way," Kurt would say, "or you're not going to get the ball."

One of the few things that hasn't changed during my 12 years is the main guy *The Arizona Republic* and azcentralsports.com has covering the team. Kent Somers covered my first press conference, and he'll probably be there for my last, unless I just quietly slip into retirement. (That's more my style.) No one is more qualified to write a book about the Cardinals. After all, the guy once got me fined $10,000.

I'll explain, but first, let me say I respect the job reporters do. My dad's a journalist, and my brother, Marcus, and I grew up watching him do his job. He took us to see all the major teams in Minneapolis: the Vikings, Twins, Timberwolves, Wild, and Gophers. But as a professional athlete, I don't like talking about myself. So when I was young, I used to leave the locker room after games even before reporters were allowed in. As I started to have success, reporters, including Kent, complained that I wasn't there to give my thoughts on the game.

So the NFL fined me $10,000. Let's just say that I now stay so long after games that I often ask reporters if the collar is up on my suit and if my tie is straight.

In this book you'll find a lot of great stories about so many interesting people. Can you imagine agreeing to buy an NFL team on a whim at a cocktail party for $50,000? That's what Charles Bidwill did. Or spending all of World War II in a Japanese prisoner of war camp, losing close to 100 pounds, and then returning home to suit up for an NFL game? The Mario "Motts" Tonelli story is incredible. Or being the so-called "worst NFL team in history to make it to the Super Bowl"? The story of that playoff run in 2008 is in here, too.

In some ways the last 12 years have gone by so fast. I've got two boys now and I spend my free time outside the facility. Guys in the equipment room give me a hard time now when I leave the locker room in the afternoon. "Fitz, how come you never help fold towels anymore?"

I'm like, "Man, I've got a family now. I have to pick up my kids from school. We have basketball practice this afternoon."

I am proud of the improvement the Cardinals have made over the past 12 years. To know I was a part of that gives me great satisfaction. The Cardinals drafted me third overall, and I've always felt there is an obligation that comes from that and to be part of the group that laid a foundation for future success.

—Larry Fitzgerald

Introduction

When did you fall in love with football? For me, that's like asking when I took my first breath.

I've been around it all my life. When I was four or five, my dad coached high school football in Oklahoma, and I have fuzzy memories of small stadiums on Friday nights. I played with cousins and neighbors in the yard, and my first experience in organized football was playing in a YMCA league, in which the weight limit was 65 pounds. I've added many years and pounds since, but I've stayed around the game.

With the exception of a couple years, I've covered the Cardinals since 1994. Buddy Ryan and I arrived at the same time, but I avoided telling Cardinals fans that they "had a writer in town." I knew better than to brag because I was following Lloyd Herberg on the beat. A great reporter, Lloyd died of cancer in the spring of 1994, leaving a huge byline to replace.

Luckily, Steve Schoenfeld, our NFL writer, was there to help me along. He introduced me to owners, agents, players, coaches, custodians, and on and on. Steve knew everyone and I would have floundered without him. We tragically lost Steve to a hit-and-run driver in 2000.

All three of us covered some lean years for the Cardinals—even lean decades. Over my 20-plus years on the beat, the one question I heard most from fans and readers was, "Don't you get tired of covering a bad team?"

I'll admit that there were some repetitive storylines. And there were many times I wondered what I was going to say that day that was different from the week before, and the week before that. But even when the Cardinals were losing, great stories were plentiful. We never knew what we were going to get from Buddy. The playoff run in 1998 was amazing.

and sandals over suits and dress shoes. Former Cardinals quarterback Jake Plummer was a teammate of Tillman's in the NFL and at Arizona State. Plummer already was a Sun Devil when Tillman, who hailed from San Jose, came to Tempe, Arizona, on his recruiting visit.

Plummer doesn't remember having much of a first impression of Tillman. "I remember him being just a guy who said 'dude' a lot," Plummer said. "He was laid-back, not presumptuous at all.

Tillman was a star at Arizona State, but few expected him to make it in the NFL. He played linebacker in college, but at 5'11" and 204 pounds, Tillman would have to play safety in the NFL. McGinnis and Cardinals defensive coordinator Larry Marmie went to ASU in the spring of 1998 to put Tillman through a private workout. It wasn't pretty. Tillman struggled through defensive backs drills, growing angrier with each setback. But Tillman insisted on going through the complete workout. McGinnis and Marmie loved what they had seen of Tillman in college, and that competitive spirit came through in the private workout. So the Cardinals selected Tillman with the third of four seventh-round picks the team had that year.

Tillman started 10 games as a rookie, and the Cardinals made the playoffs for the first time since 1975. In two of his next three seasons, Tillman became the team's regular starting safety. But like many other Americans, Tillman's life changed on September 11, 2001. It was a Tuesday, normally a day off for the Cardinals. But Tillman was among a handful of players who showed up at the team facility for work that day. Like most other Americans, he watched as news unfolded of the terrorist attacks on the country.

In an interview with azcardinals.com the next day, Tillman spoke passionately about his love for the country and the debt he felt he owed. "Times like this, you not only stop to think about how good we have it," he said, "but what kind of system we live under, what freedoms we're allowed. And that wasn't built overnight. My great-grandfather was at Pearl Harbor, and a lot of my family has gone and fought in wars. And I really haven't done a damn thing, as far as laying myself on the line like that. So I have a great deal of respect for those that have and for what the flag stands for."

Fiercely loyal, in the spring of 2001, Tillman declined to pursue a five-year, $9 million offer from the St. Louis Rams because he felt

A free spirit off the field, Pat Tillman displays his on-field intensity in 1998 after tackling New Orleans Saints running back Lamar Smith for a loss.

loyalty to the Cardinals coaches who had taken a chance on him. Tillman amassed 70 tackles in 2001 and helped a rookie, Adrian Wilson, who Tillman knew was likely to replace him in 2002. The Cardinals wanted Tillman back, however, because he would have played an important role on special teams and in passing situations.

The Cardinals tried to re-sign Tillman that offseason, ultimately offering a three-year deal worth about $3.6 million. They

The Tillman Cover-Up

Pat Tillman was not perfect. His family would be among the first to tell anyone that. Pat would, too, because he did not lie. So it's sadly ironic that his death prompted the Army and government he served to produce a series of lies designed to cover up how the former Cardinals safety was killed in Afghanistan.

An Army Ranger, Tillman was killed on April 22, 2004, about two years after he left a successful football career to enlist, along with his brother, Kevin, who played minor league baseball. Immediately, the powers that be spun a narrative that Tillman had died while charging up a hill to protect fellow Rangers. He was awarded the Silver Star. Later, the truth emerged, mostly because of the dogged determination of Tillman's mother, Mary. He died of fratricide—killed by friendly fire.

Kevin was in a convoy about 15 minutes behind Pat and didn't see the incident. According to witness testimony years later, a battalion commander ordered that Kevin not be told the truth about how Pat died. Kevin was told that Pat had been shot and killed by enemy soldiers. Pat's uniform was burned, as was his journal.

About three years after his brother's death, Kevin testified at a congressional hearing. It was the first time he spoke publicly about Pat's death and how the truth had been covered up.

It was an attempt to deceive the Tillman family and the rest of America. The Army had been the center of a handful of embarrassing incidents at the time, and the decision was made that the truth about Tillman's death would not be told. "To our family and friends, it was a devastating loss. To the nation it was a moment of disorientation. To the military it was a nightmare," Kevin said. "But to others within the government, it appears to have been an opportunity."

thought it was curious that they couldn't get Tillman to sign, considering the lack of interest from other teams. Maybe, they reasoned, Tillman would re-sign after he was married that spring. "The Cardinals were super with him," Tillman's agent, Frank Bauer said at the time. "They made nice offers and were patient. Most clubs would say the guy is whacked."

Among Tillman's friends, word started to leak that spring that Tillman was joining the Army. One acquaintance asked Plummer to try and talk Tillman out of it. "I kind of chuckled," Plummer said. "Nobody was going to talk him out of it. If his wife wasn't going to talk him out of it, what chance did I have?"

Cardinals defensive tackle Russell Davis was at home Thursday when his wife yelled to him that Tillman had just signed. "That's good," Davis said.

"With the Army," his wife said.

Tillman's decision to reject millions of dollars to serve his country became one of the biggest stories in the country. Every major news outlet called seeking interviews. Every one received the same answer. Pat's not talking about it. He's not doing it for publicity and he wants to be considered no different than any other soldier.

A few days after McGinnis announced Tillman's news, Tillman visited the team's headquarters to complete some paperwork and say good-bye to team employees. After talking to those in the media relations department, Tillman exited through the press room. "If you ever decide to talk about your decision, don't forget your local beat writer," I said.

"I appreciate that," Tillman said, "but it's not going to happen."

On April 22, 2004, Pat Tillman was killed in action in Afghanistan. A nation mourned, and hundreds of Tillman fans visited the Cardinals facility where an enormous memorial stood for weeks.

Tillman's sacrifice resonated with people throughout the world. That's just part of his legacy, Plummer said. Just as important as Tillman serving his country was the way he treated others, including friends. "Pat always seemed to find the time to connect with people he cared about," Plummer said. "He did his part to make friendships last. There are times people say, 'I haven't been able to call you. I'm so busy.' But Pat always found the time to pick up the phone. He treated people with respect. He'd look you in the eye when he talked to you. He was genuine. Those are the traits you hope your kids have."

2 Super Bowl XLIII

With 2:37 left in Super Bowl XLIII, the team dubbed the worst team to ever make the NFL playoffs led 23–20. For a Cardinals fan, this was the point the alarm went off, spoiling the pleasant dream. Or their mothers woke them for school. It's when they hit the snooze alarm or begged for five more minutes. But this was real.

It was February 1, 2009, and the Cardinals were within minutes of their first NFL title since 1947. The Cardinals weren't supposed to be anywhere close to Tampa, Florida, on February 1. They won the NFC West, but they hobbled into the playoffs with a 9–7 record. They lost four of their last six regular season games, and three of the losses were by three touchdowns or more. So while the Cardinals took offense when NBC's Cris Collinsworth called them the worst postseason team ever, it was hard to argue. "We had a team of underachievers, a bunch of cast-offs, and guys that believed in each other," safety Adrian Wilson said. "That's the main thing I'll take away from that team."

The Cardinals had surprised everyone, including themselves, by beating the Atlanta Falcons, Carolina Panthers, and, finally, the Philadelphia Eagles to advance to the first Super Bowl in franchise history. Coach Ken Whisenhunt was among the few people who believed. When the Cardinals had stayed in Virginia the week between games against Washington and the New York Jets, Whisenhunt said it would be good preparation if the team made it to the Super Bowl. Reporters rolled their eyes and tried to hide smirks. "I felt like there were a number of pieces in place there— from talent to a new stadium to an ownership that was committed to doing some of the things to win," said Whisenhunt, who was in his second season. "I've said this before. I was naive enough to think we could win in our first year."

Quarterback Kurt Warner had resurrected his career a second time. And Larry Fitzgerald was enjoying the best postseason performance of any receiver in history. In Tampa, however, the Cardinals played the first half like a team on a big stage for the first time. They dropped passes. They were penalized for 106 yards. And when they finally calmed down and put together an offensive drive, it ended with Pittsburgh Steelers linebacker James Harrison returning an interception 100 yards for a touchdown on the last play of the half.

That play would have crippled most teams. Warner threw a slant to receiver Anquan Boldin, a play that had worked for Arizona all year. Harrison was supposed to blitz, but he read the play, freelanced, and started racing with the ball down the Cardinals sideline. "I couldn't see him around our linemen and the pressure," Warner said. "I thought I had Anquan for a second, but he jumped in there and made a play."

Several Cardinals gave pursuit. Fitzgerald would have caught Harrison, but Fitzgerald ran into the back of teammate Antrel Rolle on the Cardinals' sideline. That put the Steelers ahead 17–7. They added a field goal in the third quarter, and it looked as if it was time to pat the Cardinals on the head and congratulate them on a gritty playoff run.

But Whisenhunt, offensive coordinator Todd Haley, and Warner adjusted. The Cardinals spread the field with receivers and went to the no-huddle attack that Warner had used so well throughout the season. Until then, Fitzgerald had made no impact on the game, catching one pass for seven yards through the first three quarters. That changed in the fourth quarter, which was highlighted by one of the most famous plays in team history. Fitzgerald beat a defender on a deep slant and burst through the middle of the field. Glancing at the stadium's big screen to see if anyone was going to catch him, Fitzgerald sprinted to the end zone. The 64-yard score gave the Cardinals a 23–20 lead with 2:37 left.

Whisenhunt, the Steelers' offensive coordinator before coming to Arizona, knew the game wasn't over. Quarterback Ben Roethlisberger had pulled out fourth-quarter victories before. "There was too much time on the clock," Whisenhunt said. "I felt maybe we could at least hold them to a field goal and maybe go to overtime."

They couldn't. Roethlisberger escaped sacks time and again. The Cardinals left receivers open time and again—or simply slipped while trying to make tackles. With 42 seconds left, the Steelers were at the Cardinals 6. Roethlisberger dropped back and then was flushed from the pocket. He rifled the ball to the deep corner of the end zone past the fingertips of cornerback Ralph Brown and into the arms of receiver Santonio Holmes.

Touchdown.

"The first read was the running back in the flat, but he wasn't open," Roethlisberger said. "Then I was going to bang it to Hines

[Ward] real quick, but someone was closing on him. So I just kind of looked left and saw 'Tone' in the corner."

But did "Tone" have his toes down? Officials ruled that he did, though many Cardinals fans still disagree. "One hundred percent I knew I had my feet down," Holmes said. "I never left the ground once I extended my hands. I stood up on my toes so I wouldn't get pushed out of bounds."

The Cardinals didn't have enough time to come back, and their first Super Bowl appearance ended in defeat. The loss pained Whisenhunt so much that he couldn't watch a replay of the game for a few years. Warner, however, was able to put it in perspective immediately after the game. "I am so proud of this football team," he said that evening. "I think that is one of the reasons why it doesn't hurt as bad as it could. These guys have exceeded expectations. We gave ourselves a chance to win a world championship, but that other team went out and won it."

3 Larry Fitzgerald

Not all Cardinals fans were happy when the 2003 season ended with quarterback Josh McCown throwing a touchdown pass to Nate Poole to beat the Minnesota Vikings at Sun Devil Stadium. The victory dropped the Cardinals from first to third in the 2004 draft, meaning they had no shot at taking Ole Miss quarterback Eli Manning. As it turned out, however, the Cardinals wouldn't have taken Manning with any selection as long as receiver Larry Fitzgerald from Pittsburgh was available.

Dennis Green, who had known Fitzgerald as a kid, was hired as Cardinals coach in January of 2004 and made no secret of his desire to draft Fitzgerald. No one looks back at the scenario and wonders, what if? That's because Fitzgerald might be the best player in franchise history. There's no question he's the best during the Cardinals' time in the desert and the most popular. "We could all see Larry's amazing talent from the first day we watched him on the field," said quarterback Kurt Warner, who became a Cardinal in 2005. "He had a rare skillset that doesn't come along very often."

Even though he nearly won the Heisman Trophy in his last collegiate season, Fitzgerald was far from a finished product when he came to the NFL. He turned 21 just before his rookie season started and, like most young people starting a new job in a strange place, he was lonely.

Fitzgerald often stayed at the Cardinals' facility long after other players had gone home but not to work on his game. "I'd stay behind and help the equipment guys fold towels," he said, "doing the same stuff I used to do when I was a ballboy with the Vikings. It was better than going home and playing video games."

Fitzgerald was no stranger to professional sports. His father, Larry Sr., was a longtime sportswriter and radio host in Minneapolis, and Fitzgerald used those connections to attend NHL, NBA, and MLB games and to get a job as a ballboy for the Vikings, who were coached by Green. "My brother Marcus and I would go to Twins games with my dad," Fitzgerald said. "We would sit in the cheap seats and gradually work our way down into the good ones." Fitzgerald grew up watching Vikings greats Cris Carter and Randy Moss catching passes from a variety of quarterbacks, including Hall of Famer Warren Moon.

Fitzgerald succeeded in high school and college because he was a superior athlete. He wasn't blessed with great speed, but he was big, strong, and had an uncanny ability to catch anything thrown close to him. A strong work ethic developed early in his NFL career. "He is a young man that is way beyond his years and he bought into the idea that he wouldn't always be able to rely on his physical ability to be the best," Warner said. "At some point he would need to truly understand how to play the game to have great success as he got older."

Time erodes skills, and some wondered if Fitzgerald's career peaked in 2011 when he caught 80 passes for 1,411 yards and eight touchdowns. He failed to reach 1,000 yards receiving over the next three seasons and he scored only two touchdowns in 2014, a career low. Fitzgerald proved doubters wrong in 2015. At age 32 he enjoyed one of his best seasons, catching 109 passes (a franchise record) with 1,215 yards and nine touchdowns. In addition he became an effective blocker, helping to revitalize the Cardinals running game.

Fitzgerald likely cemented his future Hall of Fame status with his performance in the playoff victory against the Green Bay Packers that season. He had eight receptions for 176 yards and a touchdown. But he will be most remembered for the 75-yard catch and run he made in overtime. That set up the winning touchdown: a shovel pass to Fitzgerald. "Great players play great in big games, and that's how you get to the Hall of Fame," Coach Bruce Arians said. "Some guys shrivel in the moment; other guys flourish in the moment. He flourishes."

4 1947 Title

There haven't been many halcyon days in Cardinals history, but December 28, 1947, was one. The day broke sunny and bright, but it was not made for football. Sleet and bitter cold from the night before had turned the football "field" at Comiskey Park into concrete disguised as sod.

It was the final game of a long and trying season for the Chicago Cardinals. Their flamboyant owner, Charles Bidwill, had unexpectedly died of pneumonia in the spring. Their punter, Jeff Burkett, had been killed in a plane crash early in the season. They were the second team in a two-team town behind the beloved Bears and their owner/coach, George Halas. But here they were, the "raggedy-ass Cardinals from the South Side," as they were often called, ready to face the Philadelphia Eagles for the 1947 title.

The Cardinals had persevered through the 1947 season, thanks to the talent the charismatic Bidwill had signed in the two previous years and the creativity and motivational techniques of coach Jimmy Conzelman. In the championship game, they built a 14–0 lead with halfbacks Charley Trippi and Elmer Angsman breaking long touchdown runs. The Eagles twice came back to within a touchdown, but Trippi and Angsman proved too much for them to overcome.

Trippi returned a punt 75 yards for a touchdown in the third quarter, and Angsman scored on a 70-run in the fourth quarter. The Cardinals won 28–21, leaving Bidwill's widow, Violet, in tears. "I wish Charles could have been there to see this," she said.

The Cardinals struggled for most of the next six decades, failing to win a single playoff game until 1975. They played for just two more NFL championships, losing both: to the Eagles in 1948 and the Pittsburgh Steelers in the 2008 season.

"It was just one helluva time and one helluva team," Jim Conzelman Jr., whose father was the coach, said in 1997 before a 50th anniversary celebrating the title. Bidwill was mostly responsible for it. A wealthy Chicago lawyer and businessman, he didn't mind spending money trying to win.

In 1946 a third professional team, the Rockets, moved into Chicago. They were owned by Jake Keshan, a former business partner of Bidwill's, and word around town was that Arch Ward, the *Chicago Tribune* sports editor who founded the new league, predicted that the Cardinals would be forced out of Chicago.

That irritated Bidwill, who loved the competition of sports and business. In 1946 the Cardinals showed they were on the verge of competing for a title. They finished 6–5, beating the Bears, the eventual NFL champions, in the season finale. "The only piece that really was missing was Trippi," Bill Bidwill said.

A starter at Georgia and an excellent baseball player, Trippi was being wooed by the new league, the AAFC and the New York Yankees. But Charlie Bidwill had forged a relationship with Trippi years earlier and signed him to a four-year deal worth $100,000, the largest contract in NFL history at the time. "He was just a fantastic owner," Trippi said in a 2015 interview. "He always extended himself to make everybody happy on the ballclub. Apparently, he paid everybody pretty good. I can testify to that."

Bidwill had already lured Conzelman, the team's coach from 1940–42, away from a job in the front office of the St. Louis Browns baseball team. Conzelman was a renaissance man with wide interests. He was one of the best speakers of his day, a better motivator than strategist. "He always made you feel like you were the most important guy on the team," Trippi said in 1997.

Conzelman knew his players, many of whom served in World War II. Some didn't plan to return to playing football after serving but were convinced otherwise by Bidwill and Conzelman. Mal Kutner, an end and defensive back, rejected Conzelman's first offer of $600 a game. "I said I wasn't playing for less than $800," Kutner said in 1997, "and he said, 'Okay.' That was a lot of money back then."

Bidwill never got to see the championship team he assembled. He was just 51 when he passed away, and even years later, many of the players from that era talk of him fondly. His death wasn't the only tragedy to strike that season.

Burkett came down with an appendicitis on a road trip to Los Angeles that year and remained behind to recuperate from surgery. Burkett took a commercial flight to return home, but it crashed into Bryce Canyon in Utah, killing all aboard. "He was supposed to arrive on Wednesday night, and a bunch of us went out there to see him when he flew in," Angsman said in 1997. "We stood there absolutely dumbfounded when we heard the plane had gone down."

The Cardinals persevered and beat the Bears for the right to play in the NFL championship. It's a team that probably should have won more titles, but Bidwill's death changed the direction of the franchise. Conzelman left in 1948 to take a job with a St. Louis advertising firm, and the front office made numerous personnel mistakes over the next few years. "The owners got sentimental over some of the players who were aging," Trippi said in 1997. "The front office at that time, I don't think they knew much about professional football. And [Violet Bidwill], she wasn't loose with the money."

In 1997 23 surviving members of the team reunited in Chicago to celebrate the 50th anniversary of the championship. Bill Bidwill presented them with rings. "It was a friendship," Phil Bouzeos, the team's equipment manager, said in 1997. "We went out together, had parties. The money didn't mean anything. We had guys who went down to the local newsstand on Tuesdays to cash their checks."

5 Kurt Warner

For a variety of reasons, every Cardinals fan is on a first-name basis with Kurt Warner.

He's the first quarterback to lead the team to a Super Bowl. He broke many of the team's significant passing records despite spending just five years with the franchise. And, just as importantly, he embraced fans, whether they were booing or cheering him.

Cardinals fans tend to forget they didn't always think fondly of *Kurt*. In 2006 they booed him after he fumbled in the last seconds of a game at University of Phoenix Stadium. And in 2008 not everyone thought Warner should have won the starting job over Matt Leinart, the 10th overall draft pick two years prior. "This seems to be the story of my life," Warner said. "Oftentimes people don't come to truly appreciate who you are or what you can do until after the fact. But I believe you also have to always be realistic and know that we didn't put a very good product on the field that first year in 2006, and the fans wanted and deserved better. My goal was to bring about that change in culture, but it wasn't happening as fast as anyone wanted. But I have always felt the biggest challenge in life and sports is to convince people that you aren't what they originally thought you were."

When Warner signed with the Cardinals in 2005, not many football experts thought he could still play. He had been benched and released by the St. Louis Rams in 2003. He had been benched halfway into his first season with the New York Giants in 2004 in favor of Eli Manning.

But the Cardinals were desperate for a veteran quarterback, and at the time, Warner was a cheap alternative. "When I signed I had great confidence in who I was as a player," Warner said. "Even though there were not a lot of teams that felt the same way, I believed that I was as good—if not better—than I had ever been."

It took Warner a while to prove it. In his first two years in Arizona, the Cardinals were lacking in many areas, including scouting, talent, and coaching. Things started to change when the team hired Ken Whisenhunt as head coach in 2007. Whisenhunt brought organization and professionalism to a franchise badly in need of it. He believed in tough love for quarterbacks, young and old. Whisenhunt and offensive coordinator Todd Haley weren't

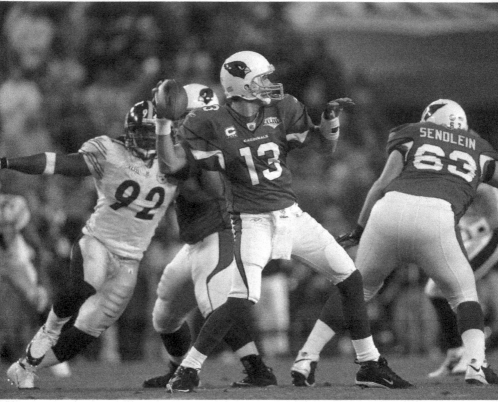

Quarterback Kurt Warner prepares to throw during Super Bowl XLIII, a game in which he threw for 377 yards and three touchdowns. (USA TODAY Sports Images)

part of the decision to draft Leinart, so they weren't going to just hand the job to him.

It also took them a while to warm to Warner, who had a reputation for fumbling and throwing too many interceptions. It was an arranged marriage of sorts. When Leinart went down with an injury in 2007, Warner replaced him. Finally a starting NFL quarterback again, Warner wasn't giving up the job easily. He suffered torn ligaments in his left elbow against the Carolina Panthers in the sixth game, but he played the next week at Washington, wearing a contraption on his left elbow that forced him to hand off right-handed.

Washington linebacker London Fletcher, a former teammate of Warner's in St. Louis, wasn't surprised. "He's finally back as a starting quarterback on a team that's a good football team," Fletcher said back then. "I don't think Kurt was going to let this opportunity slip away."

He didn't. But developing a comfort level with Whisenhunt and Haley took time. All three men could be stubborn, and each had firm ideas about how to move the football and score. Those ideas didn't always mesh. To their credit each compromised. Warner worked on securing the ball better. And Whisenhunt and Haley gradually adjusted the offense to highlight Warner's skills. They spread the field with receivers and let Warner operate much like he did while helping the Rams advance to two Super Bowls. "What made the relationship between 'Wiz,' Todd, and myself work was trust," Warner said. "We all had egos and probably thought we were smarter than the other guy. That is commonplace in the NFL. Both Wiz and Todd gave me great flexibility to shape the offense around my skills and what I saw on the field. They gave me a great deal of input every week and often on Sunday afternoons to call what I felt most comfortable with, believing that I would make it work."

Warner had to compromise, too, to make the relationship work. For example, when the Cardinals were preparing to play the Chicago Bears in 2009, Whisenhunt installed a play that called for Warner to hold the ball for a long time. Warner hated the play, which the Cardinals didn't run well in practice. "I told [Whisenhunt] over and over that week that I really didn't like it and that I hoped he didn't call it," Warner said. "He spent the week trying to convince me because it was something he had success with in the past."

In the second quarter, the Cardinals were on the Bears 17-yard line. Whisenhunt called the play. "I am sure I looked over to the sideline and shook my head," Warner said. "But I called the play, and sure enough, it worked to perfection and I threw a TD to Fitz. As I ran to the sideline, Wiz had the biggest smile, and I had to give him a high-five and tell him, 'Great call!'"

Warner was demanding of coaches and teammates. He and Haley texted each other constantly at all hours of the day or night. From his days leading the Rams to Super Bowls, Warner learned what it took to achieve greatness. And in 2007 and 2008, he often was disturbed by what he saw as a lack of maturity by the Cardinals. "All of the little things—the preparation, the attitude, the practice habits, the ownership in the product placed on field, the importance of character in success, and the mentality that life is about finding solutions, not looking for excuses," Warner said. "To watch all of this take shape over the years and to see the surprise of everyone as we headed down to Tampa for the Super Bowl was awesome."

Oddly, Warner was allowed to test his value in free agency the following spring. The San Francisco 49ers, a bitter rival of the Cardinals, brought him in for a visit, making Cardinals fans nervous. The Cardinals eventually re-signed Warner to a two-year contract through 2010.

Warner played only one more season. By the end of 2009, he was beat up. He had young kids at home, and his wife, Brenda, could see the toll football had taken on her husband.

So early in 2010, Warner announced his retirement. In 2014 his name went up in the Ring of Honor at University of Phoenix Stadium, where nearly a decade before fans had booed him. "I definitely felt the irony, knowing that many of the people cheering were the same ones who booed me off the field not so many years ago," Warner said.

Warner stayed in Arizona after retirement and continues to be active in community affairs through his foundation and even serves as offensive coordinator for his son's high school team. *Kurt* remains one of the most popular players in team history and feels a sense of pride at how far the franchise has come since his arrival. "I am most proud of the impact that I had off the field that translated to the product we placed on the field," Warner said. "When I arrived there was a culture of losing. No one ever stepped on the field expecting to win—whether in practice or in games. I don't know if anyone understands how hard it is to convince an organization and a group of players that the past doesn't have to affect the present and the future."

6 Charles Bidwill

After seven years Dr. David Jones was tired of owning a professional football team. By 1932 the Cardinals had become a financial pain, for which the doctor had found no relief. Then came a dinner party aboard the yacht of wealthy lawyer and businessman Charles W. Bidwill.

As the story goes, Jones bemoaned his team's status. It was losing money, and the prospects of a turnaround didn't look good in a city that loved the Bears and tolerated the Cardinals.

Bidwill's wife, Violet, suggested Jones sell the club to her husband, who owned part of the Bears and once helped owner George Halas during hard financial times. Bidwill and Jones struck a deal. For $50,000 the Cardinals were Bidwill's, and they belong to his descendants today.

In later decades the name Bidwill became synonymous with being cheap. That would have surprised Chicago sports fans in the 1930s and '40s, however, because Charles Bidwill didn't mind writing big checks. Bidwill would have preferred to buy the Bears, but Halas always refused to sell. So Bidwill tried to compete for the hearts—and wallets—of Chicago football fans. As an owner of a printing company and a racing business, Bidwill had made a fortune and he didn't mind spending some of it to win football games. "He was just a fantastic owner," said running back Charley Trippi, who is in the Pro Football Hall of Fame. "He always extended himself to make everybody happy on the ballclub. He always made you feel like you were the most important guy on the team."

Known as "Blue-Shirt Charlie" for his fondness of wearing blue shirts with suits, Bidwill supposedly knew Al Capone, though that was not unusual for Chicago businessmen in that time.

Bidwill loved the thrill of competition. What's the use of having money, he once asked, if you can't have fun with it? "The new boss of the Cardinals is now perhaps the city's most active athletic figure," wrote Arch Ward, sports editor of the *Chicago Tribune*. "He loved the action of football and racing," Charles "Stormy" Bidwill, one of Bidwill's two sons, said several years ago.

When it came to football, the action didn't include winning seasons or profits. The Cardinals continued to flounder, much to Bidwill's consternation. When World War II ended, a new league, the All-American Football Conference, was created, and a third team, the Rockets, set up shop in Chicago. This didn't sit well with Bidwill, who had already spent considerable money to rebuild the Cardinals.

Jimmy Conzelman had returned as coach. Stars such as tailback Paul Christman, running back/defensive back Marshall "Biggie" Goldberg, fullback Pat Harder, and another runner, Elmer Angsman, had been signed. That led to a turn in fortunes in 1946.

The Cardinals finished 6–5, only their second winning season under Bidwill.

Then Bidwill made his biggest move. Trippi, an All-America halfback at Georgia, was the most coveted dual-sport athlete at the time. The New York Yankees of the AAFC wanted him. So did baseball's Yankees. Bidwill courted Trippi for a long time, and the two struck up a strong friendship. It paid off. The Cardinals signed Trippi to a four-year deal worth $100,000.

Before the Cardinals had played a down, the backfield of Christman, Trippi, and Harder was being called the "dream backfield," and the "million-dollar backfield."

The Cardinals beat the Bears, the eventual champions, in the final game of 1946. With Trippi winning a championship was the only goal, and Bidwill was ecstatic after signing him. "Sometimes, you hold on to a dream so long, it isn't a dream anymore," Bidwill told reporters after signing Trippi in January of 1947. "This is the Cardinals' year. This is the dream come true. I can hardly wait."

Bidwill was right. 1947 was the Cardinals' year. His dream did come true. Cruelly, however, he didn't get to see it. He died of pneumonia in April of 1947. He was only 51. The team took it hard. "He was a magnificent person," Goldberg said in an interview in 1997. "When I was in the service, he saw that my wife was taken care of. He wanted to continue to pay me my salary, but I wouldn't let him."

Bidwill left behind his wife, Violet; two sons, Stormy and Bill; and a team that was built to win championships. One of a handful of men who helped the NFL survive through lean years, he was inducted into the Pro Football Hall of Fame in 1967.

After the Cardinals won the 1947 championship, Violet Bidwill expressed the unanimous sentiment of everyone connected with the team. "I wish Charles could have been here to see this," she said through tears.

7 University of Phoenix Stadium

Founded in 1898, the Cardinals are the world's oldest professional football franchise still in existence. So it's ironic that it took them until 2006 to play a game in a home of their own: University of Phoenix Stadium. For years the Cardinals were the equivalent of basement tenants.

In Chicago they played at Comiskey Park, the home of baseball's White Sox. In St. Louis they shared Busch Stadium with the baseball Cardinals. And for their first 18 seasons in Arizona, they played in Sun Devil Stadium, which was owned by Arizona State University. At Sun Devil Stadium, the team often struggled to attract even 30,000 fans. The first six weeks of the season could be miserably hot, especially sitting on aluminum bleachers. And it was hard to pay big money to watch a football team that was usually among the NFL's worst. The Cardinals had just one winning season in 18 years at Sun Devil Stadium.

It's not a coincidence the team's fortunes turned once they had a home of their own. "The new stadium made a huge difference for both the fanbase and for the team," said Kurt Warner, who was with the team before and after it moved into the new home. "It was as if the stadium gave us all a new start and a home that we were proud of. Both groups seemed to take ownership of our 'house,' and it brought with it a sense of pride that we all wanted to represent on Sunday afternoons. It never had the history of losing that seemed to be connected to the Cardinals and Sun Devil Stadium, so it gave us a chance to write a new history."

The opening of the $450 million stadium provided a pivot point for the franchise. The Cardinals have sold out every game since moving in. In the first nine years at University of Phoenix

Stadium, the Cardinals had four winning seasons and three playoff appearances.

Most importantly for the Cardinals, it's a home of their own. The stadium has provided more money to the team, and

It's Nice, But What Do We Call It?

What's in a name? Well, in the case of University of Phoenix Stadium, it's $154.5 million over 20 years. That's how much the Cardinals receive for the naming rights to the stadium that opened in 2006.

It was an interesting, and ironic, choice for a title sponsor. The University of Phoenix, which offers classes online and has numerous campuses, does not have a football team. And the stadium that bears its name is in Glendale, not Phoenix. When the naming rights deal was announced in August of 2006, local residents seemed underwhelmed. That's not a surprise, since it takes everyone a while to grow accustomed to a new name.

Plus, University of Phoenix Stadium is a mouthful of words that don't exactly roll off the tongue. The name of the new stadium was the subject of much speculation, intrigue, and grandstanding in the year before it opened. Late in the process, owners of an upscale Scottsdale Mexican restaurant, The Pink Taco, offered the Cardinals $30 million for the naming rights.

If the offer was done to gain the restaurant publicity, it worked. The owners raised a fuss that the Cardinals didn't seriously consider their restaurant's name, which is sexually suggestive. Team officials were a bit irritated they had to even respond to the idea. "There is zero chance of this happening," a team official said in the summer of 2006.

In late August of that year, the Cardinals and the University of Phoenix announced their agreement. It was officially approved a few weeks later, and on October 8 against the Kansas City Chiefs, the Cardinals played their first game under the stadium's new name. Before that it was known as Cardinals Stadium.

Overall, the stadium has been very good to the Cardinals. Counting playoffs, they were 56–28 there from 2006 through 2015. At Sun Devil Stadium, they went 63–80 from 1988 through 2005.

management, led by team president Michael Bidwill, who have been smarter at spending over the last several years. For a change the Cardinals are the most popular team in the stadium on Sundays.

That's dramatically different from their first 18 years in Arizona. "It was difficult playing in Sun Devil Stadium for many different reasons, but I believe the biggest was that it didn't feel like a home stadium to us," Warner said. "The small locker room with no Cardinals flair to it, the walk that seemed like a half-mile just to get to the stadium or back at halftime. Then you factor in the heat element—which probably affected the fans more than anything—and it felt more like a neutral site. It never felt like home to the players, and I believe the fans felt the same way. They didn't look at a game in that stadium as a Cardinals game, but more of a football game, and that is why the building would be half full and full of fans from other teams."

It didn't help that the Cardinals put a poor product on the field for most of those 18 seasons at Sun Devil Stadium. They didn't give local fans many reasons to sever their allegiances with teams they had cheered for since childhood. Sun Devil Stadium, though, didn't bother some players as much as others. "It wasn't that hard for me," said fullback Larry Centers, a Cardinals player from 1990 to 1998. "I came from a small school [Stephen F. Austin]. I was happy to be in a pro setting. I would hear guys mumble and grumble about the conditions, how far the walk was to the field, that so many fans of the other team were there. My response was: 'We haven't given them any reason to root for us.' Everybody wants to be a part of a winner. Win ballgames and switch that around."

The Bidwill family, which owned the team, found that difficult to do. With no stadium of their own, the Cardinals couldn't afford to compete with many other NFL teams. Michael Bidwill vowed that the Cardinals would spend money made from a new stadium on players.

Success didn't come immediately when University of Phoenix Stadium opened, but it didn't take long. And when the Cardinals made the playoffs in the 2008 and 2009 seasons, there was a dramatic transition among fans in Arizona.

Cardinals license plates became popular. No longer were people reluctant to wear apparel with the team logo or to openly root for the Cardinals. "I believe it gave everyone a jolt in excitement," Warner said. "Even if your main objective as a fan was to go and check out the new stadium, the energy and buzz about the Cardinals and University of Phoenix Stadium definitely was felt by the players. We finally felt like we were an NFL franchise."

8 Larry Wilson

Larry Wilson might be the greatest player in Cardinals history, but it sure didn't look that way on August 26, 1960, in Charleston, South Carolina. The St. Louis Cardinals were playing the Baltimore Colts in an exhibition game, and Wilson, a seventh-round pick out of Utah, was seeing his first professional action. Drafted as a halfback, Wilson had been moved to cornerback and here he was facing Colts quarterback Johnny Unitas and receiver Raymond Berry. "The first time they threw to Raymond Berry, I was 10 yards behind him, and he wasn't fast," Wilson said, laughing. "He changed my career right quick. They moved me to safety, and then things started rolling in the right direction."

Wilson played safety as well anyone in NFL history. He finished his career with 52 interceptions, 800 return yards, and five touchdowns. He made All-Pro five times, played in eight Pro

Bowls, and was inducted into the Pro Football Hall of Fame in 1978. He was named to the NFL's 50th and 75th anniversary teams.

Wilson was a member of the Cardinals organization for 43 years, as a player, coach (briefly), general manager, and in various other executive roles. That professional career got its start on November 30, 1959, when the Cardinals drafted Wilson, who played both offense and defense in college. Soon after the draft, Cardinals executive Bill Bidwill flew to Salt Lake City and offered Wilson a contract with a salary of $7,500, including a $500 advance. "I said, 'Well, I was drafted by Buffalo, and they're coming in tomorrow. I'd kind of like to listen to what they have to say,'" Wilson said.

Bidwill was agreeable, and the next day, Wilson met with Bills owner Ralph Wilson. The Bills offered him $7,500, too, but balked at paying anything in advance. "So I went with the Cardinals," Wilson said.

Growing up in Rigby, Idaho, and playing at Utah, Wilson had lived a sheltered life. He had no idea if he could play in the NFL and was especially concerned after that disastrous start against the Colts. But the Cardinals smartly moved Wilson to safety, and veteran defensive back Jimmy Hill mentored Wilson. "From Rigby, Idaho, to Utah, I hadn't been around too many black guys," Wilson said. "As a matter of fact, zero. Here was Jimmy Hill, one of the nicest guys you'd ever want to meet. He took me underneath his wing. He was a guy who played all over, so I kind of watched what he did. I owe so much to him, it's ridiculous."

It didn't take the coaching staff long to recognize Wilson's talents. In the early 1960s, Chuck Drulis, a defensive assistant, was looking for a new wrinkle. Offenses were having no trouble blocking linebackers when they blitzed, so Drulis came up with the idea of blitzing Wilson, the free safety.

It was called the "Wildcat" blitz and it worked right away. "We started it out in New York," Wilson said. "Coach Drulis came up to me before the game and said, 'When you get in there and hit the guy, kind of jump up and put your hands over your number so they don't know who you are. So we started hiding me all over, and it went on from there. It turned out to be a lot of fun. Of course today, they blitz everybody."

If there was a player who symbolized the NFL of the 1960s, it was Wilson. Slightly built, he was a ferocious hitter who never took cheap shots. Rookies at their first training camps were often left aghast when they caught their first glimpse of Wilson without his teeth in. "That's probably the best thing to happen to me in pro football," Wilson said of losing his teeth. "It saved me thousands of dollars. I didn't have to go see the dentist. If something was wrong, I'd just take them into the place they repaired them, and they fixed me up."

In 1965 Wilson cemented himself in NFL lore by playing with casts on both hands. Legend has it that he played with either two broken wrists or two broken arms, depending upon the account you read. "My wife gets so tired of it," Wilson said. "She says, 'Larry, I swear to God you were out there in a body cast.'"

So what's the truth?' "I broke both middle fingers in a game," Wilson said. "They put casts on up to my elbows and put this little wire thing over it. Back then, if you could run, you could play, and I wasn't running on my hands." So on November 7 against the Pittsburgh Steelers, Wilson played a game with casts on both hands and even intercepted a pass.

As the years passed, Wilson went from the naïve rookie to the grizzled veteran. And he mentored young players, just as Hill had helped him. One of those youngsters was cornerback Roger Wehrli, who went on to have a Hall of Fame career of his own. "One of the greatest players the game has ever known," Wehrli said. "I learned so much from [Wilson] in the early years of my career. He showed me how to play through pain, how to never give up. He talked about the mental toughness to play hard, no matter the circumstances, and was a great help to me the first few years. Because of our friendship and my respect for him as a great teammate, I asked him to be my presenter at the Hall of Fame enshrinement ceremony."

9 1948 Title Game

On the last Sunday before Christmas in 1948, Philadelphians woke to a heavy snow falling, surprising nearly everyone. The day before had been unseasonably balmy, and the Chicago Cardinals practiced in shirtsleeves in their final preparations to play the Eagles at Shibe Park. Cardinals quarterback Paul Christman woke Sunday morning and parted the curtains in the hotel room. He turned to his roommate, end Billy Dewell, and said, "Don't look outside."

The weather was a big deal for the Cardinals, who were seeking a second consecutive championship. They were fast and scored a lot of points. Being able to run and change directions without slipping was vital.

They were the NFL's defending champion and had proven their mettle during that title season. Before the 1947 season started, Cardinals owner Charles Bidwill died suddenly of pneumonia. During the season punter Jeff Burkett was killed during a plane crash. Tragedy would visit them again in 1948. "What happened in '47 kind of rubbed off on that '48 team," said running back Charley Trippi. After a victory over the Eagles on Opening Day, Cardinals tackle Stan Mauldin collapsed in the locker room and died of what was believed to be a heart attack. His death impacted the whole league. The Eagles, for instance, decided that if they won the championship, they would award a full player's bonus share to Mauldin's widow.

As snow fell that Sunday in 1948, some wondered if the game would be played as scheduled. But a heavy snowstorm, bordering on a blizzard, wasn't going to deter commissioner Bert Bell. ABC was broadcasting the game. Newsreel cameras were there. Tickets had been sold. The game went on. Some Cardinals didn't think it was fair to play on a day when snow obscured yard lines and goal lines. Others were more philosophical. "When you're in Chicago, you learn to play in all kinds of weather," Trippi said.

The Cardinals championship the year before had been won on a Comiskey Park Field that was a sheet of ice. The 1948 game would be a slog through the snow. "You couldn't even see the yard markers," halfback Marshall "Biggie" Goldberg said. "The game should have never been played."

The Eagles' star running back, Steve Van Buren, almost didn't play. When he woke up to see the snow, Van Buren figured there was no way the game would be played. He went back to bed and fell asleep. Only a phone call from Eagles coach Greasy Neale convinced Van Buren the game would go on. "Get to the park, for God's sake," Neale said. Van Buren hustled off to the trolley and made it to the park.

Those who arrived early enough could watch players from both teams helping clear the snow. "We all chipped in," Trippi said. Nearly 29,000 fans made it to the park that day, but they could barely see the game through the snow. And given the field conditions, neither offense could do much. The Eagles had a touchdown called back early in the game, and there was no score at halftime. It looked as if one turnover, one field goal, or one other big play would be the difference.

It was.

Late in the third quarter, there was a bad exchange between Cardinals running back Elmer Angsman and backup quarterback Ray Mallouf, who played much of the season after Christman suffered a broken hand. The Eagles recovered at the Cardinals 17 and moved to the 5. They handed the ball to their star, Van Buren, who crossed a snow-covered goal line for the game's only score. "It was a crime we lost that game," Cardinals returner Red Cochran told Joe Ziemba, author of *When Football Was Football.* "We had a much better ballclub in '48 than '47. We had beaten the Eagles twice going into that game. We were averaging 33 points per game and we were shut out, so you know something was wrong."

It would be 60 years before the Cardinals returned to the NFL's championship game. The Cardinals organization altered course after the 1948 season. Conzelman resigned and returned to private business in St. Louis. The team missed Charles Bidwill's charisma and willingness to spend money on talent. The club also had trouble letting go of older players who had helped them to consecutive championship games.

But for two years, the Cardinals were at the top of the NFL. The coach's son, Jim Conzelman, Jr., hung around that team daily. "It was just one helluva time and one helluva team," he said in 1997.

10 Moving to the Desert

In the mid-1980s Phoenix powerbrokers tried in vain to entice a few NFL owners to move a franchise to the desert or, failing that, to convince the league the area was perfect for an expansion team. Colts owner Robert Irsay flirted with Arizona before moving his team from Baltimore to Indianapolis. Philadelphia Eagles owner Leonard Tose had a deal in place to move the team to Phoenix but backed out when word leaked to the press.

On Friday, January 15, 1988, the flirtations finally ended. St. Louis Cardinals owner Bill Bidwill announced he had selected Phoenix over Jacksonville and Baltimore as his team's new home. "I made up my mind on Wednesday," Bidwill said at the time, "and I may still have had some reservations at that point in time."

Three months later NFL owners overwhelmingly approved the move. Six months after that, the Cardinals played their first home game in Arizona (and lost 17–14). "It was stressful, particularly for guys like me who had been [in St. Louis] for some time," said former receiver Roy Green. "You became entrenched in the community. I had two daughters in school. I had a radio show there."

The Cardinals never had their own home in Chicago. That's why they moved to St. Louis in 1960. They spent 28 years in St. Louis but never had their own stadium there. It had been talked about since their arrival in 1960, but the Cardinals remained tenants—first at Sportsman's Park and then at Busch Stadium. In St. Louis the Cardinals baseball team was the most popular sports franchise, and the Cardinals football club again found itself battling for the public's attention. "When you go to St. Louis, they talk about the baseball team," said Larry Wilson, a player and executive with the football Cardinals for 43 years. "They don't talk about football or hockey; it's baseball. You fight that the whole time. You've got to be something special in order to get on the front page of the newspaper."

In 1988 Phoenix was a burgeoning metropolis. Bidwill was attracted by the area's growth, as well as a more lucrative stadium arrangement at Arizona State's Sun Devil Stadium than the one he had in St. Louis. Phoenix businessmen and politicians promised to work toward building a new domed facility downtown.

For the Bidwill family, the decision was a relief. Bill Bidwill agonized over the move, and some people in St. Louis were upset about the team leaving. Quarterback Neil Lomax had to listen to angry callers during a radio show with former Cardinals great Dan Dierdorf. Bidwill and his family heard much worse. Beginning the previous November, Bidwill received death threats and started watching games from somewhere other than his usual box. Bidwill admitted making the decision removed a heavy weight from his shoulders. "Hell, yes," he told *The Arizona Republic* at the time. "God almighty, it was a release."

Soon after the announcement, the team started public relations work in Arizona. Over the next few months, players arrived for appearances, and many had the same reaction as former fullback Ron Wolfley. "I'll never forget flying in and thinking, *My gosh, look at the mountains*," he said. "It just blew my mind. It was in the winter, and I remember I got out and felt that sunshine on my skin and not a cloud in the stinking sky and it was so dry. It was a sensation I've never felt before. I fell in love."

Arizona didn't immediately love the Cardinals back. Acting on advice from Phoenix officials, the Cardinals priced tickets 50 percent higher than the NFL average. That turned some fans off. The team couldn't even sell tickets until the summer because of a lawsuit brought by a group of local people. "It's almost become a theater of the absurd," Cardinals attorney Thomas Guilfoil said at the time. The hardship has been "enormous," Guilfoil said. "In a very real sense, the antics of these people have cost the football Cardinals hundreds and hundreds and hundreds of thousands of dollars."

There wasn't much of a honeymoon when the team started playing football that fall either. Attendance was decent, but by midseason players were pleading with fans to show up.

Still, life was better in Arizona than St. Louis for the Cardinals. A new, state-of-the-art training facility was being constructed in Tempe. And there was the promise of a stadium being built downtown.

The Bidwills' pursuit of a stadium lasted for most of the next two decades, and when the domed stadium finally was constructed, it was in Glendale, not Phoenix. No matter, the Cardinals, nomads of the NFL, finally had a home of their own. "It's amazing what's happened over the last 20 to 30 years," said Wilson, who retired as an executive in 2003. "What makes it so great: it's kind of a community effort now. Everybody is kind of behind it. It has just been so gratifying sitting back and watching this happen."

11 Jake the Snake

Like many young people who just finished college, Jake Plummer thought it might be a good thing to begin his professional career away from home. He had just spent four seasons at Arizona State, and while Plummer loved his time in Tempe and greater Phoenix, starting his NFL career in a different big city was alluring. "Just for the excitement," Plummer said. "I wanted to get away, get a fresh start."

But Plummer was far from despondent when the Cardinals took him in the second round in 1997. He would be playing in the same venue, Sun Devil Stadium, that he did at ASU and in front of many of the same fans who had watched "the Snake" grow up in the previous four seasons. "It ended up being a real blessing," Plummer said. "I had a whole lot of fans who were going to root for me, who were going to let me have my struggles."

And there were struggles. In six seasons as a starter, Plummer only once finished with more touchdowns than interceptions.

He had a penchant for making silly mistakes early in games and then fantastic plays to rally his team late. "I got a lot of breaks," Plummer said. "If you were to put me on the Jets for a couple of those seasons, I would have been long gone. In those six years with the Cardinals, I had the faith of the ownership and the fanbase."

With Plummer, Cardinals fans had hope for the future. From 1950 to 1990, that was not often the case. The Cardinals went to the playoffs in 1998 for the first time since moving to Arizona a decade earlier. It was Plummer's second season and his first as a full-time starter, so the future of both the quarterback and franchise looked bright.

The Cardinals went 9–7 in the regular season, and in seven of those nine victories, Plummer led comebacks. His three rushing touchdowns in Washington on November 22 were the most by an NFL quarterback since Archie Manning in 1977. The Cardinals had to win their final three games that year to earn a playoff berth. They did it, drawing the largest viewing audiences in the history of three Phoenix television stations—the CBS, FOX, and ABC affiliates.

Led by Plummer the Cardinals had captured the imagination of Arizona fans. Everyone was giddy, including team ownership. In late December Arizona signed Plummer to a four-year contract extension worth nearly $30 million, including a $15 million signing bonus, the largest in NFL history. "This is a Christmas present to our fans," owner Bill Bidwill said.

The Cardinals were more popular than ever in Arizona, and "the Snake" was a big reason why. "That was huge for the organization," Plummer said of the playoff year. "We were finally getting a little publicity and a little credit for the kinds of players we had."

Critics of the deal correctly pointed out that the team signed Plummer at least a year before it had to. The only reason to do it so early, they said, was to help win support for a new stadium. The new contract made Plummer the focal point of criticism whenever things went wrong over the next four years. When players left in free agency, it was because the team couldn't afford to pay them because of Plummer's new deal. When Plummer struggled, it was because he felt the pressure of the hefty contract.

From 1999 through 2002, the Cardinals went 21–43. Early in 2003 management decided it was time to move on from Plummer, even though no heir apparent was on the roster. The Cardinals declined to put the franchise tag on Plummer, and he signed with the Denver Broncos.

In Arizona Plummer missed only two games in six years, but the Cardinals were 30–52 in games he started. In four seasons in Denver, Plummer proved the problems in Arizona had more to do with organization dysfunction than his perceived lack of development.

The Broncos went 39–15 with Plummer starting. After the 2006 season, Plummer abruptly retired at age 32. He was healthy, but he was just tired of football. Today, he lives with his family in the Denver area and travels to Phoenix often. He occasionally takes in a Cardinals game and looks back fondly at his years with the team. "Those were tough years, and it took a lot out of me," Plummer said. "But the Bidwill family treated me very well. A few years ago, I thanked Mr. Bidwill for all that he had done for me and my family. I'm still living off of that money. You have to thank a guy who allowed you to live such a comfortable life."

12 Two Hail Marys and a Hail, Larry

You could ask more from a sporting contest than what the Cardinals' 2015 divisional playoff game against the Green Bay Packers delivered. But you would be fairly labeled as a greedy malcontent. What other football game has ever had three coin tosses, two Hail Marys (in the same possession), questionable coaching strategy, a dynamic play to start overtime, and a game-winning touchdown that had only been practiced for, oh, about six months before being debuted?

If you weren't moved by the Cardinals' 26–20 overtime victory that day, you either didn't watch or don't have a pulse. Minutes after the game ended, Cardinals defensive tackle Frostee Rucker was asked to describe his reaction. "I don't know what to say," he said. "I don't even know my social security number."

Drama in postseason games against the Packers has become a tradition for the Arizona Cardinals. In the 2009 season, they beat the Packers in overtime during the wild-card round. Quarterback Kurt Warner had more touchdown passes (five) than incompletions (four) that day, but it took a fumble return by linebacker Karlos Dansby in overtime to win it for Arizona.

The 2015 game was even more incredible, and things became really exciting with about 11 minutes left in regulation. The Packers led 13–10. The Cardinals offense, ranked first in the NFL, had moved the ball only sporadically all day. But it began to click at the most opportune time. Quarterback Carson Palmer completed passes to convert third-down situations on three occasions. That brought the Cardinals to the Packers' 9-yard line. On first down Palmer threw hard to receiver Larry Fitzgerald on a slant. Cornerback Damarious Randall deflected the ball, which popped over the head of receiver John Brown and into the hands of teammate Michael Floyd for a touchdown. The Cardinals led 17–13 with 3:44 left. "It was a gift from God," Floyd said.

It looked like the Cardinals had clinched victory when they stopped the Packers on four downs and took possession at the Packers' 24-yard line with 2:38 remaining. But nothing in this game was simple and easy. On second down Palmer threw incomplete to Fitzgerald, who had man coverage on the outside. In that situation the vast majority of coaches would have ordered a running

On the first play of overtime of the divisional playoff game, Larry Fitzgerald runs through the Green Bay Packers defense for a 75-yard gain.
(USA TODAY Sports Images)

play to take the clock down to two minutes. Not Bruce Arians, who employed the self-described "no risk-it, no biscuit" philosophy.

The Cardinals settled for a field goal, which gave them a 20–13 lead with two minutes left. Enter Aaron Rodgers and the Packers. A sack and two incompletions left the Packers in a fourth-and-20 situation at their 4-yard line. Cardinals defensive coordinator James Bettcher wanted to play it safe, calling for a prevent defense. "No," Arians told him. "Go after him."

The Cardinals blitzed Rodgers from his right, forcing him to scramble left. He heaved the ball toward receiver Jeff Janis, who inexplicably had been left open by cornerback Justin Bethel.

That play gained 60 yards, and the Packers had life. Two plays later the Packers were at the Cardinals 41. With only five seconds remaining, they had time for one play. Again, the Cardinals blitzed. Again, Rodgers rolled to his left and threw deep. This time Janis was covered by two Cardinals: safety Rashad Johnson and cornerback Patrick Peterson. Somehow Janis caught the ball between the two of them.

Touchdown. Tie score. Overtime.

The captains met referee Clete Blakeman at mid-field for the coin flip. "Heads," Rodgers called. Blakeman tossed the coin, but it never flipped. "It went up like this," Cardinals long snapper Mike Leach said, as he raised a flat hand, "and then it went down like that."

Tails, Cardinals ball. Or so everyone thought for a second. The Packers complained, and Blakeman quickly grabbed the coin to toss it again. The Cardinals weren't happy, but Blakeman flipped it again. It was still tails and still Cardinals ball.

After a touchback the Cardinals took possession at their 20. On first down Palmer dropped back to pass and moved slightly to his right because of pressure. With no receivers open, he bumped into right tackle Bobby Massie, who was continuing to block. Palmer spun and looked to his left, where Fitzgerald stood uncovered.

Fitzgerald caught the ball and sprinted up the visitor's sideline. He cut back to avoid tacklers and stiff-armed another Packer. It looked he was going to score to end the game, but he was tackled at the 5. "He's the heart and soul of this team," Leach said. "He was on a mission."

Fitzgerald wasn't done. On second down he lined up in a tight formation, near the tight end. Palmer took the shotgun snap and shoveled the pass to Fitzgerald, who cut quickly up the middle for a touchdown. Game over. The headline in *The Arizona Republic* the next day read: "Hail, Larry."

Palmer said the play call was phenomenal. Fitzgerald, who finished with eight catches for 176 receiving yards, said his "eyes lit up in the huddle" when it was called. "We've been saving that little shovel pass for about 18 weeks," Arians said, "and it finally was the right time to use it."

It was the Cardinals' first playoff victory since that 2009 game against the Packers. And it was Palmer's first as a starting quarterback and Arians' first as a head coach. "I went over and wiped Carson's off his back, and he brushed mine off my back," Arians said the day after the game. "Those monkeys are good to get rid of."

13 Mario "Motts" Tonelli

Mario "Motts" Tonelli played parts of just two seasons for the Chicago Cardinals and didn't make much of an impact in those appearances, but what Tonelli endured between those two seasons, from 1940 and 1945, is very noteworthy. He survived the Bataan Death March and four years in Japanese prison of war camps.

Tonelli entered the service as a strapping 200-pound fullback. When the war ended, he weighed about half that.

Tonelli's amazing story began years before he donned a Cardinals or military uniform. At age six Tonelli suffered third-degree burns over 80 percent of his body when he accidentally tipped a burning garbage can on himself. Doctors told Tonelli's Italian-immigrant parents that their son might never walk again, but Tonelli's father wouldn't accept that. Using a door and some wheels, Celi Tonelli built a gurney that allowed young Mario to move about and regain his strength.

Tonelli not only walked again, but he also ran. And he did it well enough on the football field and track to draw the attention of the nation's biggest schools. Tonelli had decided to attend Southern California until Notre Dame coach Elmer Layden showed up at the Tonelli's home in Chicago with a priest who spoke Italian. That convinced Tonelli's mother, Lavania, that her son should be going to Notre Dame. Tonelli became a star there and made national headlines with a 77-yard run against Southern California that helped the Fighting Irish win the national championship. Cardinals owner Charlie Bidwill offered Tonelli a contract worth $4,000 for the 1940 season.

The war in Europe had yet to touch the United States, but it was clear where events were heading. Tonelli was among many young men who decided to sign up for a one-year hitch before resuming their lives. Then Pearl Harbor was bombed. Clark Field in the Philippines, where Tonelli was stationed, was next. With little food, ammunition, and medicine, the U.S. forces of around 10,000 on Bataan had no choice but to surrender.

Already starving and sick, the prisoners were forced to march mile after mile, day after day. Tonelli watched as soldiers collapsed and died along the way. Some were killed by Japanese soldiers, who also walked up and down the line of prisoners, confiscating anything of value, including money and jewelry.

One noticed that Tonelli was wearing a Notre Dame class ring and demanded Tonelli hand it over. Tonelli refused until he was threatened with a bayonet. "Give it to him," another soldier advised. "He'll kill you."

So Tonelli did. But a few minutes later, a Japanese officer approached and asked in perfect English: "Did one of my men take something from you?"

"Yes, my graduation ring from Notre Dame," Tonelli replied.

The officer handed it back to Tonelli and advised him to hide it during captivity. "I went to the University of Southern California," said the officer, who remembered Tonelli's 77-yard run against the Trojans.

Tonelli remained a prisoner for the next four years. He survived bouts with malaria and intestinal parasites. He lived through being transported on "Hell Ships," in which prisoners were crammed in cargo holds with their food delivered via the same buckets that carried their waste out of the hold.

When Tonelli arrived at the new prison camp, he was given a uniform that included a cap with a number on it. It was 58, his number at Notre Dame and with the Cardinals.

Tonelli figured it was a sign that he was going to survive. He did—barely. He was hospitalized upon his return to Chicago in 1945, where he was visited by Bidwill.

Tonelli wanted to play football again even if it was for one down. That seemed impossible given his physical condition. "He did something for me, for which I will always be grateful," Tonelli told Joe Ziemba, author of *When Football Was Football*, a history of the Chicago Cardinals. "Back in those days...you had to play both before and after the war in order to get credit for your pension for the seasons you missed during the war." By signing and being active for one game against the Green Bay Packers in 1945, Tonelli received credit for the four seasons he missed while a prisoner of war. "I will always be grateful to the Bidwills," Tonelli said.

Tonelli's return in 1945 was trumpeted by Chicago newspapers, but the years in prison camps had taken a physical toll. Numerous reports have Tonelli playing against the Packers. But according to researchers at the Pro Football Hall of Fame, Tonelli's name on the boxscore is scratched out with pencil, indicating he wasn't going to play.

After football Tonelli entered politics in Chicago, becoming the youngest of the board of commissioners in Cook County history. In all, he devoted 42 years to public service, retiring in 1988. It was only in his later years that Tonelli talked about his war experiences, and even then he did it not to brag but to remind Americans that a price was paid for their freedom.

A few months before his death in 2003, Tonelli was inducted into the Italian American Sports Hall of Fame. Here's how his obituary in the *Chicago Sun-Times* described Tonelli's appearance: "For four hours other sports greats basked in the spotlight, recounting their own glory. At nearly midnight Mr. Tonelli shuffled up to the microphones. He squinted at the bright lights, his voice soft and raspy in the microphone. He merely asked the audience to pray for America's soldiers and expressed his love for his country. The moment brought a crowd to its feet in tears."

14 The 1998 Regular Season Finale

For Bill Bidwill the tears came first. They were shed at Sun Devil Stadium in the early evening of December 27, 1998, and the drops were filled with the frustrations of 23 Cardinals seasons without a playoff berth. The ice cream—three scoops instead of the usual two

Bidwill enjoyed after a normal come-from-behind victory in the regular season—came later, just before bedtime.

The 16–13 win against the San Diego Chargers in the 1998 season finale was no ordinary victory. It earned the Cardinals a playoff berth in a non-strike year for the first time since 1975.

In the minutes afterward, the normally stoic Bidwill clutched a game ball, sharing a sense of disbelief with die-hard fans of his team. "I'm going to have to see it, or read about it [today], and then pinch myself to know that it happened," Bidwill said.

It happened, but barely. The Cardinals finished 9–7, their first winning season since moving to Arizona a decade before. Nearly every win came in dramatic fashion. Seven of the nine victories were by a combined 18 points, justifying the team's nickname of "Wild Cards."

The victory over San Diego was the ninth time in 26 games that quarterback Jake Plummer had led the Cardinals to victory after they had been tied or behind in the fourth quarter. "I'd get us in trouble but was able to help bail us out," said Plummer, who signed a contract worth $30 million in the last week of the regular season.

Fans were giddy after the San Diego game, and some stormed the field. One fan cracked his head open when he tumbled over the fence and hit an electric cart. Another was hit in the cheek, and a television reporter from San Diego lost her shoes in the chaos. "Guys were tugging at me and trying to take my helmet," said fullback Larry Centers. "They were almost as tough as the San Diego defense." Other fans just stood there in disbelief, as did Bidwill and some of the Cardinals players. "I didn't know how to feel," said Centers, who was drafted by the Cardinals in 1990. "I had been busting my butt for so long."

The moment didn't seem possible in early December. The Cardinals had lost two consecutive games to fall to 6–7, and they needed to win their last three games to have a chance at the wildcard. They did it in typical Wild Cards fashion. First, they overcame a seven-point deficit to beat the Eagles 20–17 in overtime in Philadelphia.

Then came another late comeback against the New Orleans Saints. The Cardinals trailed 17–16 when they took over at their 8-yard line with 1:21 left. Plummer hit receiver Frank Sanders for 25 and 28 yards to bring the Cardinals to the New Orleans 44. Two plays later Plummer scrambled up the middle for 21 yards to set up Chris Jacke's game-winning field goal on the last play of the game. That victory set up the importance of the season finale.

A Jacke field goal was the difference in that game, too, but it was the defense and special teams that won it. Cardinals safety Kwamie Lassiter intercepted four of quarterback Craig Whelihan's passes. And after the Chargers tied the game with 16 seconds remaining, Eric Metcalf returned a kick 46 yards to the Chargers 44. "They squibbed it pretty deep," Metcalf said. "I don't know if they were playing for us to do a middle return. That's what you normally do on a squib. But I know a lot of people thought we were just going overtime."

Six seconds were left. Plenty of time for Plummer to hit Sanders with a 10-yard pass and set Jacke up for the 52-yard field goal that gave the Cardinals the victory. Several of the Cardinals veterans couldn't believe what had just happened. "Are we really in the playoffs?" Centers asked at the time. "Are they going to make a bad call and tell us tomorrow that we're not in the playoffs after all?"

15 Bill Bidwill

In many ways Cardinals owner Bill Bidwill is a simple man. He loves history, cars, food, his family, and telling stories of what the NFL—and life—were like 70 years ago. But in many ways, Bidwill could be confounding when he was running the Cardinals. While he reveled in telling tales of the past, he was never much one for shedding light on the present. Whenever reporters asked him about current events with his team, his reply often was a smile, a shrug, and uplifted palms, as if to say, "darned if I know."

Bidwill was part of the NFL from his youngest days. He served as a ballboy in the 1940s when his father, Charles, owned the team. Bill and his brother, Stormy, assumed responsibility for the team soon after it moved to St. Louis, and Bill became sole owner when he bought his brother out in 1972. For most of his long career, Bidwill's name was synonymous with losing. He had a reputation for being cheap and accepting losing, as long as the team made money. Given the Cardinals' history of futility for most of 60 years, the labels were not inaccurate.

But neither do they present a 360-degree view of the man. Bidwill was generous, often donating to charities under the condition that the gifts remain anonymous. He did that in St. Louis and in Arizona. It's also a myth that winning wasn't important to him. He proved that when the team made it to the playoffs in 1998. From 1988 to 1998, the Cardinals had just one winning season in Arizona. They went 9–7 in 1998, clinching a playoff berth in the final game.

Bidwill clutched a gameball as he watched fans celebrate at Sun Devil Stadium that day. He could not hide his tears. "I'm going to have to see it, or read about it, and then pinch myself to know it happened," he said at the time.

As much as he loved the NFL and the Cardinals, Bidwill often appeared to have little clue about how to run a team. Employees, including players, weren't sure which Bill Bidwill was going to pass them in a hallway on a certain day: the one with a big smile and a hearty hello or the one who kept his head down to avoid personal contact. "That's the way he was," said Hall of Fame tackle Dan Dierdorf. "I always had a good relationship with Bill. He had some social-skill problems, okay, but no one who ever knew him would question that the man had a deep love of the National Football League. He realized the role his father played in the NFL and he was very proud of the fact the Bidwill family was one of the founding families of the NFL. He would have done anything for the league."

In Bidwill's later years, he became close with receiver Larry Fitzgerald, but that had more to do with Fitzgerald's outgoing personality. The young receiver loved to tease his owner, often hugging him and patting down Bidwill's pockets at the same time. It was an inside joke because no Cardinal was ever paid more by the Bidwills than Fitzgerald.

Other players did not find him so endearing. Former quarterback Jim Hart once went into Bidwill's office to ask for a raise. Bidwill took a seat behind his desk and took out an egg timer. "You've got three minutes," Bidwill said.

Dierdorf had a different relationship with the owner. "He didn't want to be close to the players," Dierdorf said. "It was a personal decision. He didn't want to be backslapping the players. That doesn't make him a bad person; that's just the way it is."

To illustrate the point, Dierdorf recalled the day he informed the Cardinals owner that he was retiring. Dierdorf's knee had given out in practice the day before, and he knew it was time. "I go into his office and sit down," Dierdorf said. "It might have been the second time in 13 years I had ever been in his office. I said, 'Now

I've got to say something. You can release me. It's well within your rights because I can't do this anymore.' He looked at me, and it was like I had just offered to take him out back and drive over him in my car. He had a stricken look and said, 'You don't think I would ever really do that?' He got up and said, 'Let's go get the PR people.' Then he stopped and said, 'It's been a wonderful 13 years.' He had tears in his eyes. I don't think many people who played for the Cardinals got to see that side of Bill Bidwill."

16 The Pottsville Curse

Any Cardinals fan who stuck by the franchise in the lean years—make that lean decades—would not dispute the assertion that the team is cursed. But by whom or what is a mystery to most of them. Some good folks in Pottsville, Pennsylvania, proudly proclaim themselves as the creators of a curse that's rooted in 1925, when the Chicago Cardinals won a disputed NFL title over the Pottsville Maroons.

That's right. Pottsville had a team back then. In fact, 1925 was the Maroons' first year in the NFL, and they were good, finishing with a 10–2 record that included a 21–7 victory against the Cardinals in Chicago. That game was billed as the NFL title game, even though there was no such thing in that day. The champion was determined by which team had the best record. That was the Maroons.

The team's owner wanted to cash in on the success. He agreed to play Notre Dame and its famous Four Horsemen in an exhibition game the following week in Philadelphia. But there was a problem. The Franklin Yellow Jackets complained to NFL president Joe Carr that Philadelphia was their territory—not the Maroons'. Carr agreed and warned the Maroons not to play the game. But the Maroons did, and Carr awarded the championship to the Cardinals.

Nearly a century later, that decision remains controversial. Sure, the Maroons had ignored Carr's warning, but the Cardinals weren't saints either. Four days after losing to Pottsville, the Cardinals beat a team called the Milwaukee Badgers 59–0. Just before the game, the Cardinals became aware the Badgers were using four players from a Chicago high school, including a 16-year-old.

Cardinals owner Chris O'Brien was fined $1,000. "Just before [the game started], I learned that there were high school amateurs on the Milwaukee team," he said in a statement. "Now I know the mistake I made was in not canceling the game right then. But there were several hundred people out there to see the game. Things were moving fast. I didn't sit down and think it out carefully."

Two days after the win against the Badgers, the Cardinals beat the Hammond Pros, who hadn't played in a game in more than a month. The Cardinals finished with an 11–2–1 mark and Carr proclaimed the Cardinals league champions, though O'Brien magnanimously refused the designation. The Cardinals didn't embrace the title until the 1930s after Charles Bidwill bought the team. And the Bidwills continued to defend the title for the next 80 years or so.

The folks of Pottsville still believe the title belongs to them. The NFL has considered the matter at least three times since 1925 and as recently as 2003. Each time the owners decided the title should stay with the Cardinals. Pennsylvania governor Ed Rendell got involved in the latest effort, but NFL owners stuck with the Cardinals by a vote of 30–2.

Siding with the Maroons, fellow Pennsylvanians, the Pittsburgh Steelers and Philadelphia Eagles, were the only dissenting votes. Owners did vote to give Pottsville an award for being one of the

NFL's pioneering communities. That placated no one. "The award is just something to keep us quiet," said Nicholas A. Barbetta, chairman of the Pottsville Maroons Memorial Committee, in 2003. "It's like winning a brand new car, then they turn around and give you a broken-down bicycle."

It's difficult to ascertain if the alleged Pottsville curse began in 1925 or in 2003, when the Cardinals were allowed to keep the title. As with most mystical things, the curse's authenticity can be questioned. The Cardinals won a championship in 1947 and played in the title game in 1948. Sure, they didn't do much in the six decades that followed, but what legitimate curse would allow a team to win even one title?

If the curse started in 2003, it's not working. University of Phoenix Stadium opened in 2006, providing the Cardinals a home of their own for the first time in franchise history. In the 2008 season, the team played in the Super Bowl. And from 2013 to '15, it won 34 games, the most in team history over a three-year period.

17 The 2015 Season

Whenever a football season ends, most coaches, including the Cardinals' Bruce Arians, look forward to their first extended downtime in months. But Arians felt different at the end of the 2014 season. The coach was so excited about the amount of talent returning that he was ready almost immediately to prepare for 2015. "I don't look at, 'What if?'" Arians said after injuries had ruined the 2014 season. "'What if?' will drive you crazy. I look at what can be, and what can be is a great football team with a few new pieces next year, but the core is here now."

Arians was right. The 2015 Cardinals fell short of "great," but they might have been the best team in franchise history. The Cardinals won the NFC West and set several single-season franchise records, including victories (13), road victories (seven), points (489), yards (6,533), and games won by at least 10 points (eight).

What they didn't do was win the Super Bowl. They played their worst game of the season in the NFC Championship Game, losing to the Carolina Panthers 49–15. "Unless the confetti is coming down on you and you're putting rings on, the season is not successful," Arians said the day after that loss. "That being said, there are a lot of good things that happened this year, goals that were met, big, big plays, big games."

Arians never attempted to manage expectations for the 2015 team. He knew the Cardinals were going to be good and made it clear that anything less than a Super Bowl ring would be a disappointment. He had every right to be optimistic. The Cardinals were in position to contend in 2014, but injuries to the top two quarterbacks, Carson Palmer and Drew Stanton, could not be overcome. The Cardinals had won 13 of Palmer's last 15 starts: 7–2 down the stretch in 2013 and 6–0 in 2014.

If Palmer returned healthy in 2015, the Cardinals were confident they were as good as any other team in the NFC. And that's what happened. Palmer returned in peak physical condition. Not only had he worked hard rehabilitating his knee, but Palmer also spent nearly the same amount of time strengthening his right shoulder. The difference was obvious from the first day of training camp.

Palmer wasn't the only key player who returned to health for the start of the 2015 season. Cornerback Patrick Peterson struggled early in 2014 and was later diagnosed with Type 2 diabetes. With that under control, Peterson lost weight and regained his speed and quickness. Defensive back Tyrann Mathieu, "the Honey Badger," had completely recovered from a severe knee injury suffered at the end of the 2013 season. Mathieu dubbed 2015 his "savage season." He explained why: "It's a mind-set," he said. "It's a mind-set to prove people wrong. I'm sure a lot of people didn't think I'd probably come back and be this good or be this effective for my team. For me it's just about proving people wrong, being accountable to my teammates and giving them my best every play, every down, and in the end, winning football games and stacking up some awards."

The Cardinals were good. They knew it and they proved it. They won their first three games by at least two scores. By mid-October they were 4–2 and entering the toughest part of the schedule. They met that challenge by winning nine consecutive games, the franchise's longest winning streak since the 1948 team won 10 in a row.

The season was filled with great stories. Mathieu played so well that he was a contender for Defensive Player of the Year until he suffered a knee injury on December 20. Palmer had the best season of his career. At 32 wide receiver Larry Fitzgerald finished with more than 1,000 receiving yards for the first time since 2010. Signed in mid-August running back Chris Johnson was on his way to a 1,000-yard season before suffering a leg injury in late November. Rookie David Johnson stepped in for Chris Johnson and showed signs of becoming a star.

But on a clear January night in Carolina, the season ended before the Cardinals expected. They were taken apart by the Panthers in every phase and looked nothing like the team that had breezed through the regular season. The disappointment was obvious afterward. The Cardinals were not some plucky team that overachieved to come within a win of making the Super Bowl.

From the minute the 2014 season ended, they looked forward to contending for a title in 2015.

Fitzgerald fought backs tears when talking to reporters after the loss in the NFC Championship Game. "You put so much pressure on yourself," Fitzgerald said. "Seven months it's been the journey, the mental strain, the focus that it requires to be able to have sustained success like we were able to this year. It's great, but it takes a great toll on you. Just sleepless nights and restless days where things don't go well. It really affects you."

18 Jimmy Conzelman

In today's NFL a head coach who sleeps at the office no more than three nights a week is regarded as a renaissance man. But at one time, and in at least one city, there was a place in the NFL for a true renaissance man. It was in Chicago from 1946 to 1948, and Jimmy Conzelman was the perfect choice by Cardinals owner Charles Bidwill to blend a team of youngsters and war veterans into a championship contender.

Football coach was only one of Conzelman's many titles. He was an accomplished actor and musician. A writer, he spent part of the offseasons on assignment for magazines such as *Collier's* and *The Saturday Evening Post*. A gifted public speaker, he gave a memorable commencement address at the University of Dayton in 1942 about young men going to war that was required reading at West Point for a time. No wonder most of his players called him "Jimmy." The term "Coach" didn't seem to fit. "I never did regard Jimmy as the smartest football coach in the world," center

The Ring of Honor

Jimmy Conzelman is one of 15 men in the Cardinals ring of honor at University of Phoenix Stadium. Here are the others:

Ernie Nevers, fullback
John "Paddy" Driscoll, quarterback/defensive back
Charles W. Bidwill Sr., owner
Charley Trippi, halfback
Ollie Matson, halfback
Dick "Night Train" Lane, cornerback
Marshall Goldberg, halfback/defensive back
Dan Dierdorf, offensive tackle
Pat Tillman, safety
Larry Wilson, safety
Roger Wehrli, cornerback
Aeneas Williams, cornerback
Kurt Warner, quarterback
Adrian Wilson, safety

But there are three others who deserve to be included.

1. Jackie Smith, tight end—Twelve former Cardinals are in the Pro Football Hall of Fame. Eleven of them are in the team's ring of honor. Smith is the exception. Why? It's apparently because of a testy relationship with owner Bill Bidwill. Smith was critical of the organization at the end of his tenure in St. Louis, something that apparently has not been forgotten. The two sides should move past those hard feelings. Smith played 15 of his 16 NFL seasons for the St. Louis Cardinals and was among the best tight ends of his generation.

2. Jim Hart, quarterback—Hart's absence is also a head scratcher. He played 18 seasons for the Cardinals—more than any other player—and is second to kicker Jim Bakken in most games played with 199. Hart made the Pro Bowl four times. He also butted heads occasionally with Bidwill.

3. Larry Centers, fullback—Centers is one of the best pass-catching running backs in NFL history. The Cardinals had many lean seasons in Centers' tenure (1990–98), and he often was one of the few reasons to watch their games. There apparently were some hard feelings when he was allowed to depart via free agency. Centers frequently visits Arizona and considers himself a Cardinal.

Bill Blackburn once said. "But he could make a player produce 150 percent when he didn't even know he had 10."

Conzelman was a player-coach for four teams in the 1920s, including champion Providence in 1928. As a coach, Conzelman didn't care much for Xs and Os. As a former player, he respected the opinions of the men he coached and he listened to them when it came to strategy. Cardinals quarterback Paul Christman and others were allowed to create and tinker with plays and strategy. Several years ago, Cardinals owner Bill Bidwill recalled one time when the experimentation backfired, and a play lost considerable yardage. A reporter asked Conzelman what he planned to do about it. "Nothing," said Conzelman, who was inducted into the Hall of Fame in 1964. "It wasn't a bad idea."

Conzelman was the perfect man hired at the most opportune time. By 1946 Cardinals owner Charles Bidwill had grown frustrated with losing. His was the second most popular team in town behind the Bears, and a fledgling league was planning to bring a third team to the city.

That didn't sit well with Bidwill, a sportsman who hated losing and appearing in small letters on the marquee. Bidwill hired Conzelman, and the two of them put together a team that won the 1947 title—the Cardinals' last NFL championship—and made it to the 1948 title game.

Bidwill was willing to spend money, signing running back Charley Trippi to a four-year deal worth $100,000, an astounding amount in 1947. Conzelman had an eye for talent and character. Running back Elmer Angsman played for Notre Dame, so he was well-known and had a reputation for toughness. In college he once practiced two days after having nine teeth knocked out against Navy. "Dad said, 'Get him. I want someone that tough,'" Jimmy Conzelman Jr. said in 1997.

Conzelman knew how to lead men, too. Running backs Pat Harder and Angsman, part of the "million-dollar backfield" enjoyed the nightlife Chicago had to offer. So Conzelman came up with a scheme to keep them in line. "He called me in and said, 'Elmer, Harder has been a tough Marine and he doesn't have that great religious background that you have. Can you keep an eye on him?'" Angsman said during 1997, the 50th anniversary of the championship team.

Near the same time, Conzelman told Harder that as a veteran he had a duty to keep an eye on Angsman, who was just a cocky kid out of Notre Dame. After a few days of sitting around and going to bed early, Angsman looked at Harder and said, "You know, if it wasn't for you, I'd be out having a good time."

"What do you mean?" Harder replied.

"Well, Coach told me to keep an eye on you."

"On me?" Harder said. "He told me to watch *you*."

They didn't spend many more nights sitting at home.

Conzelman was a master at motivation and he wasn't above using corny props and stories to make his point. Before games he often told players to "turn it on." To emphasize that point, he once had a giant replica of a faucet brought into the locker room. "Jim gave us pep talks that were kind of laughable," Trippi said. "He wanted us to enjoy them and take part in his speeches. And we did."

But the good times didn't last for the Cardinals. After the 1948 title game, Conzelman resigned to take a job with an advertising firm in St. Louis, a big reason the franchise wasn't able to sustain success. "He was like a father to us on the football field," Trippi said. "Jim was just one of a kind. I would love to see everybody in football have a coach like that at one point in their careers."

19 Memorize Dennis Green's Monday Night Meltdown

Longtime Cardinals fans have scars from the franchise's decades of struggles. Broken so many times, their hearts are held together by an epoxy made of hope, stubbornness, and perhaps, most important of all, a sense of humor. If newer fans want to fit in with this grizzled bunch, developing a sense of the team's history, at least in Arizona, is essential. And nothing will show your passion like memorizing coach Dennis Green's tirade after the Cardinals blew a 20-point lead and lost to the Chicago Bears on *Monday Night Football* in 2006.

First, some background. The Cardinals played the Bears in the third preseason game that year. They played pretty well, too, beating the Bears, who were a much better team. But it was preseason, and to most people, that meant nothing. But it did to Green, as you will be able to tell by his tantrum.

The regular-season contest against the Bears was the first Monday night game at University of Phoenix Stadium, which had opened that year. The Cardinals were 1–4 entering that game but believed a victory against the Bears could change their season. And for the first half, the Cardinals looked like a new team. Rookie quarterback Matt Leinart was sharp, picking apart the Bears with short, accurate passes. The Cardinals led 23–3, comfortably on their way to an upset.

Or so it appeared.

They collapsed in the second half, thanks in part to turnovers and Green becoming conservative on offense. The Bears won 24–23, which prompted Green's meltdown.

His press conference afterward began slowly with Green giving perfunctory answers to expected questions. Then, someone asked

Green this question about Bears quarterback Rex Grossman: "You forced Rex into four picks and two fumbles. What did you see about the Bears to shut them down that way?"

That query launched one of the greatest meltdowns by a coach in NFL history, a reason to visit YouTube.com, and even a Coors Light commercial. "The Bears are who we thought they were," Green said. "They're what we thought they were. We played them in preseason. Who the hell takes the third game likes it's bullshit? Bullshit!"

With the rare back-to-back expletives, Green was just warming up: "We played them in the third game. Everybody played three quarters. The Bears are who we thought they were! And that's why we took the damn field. Now, if you want to crown them, then crown their ass!" said Green, who slapped the microphone in front of him. "But they are who we thought they were! And we let 'em off the hook!"

After a few seconds of silence, a Cardinals spokesman ended the news conference, and Green left the room.

20 Charley Trippi

In early 1947 Charley Trippi was a wanted man, and no wanted Trippi as badly as Chicago Cardinals owner Charles Bidwill. Bidwill was a year into building the Cardinals into a winner, and while progress had been made, acquiring Trippi would make the franchise an instant contender for the NFL title. Bidwill got his man, signing Trippi to a four-year, $100,000 contract, an astounding amount at the time.

No one complained that Bidwill had overpaid, and the owner was ecstatic to sign Trippi. According to *When Football Was Football*, an excellent history of the Chicago Cardinals, Bidwill told reporters: "I would like to say this means a championship for the Cardinals, but you know that's going too far. They'll know we're in the league anyway!"

People found that out quickly. The Cardinals won the NFL title in 1947 and lost in the 1948 championship game. Trippi was the final piece. He scored two long touchdowns in the 1947 championship game and ended up playing nine years for the Cardinals and then serving as an assistant coach for several more. "Back when I played, we just enjoyed playing football," Trippi said. "Money was secondary because a lot of players didn't make a lot of money playing football back then."

Trippi did and he was worth every penny. The Cardinals drafted Trippi in 1945 and desperately wanted him when he was released from military duty. The problem was that so did two New York Yankees teams, the baseball variety and the Yankees of the new All-America Football Conference. Trippi, who played at Georgia, was well-known throughout the country and would help at the ticket office. He could help on the field, too.

Bidwill knew that and he turned on the charm and opened his checkbook to get Trippi. He established a relationship early with Trippi. The two men made an instant connection, and Trippi soon gave Bidwill his word that he would sign with the Cardinals. "My dad is the kind of person, who if he had made someone a promise or had a gentleman's handshake to do something, then by God, he was going to do it," said Charles Trippi Jr. "No matter what else came up."

In 1947 it was money that came up. The football Yankees reportedly offered Trippi more than the Cardinals, but he had made a promise to Charles Bidwill. "Nobody in the Cardinals organization had any contacts with Trippi outside of Charlie," team president Ray Benningsen said, according to *When Football Was Football*. "It was his greatest victory."

Trippi made far more money than his teammates, but he was readily accepted because of his humble nature and his talent. Growing up, Trippi Jr. rarely heard his father talk about his football exploits, even though Trippi Sr. is in the Professional and College Football Halls of Fame. And that's even though he played halfback for five seasons with the Cardinals, quarterback for two, and defense for another two. He averaged 5.1 yards per rush, still the highest average in Cardinals history. "I remember he took me to a Falcons game in Atlanta when I was 12, 13 years old," Trippi Jr. said. "We were in the press box and enjoying the game, having lunch. Just before halftime, he said, 'Sit here, I have to go somewhere.' Next thing I know he's down on the field, receiving an award."

21 Dan Dierdorf

Decades ago the NFL draft was a quiet affair, which is hard to believe given that it's practically a national holiday today. It wasn't broadcast, and camera crews didn't show players waiting anxiously, surrounded by families. In 1971 Dan Dierdorf's draft day experience was typical. The phone rang. It was the St. Louis Cardinals, telling him he'd been taken in the second round with the 43rd overall pick. That was about it for excitement. "I'd never been to St. Louis before," Dierdorf said. "I grew up in in Ohio, went to college at Michigan. I was a Cleveland Browns fan and I just remember

Long before he became a famous announcer, Dan Dierdorf was a ferocious offensive tackle for the St. Louis Cardinals. (USA TODAY Sports Images)

the Browns played the St. Louis Cardinals a lot. And the Cardinals seemed to win most of those games. So I didn't like the Cardinals. They beat up on my Brownies."

Dierdorf spent the next 13 years playing on the Cardinals offensive line. He played mostly right tackle but a little left tackle, too, and some guard and center in a pinch. One of the bigger players of his time, the 6'3", 275-pound Dierdorf made the Pro Bowl six times and was All-Pro five times. He is in the team's ring of honor and was inducted into the Pro Football Hall of Fame in 1996. In his induction speech, he summed up his playing style. "I look at the first couple of plays as being of extra importance," he said. "In those first few plays, I try to remove any thought my opponent might have had that that was gonna be his day."

Dierdorf possessed a rare blend of size, quickness, speed, and power. With the Cardinals in the 1970s, he anchored an offensive line that led the NFL three times in fewest sacks allowed.

Asked to describe Dierdorf as a player, former quarterback Jim Hart's first words were, "Holy mackerel! Left defensive ends didn't get in my face often, even the likes of the Cowboys' 'Too Tall' Jones. Those ends didn't get in because Dan was just so strong. He didn't even lift weights that much in his career. We didn't have any weights for many years. We didn't have a weight room until later in the '70s, and it was an old closet down in the bowels of Busch Stadium."

Dierdorf played both guard and tackle his first two seasons and settled in at right tackle during his third. By the mid-1970s, he was the leader of perhaps the NFL's finest offensive line.

In 1975 the Cardinals set an NFL record by allowing only eight sacks in 14 games. That's even more remarkable, considering they had perhaps the most sophisticated passing attack in the NFL. They passed 355 times that year, an average of more than 25 a game.

Omo and the Machine

John Omohundro and Jim "the Machine" Shearer spent the better part of four decades with the Cardinals, and within the NFL, their names were almost legendary. Yet, most Cardinals fans probably had no idea who they were. Such is the fate of an athletic trainer, and "Omo" and "the Machine" were quite happy to work behind the scenes.

They did far more than tape ankles, fill ice bags, and help injured players to the sideline. Omohundro and Shearer were friends and confidants to countless players over the decades.

Omohundro came to the Cardinals in 1967 and retired 41 years later. He hired Shearer in 1974, and Shearer retired 39 years later. Both could write a series of books about their experiences. "I promised the players I wouldn't do that," Omohundro said, laughing.

That's a "damn good thing," said former Cardinals tackle Dan Dierdorf. "We don't need Omo spilling the beans on any locker room secrets."

The two athletic trainers had dramatically different personalities; perhaps that's why the combination worked so well. Omohundro was quick to smile, joke, and make a bad pun. There weren't many people he didn't like, and most everyone liked him in return. Shearer was crusty and possessed an acerbic wit. If Shearer didn't give you a bad time, it meant he didn't like you.

Like Omohundro, Shearer was well-known throughout the NFL. But hardly anyone ever called him by his given name. He was always "the Machine," or just "Machine." According to Dierdorf, a masterful move by Omohundro was behind the nickname. Players had to have their ankles taped before practices, and Omohundro, who was excellent at taping, would intentionally tape a little too tight so the player would get a slight nick in the back of his Achilles. It wasn't long before players started opting for Shearer to tape their ankles, not Omohundro. "If 50 guys were getting their ankles taped, 40 went to 'Machine,' and the other 10 dummies went to Omo," Dierdorf said.

So Shearer had to work faster and players nicknamed him "the Machine" because of how quickly and efficiently he could tape. "John was a brilliant man," Dierdorf said. "He could stand there and tell stories and laugh while 'Machine' was working his ass off. Thus, 'the Machine' is born."

Dierdorf didn't miss a game until 1977, when he suffered a broken jaw. A knee injury forced him to miss most of the 1979 season, but he made the All-Pro team in 1980. By 1983 Dierdorf's knees were shot. During practice one day midway through the season, a knee gave out while he executed a simple one-on-one block. "I went home and told my wife, 'That's it,'" Dierdorf said.

The next day, Dierdorf informed owner Bill Bidwill, who asked Dierdorf if he was sure.

Dierdorf said he was, and Bidwill headed for the door to tell people in the public relations department. "He stopped and looked at me and said, 'It's been a wonderful 13 years,'" Dierdorf said. "He had tears in his eyes. I was so moved by that."

After their retirements Dierdorf and Hart opened a line of restaurants in the St. Louis area, most notably a steakhouse called Dierdorf and Hart's. "He's responsible for Dierdorf and Hart's restaurant being open for 30 years," Hart said. "He's got a business sense like you wouldn't believe."

Hart laughed when recalling the "research" that went into the two players entering the restaurant business. On many road trips, the two would try to find a nice steakhouse and then talk about opening a place after they retired. "We'd taste the steak and think, *We can do better,*" Hart said. "And we always wanted the beer to be colder. That was what we wanted in a place: cold beer and a good steak."

Dierdorf became even more well known nationally after retiring as a player. He was an analyst on NFL broadcasts, including on *Monday Night Football*, for ABC and then CBS from 1985 to 2013, when he announced his retirement from the booth. The retirement didn't last long. In 2014 Dierdorf became part of the broadcasting crew for his alma mater, Michigan. "This is the only broadcasting job that I would have considered after retiring from network television," he said.

22 Cardiac Cardinals

No one is sure exactly when the phrase "Cardiac Cardinals" was first used or who coined it. But it sure fit the St. Louis Cardinals teams of the mid-1970s. They featured high-powered offenses and a knack for taking games down to the final seconds and winning them. In 1974 the Cardinals won five of their first seven games by a touchdown or less. They clinched the NFC East title by beating the New York Giants in the final game of the season.

In 1975 eight of their games went down to the final minute. The Cardinals won seven of them, including one against Washington when receiver Mel Gray caught a controversial touchdown pass from Jim Hart. Dubbed the "Phantom Catch" because it was questionable whether Gray had it long enough to count, the score sent the game into overtime, and the Cardinals won 20–17. "Even when we didn't win, there was a lot of entertainment value, and I think that's important," said Hall of Fame offensive lineman Dan Dierdorf. "Fans, even back then, what they wanted is for you to be competitive. They liked to believe when you got to the stadium, you got a chance to win and that you're going to be in it in the fourth quarter. And those teams were exciting. We may have lost the game, but, by God, we lost 35–31."

The Cardinals of the mid-1970s were exciting partly because they didn't play the game like everyone else. Coach Don Coryell believed in the passing game and he had threats at every position: Jim Hart at quarterback, Terry Metcalf at running back, Mel Gray at receiver, J.V. Cain at tight end, and a great offensive line led by Dierdorf, Tom Banks, and Conrad Dobler.

Coryell didn't think like every other coach. For instance, the Dallas Cowboys were using their "flex defense" in those days, which featured lineman Randy White lining up a few yards off the ball. On running plays offensive linemen had trouble reaching White, who used the extra time and space to determine where the plays were going. "Don Coryell took one look at that and said, 'Why are we trying to run the ball? Let's just throw the ball on first down,'" Dierdorf said. "And we tortured the Cowboys. Our guards were the happiest guys in the world. You want to stick Randy White and Harvey Martin two yards off the ball? We'll throw it. Don wasn't afraid to do things like that."

From 1974 through 1976, the Cardinals won 31 games. Hart had his best seasons in the NFL, as did Gray. Metcalf became perhaps the league's most versatile weapon during the time.

But those teams didn't win a playoff game. They had the bad luck to never play at home in the playoffs and they were never stout enough on defense to contain elite offenses.

All the players appreciated Coryell's brilliance, but there was no question he was an offensive coach. "His type of offense was a perfect fit for the personnel we had on the Cardinals," said former cornerback Roger Wehrli. "He had a great offensive mind and in fact paid little attention to the defense. He knew he had a defense, but I'm not sure he knew all our names. Did I mention he had a great offensive mind?"

The Cardiac Cardinals flatlined later in the decade because of poor drafting, other poor personnel decisions, and Coryell's departure after the 1977 season. "The teams of the mid-70s were as good as any team in the league," Wehrli said. "We were known as the Cardiac Cardinals, but we probably lacked maybe one or two players to get further in the playoffs consistently."

23 Bruce Arians

Bruce Arians' football philosophy is as bold and unique as his sense of fashion. He loves wearing Gatsby hats and throwing deep. He favors designer eyewear and provocative play calls. He rarely wears beige or plays it safe in games or most anything else in life. "No risk-it, no biscuit," he likes to say.

That's how Arians coaches football, plays golf, and attacks life. Cowards lay up when confronted by water and always run the ball on third and inches. Not Arians. It's probably one reason he was an assistant in the National Football League for 20 years before anyone interviewed him for a head coaching job. "Honestly, he was overlooked for years," said his wife Christine. "He didn't even get an interview. I always said it's because the man has no idea how to play politics. He doesn't sugarcoat. And when it comes to football, he truly believes he's right."

Judging from Arians' first three seasons with the Cardinals, it's hard to believe the man is ever wrong. The Cardinals won at least 10 games in three consecutive seasons for the first time since 1974–76 and qualified for the playoffs twice. In 2015 the Cardinals won 13 games, a franchise record for victories in a season.

Before taking the Cardinals job, Arians had coached 38 years, including coaching running backs for Paul "Bear" Bryant at Alabama, and had one stint as a head coach: at Temple for six years. He had some success at Temple but not enough, and the job took a toll. Arians didn't know how to delegate responsibility and ended up sick with migraines. "I was head coach, offensive coordinator, quarterback coach, recruiting coordinator, and chief fund-raiser," Arians says. "I wore every hat."

Arians learned from that experience, and he hasn't had a migraine since Temple fired him in 1988. He was a wishbone quarterback at Virginia Tech, so it's ironic that he's become known as a quarterback whisperer in the pass-happy NFL. Over the last two decades, he's coached some of the game's best quarterbacks, including Peyton Manning, Ben Roethlisberger, Andrew Luck, and Carson Palmer.

For years it was an impressive resume largely ignored by owners when they searched for head coaches. It took a twist of fate and a fairy-tale season for him to become a head coach in the NFL. After the 2011 season, Arians was fired as offensive coordinator by the Pittsburgh Steelers, reportedly because ownership thought he passed too much and wasn't tough enough on Roethlisberger.

The Steelers announced that Arians was retiring, which was sort of true in that Arians and Christine had no plans. They were in the midst of moving from Pittsburgh to their "forever home" in Georgia when Arians' cell phone rang. It was Chuck Pagano, the new Indianapolis Colts coach, asking if Arians was really retiring or was interested in coaching.

Pagano knew the answer. So did Christine. "Oh, no," Christine said in the car that day. "You're going to take that job."

He did. And when Pagano was diagnosed with leukemia early in the season, Arians went from offensive coordinator to interim coach. He guided the Colts to a 9–3 record and was later named the 2012 Coach of the Year.

As a head coach, Arians was as brash, cocky, and demanding as he was as an assistant.

One day in practice early that year, Arians, the offensive coordinator, dressed in black from head to toe. "You look like you're going to a funeral," Colts cornerback Jerraud Powers said.

"I am," Arians responded.

"Oh, yeah. Who died?"

"You did. Because we killed you fuckers yesterday."

Arians has coached that same way with the Cardinals, which doesn't surprise his son, Jake, who for years has met him at the Senior Bowl in Mobile, Alabama. While there, Arians often vowed that he would never change if fortunate enough to become an NFL head coach. "He would always point out the guys who had changed when they became head coaches," Jake says. His dad referred to it as "taking the pill."

Arians has never taken the pill. He is loud in practice and profane on the field and in the meeting rooms. Don't take it personally, he tells his players. "I like you as a person," he says, "it's your football that stinks."

"Guys get ticked off about it, but that's just his way of making us keep the edge," said Powers, who signed with the Cardinals in 2013. "Even though we're out there competing for ourselves and want to do great, in the back of our heads, we're trying to do stuff so we can go back and be like, 'Now, what are you going to say?'"

Arians is harder on quarterbacks than anyone, but he also develops a stronger connection to them than other players. That's a necessity, he says, because the NFL is a quarterback-driven league. "He's as smart of football mind as there is in the game," Palmer said. "He doesn't waver, he doesn't change week to week. After a win it's the same as after a loss. You've got to be ready to be chewed out after a win or a loss. He wants to put that pressure on you, that kind of tough-minded, never-good-enough mentality because he knows that's what it takes to win."

The marriage between Arians and the Cardinals has worked out so well that it seems a higher power must have been at work. And maybe it was, if you consider desperation—or something close to it—a higher power. Both sides looked at other options in January of 2013 before finding themselves out of potential dance partners. Arians thought he was going to get the Chicago Bears job and didn't. Meanwhile, a handful of other teams cancelled interviews. The Cardinals talked to other candidates, but interest wasn't always reciprocated. The Cardinals and Arians fell into each other's arms over dinner.

Team president Michael Bidwill had to laugh when Arians dropped three f-bombs in one sentence. Bidwill and general manager Steve Keim were smart enough to quickly reach a deal with Arians. Two years later Bidwill signed Arians to a new contract. "He probably doesn't meet central casting for that proto-typical NFL coach, but that doesn't matter to our players, it doesn't matter to our fans," Bidwill told *The New York Times*. "What matters is we've got a great football coach."

Back-to-Back NFC East Champs in 1974 and 1975

The Cardinals won only one of their last seven games in 1973, but, oddly, there was no shortage of optimism among the players as they reported for training camp in 1974. They had a coach, Don Coryell, in whom they had great belief. They had the makings of a dominant offensive line, one of the league's best quarterbacks in Jim Hart, a great tight end in Jackie Smith, and a dynamic all-around offensive threat in back Terry Metcalf.

As it turns out, the players knew what most of their fans didn't: a new era of Cardinals football was dawning. The Cardinals won the NFC East title in 1974 and made the playoffs for the first time since 1948. They followed up that up with another division title in 1975, finishing 11–3, the team's best record since going 11–1 in 1948. "We were in the NFC East when the NFC East was the NFC

East," said Dan Dierdorf, the team's Hall of Fame lineman. "If you won the NFC East, that's because you beat Roger Staubach and the Dallas Cowboys. If you won the NFC East, it's because you beat Sonny Jurgensen and the Washington Redskins. You did not win the NFC East by going 7–9 like you can now. This was a division filed with Hall of Fame players and iconic franchises."

The NFL's playoff format was different back then. Today, division winners are assured of playing their first postseason game at home. The 1974 and 1975 Cardinals, however, had to go on the road for their first playoff games. That contributed to those being their only playoff games. In 1974 the Cardinals had to travel to Minnesota for the divisional playoff game. At Metropolitan Stadium that day, it was 19 degrees with a windchill of 9 degrees.

The Cardinals stayed close in the first half, scoring first on a 13-yard pass from Jim Hart to receiver Earl Thomas. The Vikings responded with a touchdown, and the game was tied at halftime. Minnesota put the game away in the third quarter, scoring 16 points, including on a 20-yard fumble return. The Cardinals defense couldn't hold up against the Vikings running attack. Minnesota ran 42 times for 199 yards with Chuck Foreman gaining 114 yards.

History repeated in 1975. In the height of their "Cardiac Cardinals" days, the Cardinals went 11–3, and Metcalf set a then-NFL record for combined yards with 2,462. But the Cardinals still couldn't get a home playoff game. They traveled to Los Angeles, where the Rams beat them 35–23. The Cardinals could not stop Rams running back Lawrence McCutcheon, who rushed for 202 yards, and Los Angeles returned two interceptions by Hart for touchdowns in the first half and led 28–9. "We always wished we could have a game at home," Dierdorf said. "There weren't as many playoff teams back then, so you're 11–3 and you still have to go on the road. That would never happen today."

It was 23 years before the Cardinals would make the playoffs again in a non-strike year. "I never won a playoff game; I only played in three," Dierdorf said. "It's just proof how hard it is to win in the National Football League and how hard it is to win consistently for a long time. That's why people like myself have admiration for franchises like the Patriots and what they've done, consistently winning every year. It's damn hard to do."

25 Moving to St. Louis

Through most of the 1950s, rumors swirled that the Cardinals were interested in migrating from Chicago to a new home where they wouldn't have to compete with another NFL team for attention. Walter Wolfner, the Cardinals managing director and second husband to Violet Bidwill, consistently denied the rumors. And late in the decade, he reached an agreement for the team to play at Soldier Field.

But the team's situation in Chicago remained tenuous. Wolfner butted heads with Chicago owner George Halas, which was not a good thing in Chicago. And CBS reportedly was pressuring the NFL to have just one team—the Bears—in Chicago. The Cardinals, meanwhile, were struggling to make it as the second team in the Second City. According to the *Chicago Tribune*, the Cardinals had trouble paying visiting teams the $30,000 they were guaranteed.

The Cardinals lasted just one season at Soldier Field. In the spring of 1960, the NFL granted Wolfner permission to move the franchise to St. Louis, which was his home. Two years later Violet died and left a three-page will. In it, she passed ownership of the franchise on to her sons, Charles Bidwill Jr., known as "Stormy," and William Bidwill, "Bill" or "Billy" to many.

Wolfner contested the will, which left him only a few oil wells in Oklahoma. In court documents Wolfner revealed that Stormy and Bill Bidwill had been adopted by Violet and her first husband, Charles Bidwill. The adoptions, he argued, were not valid. The two sons were stunned; no one had ever told them they were adopted. Wolfner petitioned the court to declare the adoptions illegal. The judge rejected that argument. In the ruling the judge wrote: "On all the evidence before it, the County Court found that the mothers had consented to the adoption, and these decrees cannot be challenged 30 years later for any of the reasons urged by Wolfner."

So Stormy and Bill inherited the team and retained their previous titles. Stormy was president, and Bill was the vice president. Stormy, the oldest, ran the team, but there were challenges. The team played at Sportsman's Park, a 34,000-seat stadium, and the Cardinals had no regular practice site. They practiced at an open field in a city park. In 1964 Atlanta tried to lure the Cardinals. But the promise of a new stadium kept the Cardinals in St. Louis, and they began playing in Busch Memorial Stadium in 1966. A record crowd of 50,673 attended a game against the Dallas Cowboys, setting an attendance record that would stand four seasons.

Over the years the relationship between Stormy and Bill reportedly deteriorated. "His idea of how to run the team and mine were different," Stormy told the *Chicago Tribune*. "The leaving wasn't easy for either of us." Bill had moved to St. Louis to run the team, and Stormy stayed in Chicago to oversee the family's racing businesses. In 1972 the brothers reached an agreement. Bill bought

Stormy's share of the Cardinals reportedly for around $6 million. And Stormy took over the family's interests in racing horses and dogs.

26 Anquan Boldin

NFL general managers and coaches spend considerable time describing to scouts what they want in players other than obvious attributes such as size, speed, and quickness. Toughness, passion, and heart are difficult to measure. From 2003 through 2009, Cardinals front-office executives could have skipped the speech and instead shown their scouts a picture of Anquan Boldin.

Everything a football team could want was inside the 6'1", 218-pound receiver the team drafted in the second round out of Florida State in 2003. "Stopwatches can't judge talent," said ex-Cardinals coach Dave McGinnis during Boldin's rookie season. "I have coached some great players in this league, Hall of Fame players, and this kid's foundation, as solid as he is, has all the attributes of all of them."

For most of his seven seasons in Arizona, Boldin was the face of the franchise. He was an impact player from his first game through his last. Boldin had 217 receiving yards in his first game with the Cardinals, an NFL record for a player in his first game. And he was a productive player long after the team traded him to the Baltimore Ravens in 2010.

When Boldin left Arizona, he held team records for career receptions, receptions in a season, and most consecutive games catching a touchdown pass. For his last six seasons, he teamed with

Larry Fitzgerald to form one of the NFL's most dangerous receiving duos. "He plays with a chip on his shoulder as if he was affronted by someone or something," Fitzgerald said.

It's odd to imagine now, but not every Cardinals decision-maker was sold on Boldin back in 2003. He had suffered a knee injury at Florida State, was leaving school a year early, and hadn't run well for scouts (4.7 seconds in the 40-yard dash). But at least three people in the organization loved him: McGinnis, offensive coordinator/receivers coach Jerry Sullivan, and scout Steve Keim, who later became the team's general manager. That trio lobbied heavily for Boldin, convincing general manager Rod Graves to take him in the second round, even though the club had drafted a receiver, Bryant Johnson, in the first.

In Arizona, Boldin was the best player on a lot of bad teams. Often, he was one of the few reasons to watch the Cardinals. Ironically, his opinion of the franchise began to sour just as it began to experience success. In training camp of 2008, Boldin vehemently criticized coach Ken Whisenhunt and management, accusing them of reneging on a promise of a new contract.

Boldin vowed never to sign another contract with the team. Whisenhunt and the Cardinals blamed the problem on Boldin's agent, Drew Rosenhaus. In the meantime the Cardinals signed Fitzgerald to another huge contract, and it was obvious the team would not be able to afford to keep both of its elite receivers.

Boldin never held out, however, and proved his toughness again in late September. The Cardinals were getting blown out that day by the New York Jets in New Jersey. It was an ugly game, the kind that both players and fans want to end as fast as possible. But the Cardinals had put up a fight in the second half and were trying to score in the final seconds. Kurt Warner threw to Boldin in the end zone. The pass was a little high, and as Boldin tried to make the catch, safety Kerry Rhodes hit him from behind, propelling Boldin toward safety Eric Smith, who was closing fast. That helmet-to-helmet hit by Smith was not easily forgotten.

The sound of the hit reverberated through the lower part of the stadium. Everyone became silent when they saw Boldin prone in the end zone. He was knocked cold and suffered several facial

Wide receiver Anquan Boldin, who recorded 586 receptions for 7,520 yards during his seven years in Arizona, makes a one-handed catch against Denver Broncos cornerback Domonique Foxworth in 2006.

fractures, as well as dental damage. At first, the Cardinals were terrified the injury was more severe than that. Seven plates, 40 screws, and three weeks later, Boldin was playing again. In his first five games back, he caught 46 passes for 513 yards and six touchdowns. "What Anquan has done is so unbelievable," Whisenhunt said at the time.

The Cardinals advanced to the first Super Bowl in franchise history that season, but Boldin wasn't happy, and it showed. He got into a tiff with offensive coordinator Todd Haley during the NFC title game and went to the locker room immediately afterward, avoiding the celebration on the field.

In the offseason of 2009, there were trade talks involving Boldin, but he went nowhere. He and Fitzgerald again finished with more than 1,000 yards receiving apiece, and the Cardinals won their second consecutive NFC West title. Everyone around the team knew it was Boldin's last season in Arizona. And in March the team traded Boldin and a fifth-round pick to the Ravens for selections in the third and fourth rounds. Oddly, Boldin spent part of the next day at the Cardinals' facility, participating in a flag football tournament to benefit Warner's foundation. Boldin took it seriously, as he did with all athletic contests, drawing up plays for a corporate-sponsored team.

Afterward, he was melancholy about leaving the desert. "To go from what we did in '03 [4–12] my rookie year to the pinnacle last year, it's definitely been a blessing, and that's what I'm most proud of," Boldin said that day. "When I first got out here, that was my main goal: to change this organization to a winning organization, one that was respected around the league. And leaving here now, I think I've done that."

27 Patrick Peterson's Happy Returns

When Patrick Peterson began playing football at age seven, coaches used him as a punt returner because it was another way to get the ball in the hands of their best athlete.

Fourteen years later, not much had changed. Peterson, 21, was in his first season with the Cardinals. Coaches still used him as a punt returner because it was a way to get the ball in the hands of their best athlete. It was astounding what Peterson did with it that 2011 season. He returned four punts for touchdowns, tying an NFL record for a single season, and he became the first to do it with four returns of at least 80 yards.

Peterson, who also started at cornerback, was selected to the Pro Bowl as a kick returner and was the only rookie to make first-team All-Pro. The Cardinals offense struggled throughout that season, and the team needed every one of Peterson's punts. Three of them proved to be the deciding margins in victories. Another, against the Baltimore Ravens, gave the Cardinals a 17–3 lead that they later relinquished. "I'm an offensive guy playing defense," said Peterson, a cornerback.

Peterson proved that quickly. In his first NFL game, he returned a punt 89 yards for a touchdown to give the Cardinals a 28–21 victory against the Carolina Panthers. "Anybody else fair catches that thing," quarterback Kevin Kolb said after the game.

Peterson's next one came against Baltimore in the seventh game, and he followed that up with one the next week in overtime against the St. Louis Rams. By then Cardinals coach Ken Whisenhunt and special teams coach Kevin Spencer were giving Peterson freedom to use his own judgment on which punts to return. "He has such a great feel and he is definitely a force," Whisenhunt said at the time. "The thing that gives you comfort is that he doesn't drop balls."

Peterson can give his father, Patrick Sr., partial credit for that. Patrick Sr. spent a lot of time working with his son on all facets of the game, including catching punts. Peterson looks natural catching the ball with his hands providing a soft landing for the ball. That was not an accident. Since his son was a child, Patrick Sr. tossed water balloons at his son, emphasizing how important it was to catch the ball in the hands, not against the body. "We also used tennis balls and golf balls," Patrick Sr said.

Why golf balls? "If he let that golf ball hit him in the nose, it's going to hurt."

Patrick Jr. also learned the art of sizing up an opponent's coverage while the ball was in the air. Instead of drifting under punts, he ran hard to where the ball was going to land. That gave him time to peek at defenders running downfield. "Once I see the gunners taken care of, I know the middle guys have to wait until the ball is punted," Peterson said. "And they are slower. Once I catch the ball, I worry about one guy at a time."

As much freedom as coaches granted Peterson that year, fielding the ball at the 1-yard line was stretching it a bit. But Peterson did in that in overtime against the Rams, and the 99-yard score gave the Cardinals a 19–13 victory to break a six-game losing streak. "I knew that was gutsy," Peterson said afterward. "I decided to catch the ball and run for my life."

The fourth return for a touchdown also came against the Rams three weeks later. The game-winning return in the first game versus the Rams capped a strange couple of minutes for Peterson. He was called for pass interference in the final seconds of regulation, setting up a 42-yard field-goal attempt by Rams kicker Josh Brown on the final play. But defensive end Calais Campbell blocked the kick to send the game into overtime. The Cardinals (2–6) stopped the Rams on the opening possession, forcing the contest's final punt. "I don't know about you guys, but I can't take much more than there was today," Whisenhunt said of the emotional swing in the final minutes.

It took Peterson just 11 games to tie the NFL record for punt returns for touchdowns and have more punt returns for scores than any other Cardinal in history. Peterson nearly broke the NFL record against Seattle in the final game of the season. Seahawks coach Pete Carroll chose to punt to Peterson, who returned one 42 yards before being tripped.

After that season Peterson's punt return statistics dropped in 2012 and 2013. He gave them up entirely in 2014 but was back on the job in 2015. "I love to have the ball in my hands," Peterson said. "I love being on the field, and being on the field that extra down means I have an opportunity to do something special."

28 Million Dollar Backfield

The Cardinals weren't very good in the late 1930s, and they were even worse when World War II depleted their roster and those of every other team. But the end of the war signaled an end to the Cardinals' misery. Players returned from service, including halfback Marshall Goldberg. Recent draft picks such as Elmer Angsman and Pat Harder, both running backs, paid great dividends.

The Cardinals went 6–5 in 1946, the year coach Jimmy Conzelman returned to the team.

Owner Charles Bidwill was fulfilling his promise to Conzelman to provide enough talent to win, but Bidwill wasn't done. In the offseason of 1947, he made a hard push to sign Charley Trippi, a star running back at Georgia. The Cardinals had drafted Trippi in 1945 before he finished his college career. Two years later he was about to become a rich young man. The Cardinals and the Yankees of the All-America Football Conference were bidding for Trippi, as were baseball's New York Yankees.

Trippi chose the Cardinals, signing a four-year deal worth about $100,000. Together that group was became known as "The Million Dollar Backfield," nearly a decade before the name was applied to the famous San Francisco 49ers group. Bidwill called it his "Dream Backfield," and it was made up of Paul Christman at quarterback; Goldberg, Angsman, and Trippi at halfbacks; and Harder at fullback.

Goldberg played on defense most of the time in 1947, but even playing football was an accomplishment for him. He was sick when he was mustered out of the service and was mysteriously losing weight. In a 1997 interview, Goldberg said doctors in Chicago diagnosed testicular cancer. He underwent surgery in March of 1946. Hardly anyone knew because the Cardinals were able to keep the news out of the press. Goldberg played three seasons and passed away in 2006 at the age of 88. Unfortunately, Bidwill never got to see the dream backfield play. The owner died of pneumonia before the season.

Harder led the league in scoring with 102 points (seven touchdowns, seven field goals, and 39 extra points). Christman passed for 2,191 yards and 17 touchdowns. Angsman scored eight touchdowns, and Trippi averaged nearly five yards per carry. The Cardinals went 9–3 that season and beat the Philadelphia Eagles 28–21 for the franchise's first NFL championship since 1925.

The game was played on a frozen field at Comiskey Park, but that didn't stop the "Million Dollar Backfield" from displaying its speed. The Eagles' eight-man line still couldn't stop the Cardinals. Trippi scored on a 44-yard run in the first quarter. Then Angsman went 70 yards for another touchdown. In the third quarter, Trippi returned a punt 75 yards to give the Cardinals a 21–7 lead. And in the fourth quarter, Angsman again scored from 70 yards out.

The Million Dollar Backfield wasn't together long. It helped the Cardinals advance to the 1948 championship game, but things fell apart after that. Conzelman resigned to enter business, and without their coach and owner, the Cardinals descended to their customary place in the NFL standings. They recorded just one winning season in the 1950s. Harder left after the 1950 season and finished his career with the Detroit Lions. Christman was sold to the Green Bay Packers in 1950. Goldberg retired after the 1948 season to pursue business opportunities. Angsman finished his career in 1952, and Trippi played through 1955.

29 Roger Wehrli

Roger Wehrli grew up in King City, Missouri, a town of about 1,000 people in the northwestern part of the state, but he wasn't a St. Louis Cardinals fans. The Kansas City Chiefs were the closest professional franchise to King City, and, besides, Wehrli favored basketball over football and track, all three of which he played in high school.

That changed after Wehrli's senior season. Missouri football coach Dan Devine offered Werhli the Tigers' last available scholarship for the 1965 season. Wehrli accepted, became a star defensive back, and eventually was chosen in the first round of the 1969 draft by the Cardinals. In 2003 he was inducted into the College Football Hall of Fame. And in 2007, his last year of eligibility as a modernday candidate, he was inducted into the Pro Football Hall of Fame.

Not bad for the kid from a small farming community.

Back in 1969 Wehrli didn't even think the Cardinals were interested in him. The Dallas Cowboys, Los Angeles Rams, and Cleveland Browns were among the teams that had contacted him—but not the Cardinals. The night before the draft, Wehrli attended an athletic banquet in St. Louis, and happened to be seated next to Charley Winner, the Cardinals head coach. Winner told Wehrli the Cardinals were looking seriously at drafting him. "My parents were hoping I'd end up close to home in Kansas City," Wehrli said, "but the Cardinals had the 19ᵗʰ pick in the first round, so that's where I ended up."

It was one of the best decisions the Cardinals ever made. Over 14 seasons Wehrli made seven Pro Bowls, five All-Pro teams, and intercepted 40 passes. Some of the greatest quarterbacks in NFL history avoided throwing Wehrli's direction. "After a while you just stopped challenging him," Cowboys quarterback Roger Staubach told the *St. Louis Post-Dispatch*. "There was no point to it. He was the best cornerback I played against. The term 'Shutdown Corner' originated with Roger Wehrli."

Quiet and unassuming by nature, Wehrli was smart enough as a rookie to watch and listen to safety Larry Wilson, an established star. "I learned so much from him in the early years of my career," Wehrli said. "He showed me how to play through pain, how to never give up. He talked about the mental toughness to play hard, no matter the circumstances, and was a great help to me the first few years. Because of our friendship and my respect for him as a great teammate, I asked him to be my presenter at the Hall of Fame enshrinement ceremony."

Wehrli's former teammates have great respect for him, too. His induction to the Pro Football Hall of Fame was way overdue in their opinion. During Wehrli's era the Cardinals were known for having a potent offensive attack but average to weak defenses. They also didn't win much; Wehrli played on only three winning teams with the Cardinals. "Roger had unbelievable speed for a white man, as everybody used to say," said former Cardinals quarterback Jim Hart. "He was a smart guy. One of the things that pissed me off—we'd played basketball in the offseason, and he'd eat two Big Macs right before we played. I'd eat one Big Mac and gain five pounds. He didn't sweat much either."

The late Charlie Sanders, a Detroit Lions tight end in the same Hall of Fame class as Wehrli, said opponents sometimes underestimated Wehrli because he was one of the few white cornerbacks in the NFL. "You would think that this was a guy you'd be able to take advantage of," Sanders said in 2007. "Those who played in my era will understand what I'm saying. You didn't typically see non-Afro Americans playing that position. But he represented very well.

"How did he get where he is right now? Basically because he brought an attitude, along with skill, along with quickness. And I give all the credit to the Cardinals for recognizing that talent and putting him into position where he could end up in the Hall of Fame."

When he was a player, Wehrli didn't even dream of making the Hall of Fame. It didn't cross his mind until the final game of Wilson's career in 1972. "There was a representative [of the Hall] there to box up his uniform to be displayed at the Hall," Wehrli said. "I thought, *How great that was that I had played with a guy that was going to be in the Hall of Fame?* In my case it was not something I thought about during my playing days."

After Wehrli retired he would occasionally be introduced as a future Hall of Famer. Over the years he made the list of nominees but not into final consideration. "After a while it kind of dropped off my radar, and I really never thought about it unless someone would ask," Wehrli said.

But in 2005 Wehrli made it to the final 15 and he was selected in 2007. "I always figured if I deserved to be there I would eventually get there," he said. "I feel honored to be a part of this special team that represents the best players that have ever played the game. I've been able to reconnect with players I've played with and against in Pro Bowls and players I've admired from different eras. And I enjoy being able to attend various events all over the country as a representative of the NFL. It's always a great honor to put on that gold jacket."

30 Carson Palmer

When Carson Palmer arrived in Arizona in 2013, Cardinals coach Bruce Arians likened his relationship with the quarterback to two old cowboys riding toward sunset in the desert.

Palmer, 27 years younger than Arians, understood the metaphor but wasn't quite ready to put himself in the same demographic as the head coach. "I don't like to use the word 'old,'" Palmer said. "You can use it when you talk about coaches. I'm into my mid-to-early 30s, and in quarterback years, that's middle of the road in my book."

In Arizona both quarterback and coach turned back the clock. Arians got his first chance to be a head coach in the NFL, and Palmer walked into the best situation of his career. Palmer was 29–9 as a starter in his first three seasons with the Cardinals and was a contender for the NFL's Most Valuable Player award in 2015. Given those statistics, the Cardinals got him in a steal. They traded a sixth-round pick to the Oakland Raiders in exchange for Palmer and a seventh-round selection.

At the time Palmer didn't have a lot of market value. He had forced his way out of Cincinnati by threatening to retire if the Bengals didn't trade him. He backed that up by sitting out the first six games of 2011. The Bengals eventually gave in, sending Palmer to Oakland. The Raiders weren't very good, and they went 8–16 in games Palmer started. "When we made the trade for Carson... there was a perception," general manager Steve Keim told Arizona Sports 98.7 FM in early 2016. "You're talking about a guy who sat out a year in Cincinnati, that maybe he was a quitter or whatever the thought was around the country. After getting to know him for three years, I haven't been around many people who are as tough mentally or as competitive as he is. I have a tremendous amount of confidence in Carson Palmer in every aspect of the game."

Palmer was not an immediate success in Arizona. Arians' offensive system is complicated and puts a great amount of responsibility on the quarterback and, to a lesser extent, receivers. Receivers usually have two or three route options on every pass play, and it's up to them and the quarterback to properly read coverages. During the first half of the 2013, many of Palmer's passes ended up nowhere near a receiver because of misreads.

Things started to click near midseason, and Palmer threw 16 touchdown passes over the final nine games. The Cardinals went 7–2 and knew they were on to something.

Palmer's 2014 season was cut short by a torn ACL, but he returned to practice in just seven months—thanks to a rigorous offseason training program.

In 2015, Palmer's 12th NFL season, he set franchise records for passing yardage (4,671) and touchdowns (35) to lead the Cardinals to an NFC West title. The Cardinals advanced to the NFC Championship Game against the Carolina Panthers. They were blown out 49–15, as Palmer played his worst game since early in his first season with the team.

Palmer had won his first playoff game the week before, but that was quickly forgotten after his awful performance against the Panthers. To his credit, Palmer accepted the criticism and said he understood people who questioned his ability to play well in big games. "There's nothing like adversity to fuel the fire," he said. "Staring over at that [Panthers] sideline, that's going to stick with me for probably the rest of my life."

As bad as Palmer was in the NFC title game, he played great during the regular season. The Cardinals, who had spent the previous three years searching for a competent replacement for Kurt Warner, weren't going to complain about Palmer. As Keim likes to note, every year there are a dozen or so NFL teams desperately searching for a quarterback. With Palmer the Cardinals were happy not to be one of them.

31 The Honey Badger

Before the 2013 NFL Draft, Tyrann Mathieu swore he wasn't going to cry after he was selected. But there he was, shedding tears when it was announced on television that the Cardinals had chosen him in the third round. And there he was, crying during a conference call with Arizona reporters shortly after. "I've been playing football my whole life," he said, "but it's different this time."

What was different was that Mathieu no longer took the game for granted. Kicked off the Louisiana State team after numerous positive tests for marijuana, Mathieu was embarrassed and humbled. He vowed that he was a changed man, but not everyone believed him. "He's proven to be irresponsible," Hall of Fame general manager Bill Polian said during ESPN's broadcast of that draft. "I don't know why you'd want him at any price."

Over the years the Cardinals rarely had taken a chance on a player with Mathieu's background. But they had a new general manager, Steve Keim, and a new coach, Bruce Arians, who believed in second chances. Arians, who was kicked out of a Catholic high school as a senior, identified with Mathieu. "We've all made mistakes in our lives, especially when we're at that age," Arians said. "To take away every opportunity? That's not what I believe in."

To Keim the risk of taking Mathieu was far outweighed by the reward. When Mathieu did play in college, he was dynamic. When healthy, he's done the same thing in the NFL.

Through three years with the Cardinals, Mathieu has exceeded all expectations despite having to fight through two severe knee injuries.

It was obvious in his first game that Mathieu was a special player. He saved a touchdown against the St. Louis Rams by punching the ball loose from a receiver. Mathieu had 65 tackles, two interceptions, and a sack before suffering two torn knee ligaments during the 13th game of the season. It was a long road back for Mathieu, who played in 2014 but clearly wasn't himself.

By 2015 Mathieu, nicknamed "The Honey Badger" at LSU, was at full strength. He dubbed 2015 the "savage season." "He has a gleam in his eye that I didn't see at all last season," Arians said.

Mathieu set astronomical goals for himself, including intercepting eight passes and finishing with 95 tackles. By midseason many of those goals looked attainable. Mathieu made plays every week as the Cardinals marched toward the most successful regular season in team history. Mathieu, who had five interceptions and 80 tackles, was being mentioned as a candidate for Defensive Player of the Year. But his season ended during a Sunday night game in Philadelphia on December 20. On the last defensive play of the game, Mathieu intercepted a pass and pivoted to head up field. Then he went down untouched. He had a torn ACL and missed the rest of the year.

The entire team was downcast, especially Arians, who admitted he had a special relationship with Mathieu. Arians was teary the day after Mathieu suffered the injury. "I love the player," he said, "but I love the person more."

Mathieu, the person and the player, has been nearly flawless since joining the Cardinals. He shows up to work with a smile, and his passion and energy for the game are infectious. And his teammates have had a positive impact on Mathieu, especially the other defensive backs. "Just being a part of something, for me that's most important," Mathieu told the team's website, azcardinals.com. "I've always been that way. It's real. I connect with them. I don't

Tyrann Mathieu jogs off the field after a 47–7 victory against the San Francisco 49ers in 2015, a game in which he recorded two interceptions, including a 33-yard Pick-6.

hide anything from them. I show them my scars. They know my personal life lows. They know when I'm doing great, they know when I'm doing bad, and I think guys respect that. I think they like working with me because most of the time I'm smiling, I'm having fun, and I'm just trying to play football."

32 The Genius

Don Coryell didn't look much like a football coach. He was 5'8", around 150 pounds, and spoke with a lisp. Yet, few men made more of an impact on the Cardinals or the NFL.

In 1973 Coryell inherited a St. Louis Cardinals team that had fallen on hard times, going 4–9–1 in consecutive years. Coryell was an out-of-the-box hire by owner Bill Bidwill, who assumed full ownership of the team the year before. Coryell was 49 the day he arrived in St. Louis. He coached San Diego State the previous 12 seasons and had no experience with professional football. "When he first came out, he took a group of us out to have dinner and talked about the situation," said Jim Hart, the quarterback at the time. "He said, 'Guys, I like to throw the ball.' I went from almost out of the league to being a quarterback again. That was pretty neat."

Coryell treated his players like men, and unlike his predecessor, Bob Hollway, he was not a dictator. Hollway used to walk between players during warm-ups, pointing out who needed a haircut, said offensive tackle Dan Dierdorf. Players learned just how different Coryell was at the first team meeting of training camp. Coryell was required to read off the list of finable offenses: what it cost for missing breakfast ($25), lunch ($50), dinner ($100), etc. When Coryell finished, Dierdorf raised his hand. "What?" Coryell said.

"Well, Coach," Dierdorf said. "When we're going out on the practice field at 7:45 or 8:00 in the morning, a lot of us aren't interested in having an omelet before a big football practice."

Coryell was silent for a few seconds. So was the room.

Finally, Coryell spoke. "I don't give a crap if you never come to any of the meals," he said.

"At that moment," Dierdorf recalled, "we would have run through a brick wall for him. He basically took the fine list and threw it away. That was Coryell. He didn't care if you put feathers in your helmet. The man only cared whether you could play football. Talk about winning over a group of guys who were micromanaged prior to that."

The Cardinals went 4–9–1 in Coryell's first season, but the players knew things were different. Their coach was small, but fiery and demanding. And his passing game was unlike anything the NFL had seen. Much of it can still be seen in the NFL today. The passing tree of routes came from Coryell. The three-number way of calling plays was from Coryell, too, as were the one-back set, the empty backfield, the H-back, and many of the tenets of what's known today as the West Coast Offense.

Coryell had a small but amazing staff of assistant coaches that included future Washington coach Joe Gibbs and Jim Hanifan, who was considered among the finest offensive line coaches in NFL history.

Coryell's time with the Cardinals was short but remarkable. The team went 10–4 in 1974 and made the playoffs for the first time since 1948. Hart was named the NFC's Player of the Year, and running back Terry Metcalf finished second. In 1975 the Cardinals won the division with an 11–3 record but lost to the Los Angeles Rams in the divisional playoffs. The offensive line, which included Pro Bowlers Conrad Dobler, Dierdorf, and Tom Banks, was among the best in NFL.

Coryell also had an eye for talent. Hart and receiver Mel Gray didn't play much the year before Coryell arrived. Coryell watched film of both of them and then made them full-time starters. Bidwill was impressed with Coryell, too, and rewarded his coach with a contract extension. But the relationship soured, and Coryell spent just five seasons with the Cardinals. Coryell sided with Metcalf in a contract dispute, which irritated Bidwill. And the coach grew increasingly frustrated that he had so little influence in personnel decisions. Coryell knew the Cardinals were not going to become a championship contender until there were upgrades on defense.

From 1974 to 1976, Coryell's Cardinals won 31 games and two NFC East titles. But by the end of 1977, Coryell had been through enough. He had to watch as personnel director George Boone drafted cornerback Tim Gray with the first pick in 1975 and quarterback Steve Pisarkiewicz with the first pick in 1977. "If things keep on course, next year we'll win four games," Coryell said in late 1977, "and in 1979 we'll win two games."

Never one to hide his emotions, Mount Coryell erupted. He ranted about his small coaching staff, the franchise's lack of direction, and the insults his wife and daughter took from some fans. Coryell expected Bidwill to fire him. He even wanted him to. Bidwill waited a few weeks and then obliged.

Coryell moved on to the San Diego Chargers. Bidwill turned to former Oklahoma Sooners coach Bud Wilkinson, who lasted less than two seasons. "Losing Coryell was probably the lowest point of my career," said cornerback Roger Wehrli, who is in the Pro Football Hall of Fame. "Some coaches have that certain ability to produce winning teams that cannot be taught. You have it or you don't. Coryell had it."

33 McCown to Poole

Based on cumulative statistics, the passing combination of quarterback Josh McCown to receiver Nate Poole would not be part of Cardinals lore. They connected for only one touchdown. But oh, what a touchdown it was. That one play, the final one of the 2003 regular season, changed the fortunes of three franchises.

It gave the Cardinals an 18–17 victory against the Minnesota Vikings but more importantly gave them the third overall pick in the 2003 draft instead of the first. It knocked the Vikings out of the playoffs and put the Green Bay Packers in the postseason. And it gave Dave McGinnis a victory in his final game as Cardinals head coach. He was fired the next day. Poole's catch was one of few highlights of the season for the Cardinals. He had been cut by the team four times and was starting just his third NFL game. "I never dropped my head," Poole said after the game.

The Vikings did after Poole's catch, but back in Green Bay, there was celebration. And the following week, Poole and his wife enjoyed a free trip to Green Bay, where they were feted and given a key to the city. McCown, who scrambled on the play and threw the perfect 28-yard touchdown pass with no time left, received a basket of Wisconsin cheese. "Nate got a key to the city," McCown joked. "And all I got was constipation."

McCown received what he called a "soft invitation" to visit Green Bay but couldn't go because his wife was about to have their third child. But he did receive Christmas cards that year from Packers fans. "They crossed out 'Merry Christmas' and wrote, 'Thanks for getting us into the playoffs,'" he said.

McCown and Poole have stayed in touch over the years. Both make their homes in the Charlotte, North Carolina, area. Their daughters are involved in gymnastics, and the two fathers bump into each other once in a while and remain connected by that play. "It's still one of my favorite moments," McCown said. "We weren't doing anything but playing ball and having fun. It was just a fun way to end the game."

Many Cardinals fans would rather have seen McCown's 166th pass attempt of 2003 fall incomplete. That would have given the Cardinals the No. 1 pick and the chance to draft quarterback Eli Manning. (Manning, though, could have refused to play for the Cardinals, as he did with the Chargers that year.)

McCown, McGinnis, and every Cardinal whose last name didn't begin with Mc could not have cared less about the 2004 draft. "With all the circumstances surrounding this ballclub, how can you not just savor the moment?" said running back Emmitt Smith, who was in his first season in Arizona. "We lost so many games here at the end like that and now we actually pulled one out, even had to go to the replay. I mean, c'mon, savor the moment."

Entering the season finale, Cardinals had lost seven consecutive games and they weren't competitive in many of them. The streak included blowout losses in Cleveland, Chicago, and San Francisco. McGinnis' departure wasn't official, but everyone knew the game against the Vikings would be his last. That's one reason there was so much emotion in the locker room afterward.

The McCown to Poole pass snatched the victory away from Minnesota, dropping them to 9–7 and out of the playoffs. But the Vikings contributed to their own demise, too. They led 17–6 with 6:48 remaining, and a playoff berth seemed assured. But then McCown led the Cardinals on a 14-play, 60-yard touchdown drive. A defensive holding called negated a sack that would have put the Cardinals in a third-and-25 situation. On third and 13 near midfield, McCown found Poole for a 37-yard gain. And the Cardinals twice converted on fourth down, including a two-yard touchdown pass to tight end Steve Bush.

Running back Damien Anderson recovered the onside kick, and a defensive pass interference call helped the Cardinals set to the Vikings 9. Two sacks later the Cardinals faced a fourth and 25 from the Vikings 28. They hurried to the line, and the ball was snapped with four seconds remaining. McCown took the shotgun snap and evaded an outside rusher. As McCown sprinted right, he motioned for Poole to move to his right, toward the corner of the end zone.

Throwing off one foot, McCown placed the ball high to Poole, who caught it over two defenders and touched one foot into the end zone before being forced out. The force-out rule has been changed since, but back then it was a touchdown.

Just like that, the Packers were champions of the NFC North, the Vikings were out of the playoffs, and the Cardinals were drafting third—not first. The latter probably didn't matter. New Cardinals coach Dennis Green fell in love with McCown and he already had close ties to the top receiver in the draft: Larry Fitzgerald. "I think Denny would have taken me No. 1," Fitzgerald said, smiling.

34 Aeneas Williams

In the summer of 1989, Aeneas Williams was many things: a junior at Southern University, an accounting major who hated numbers, Achilles Williams' little brother, and the youngest son of Lawrence and Lillian Williams. What he was not was a college football player. And for the previous three years, many people close to him could not figure out why. "Neekie," family and friends would ask, using a family nickname, "why are you not playing football?"

In the summer of 1989, Williams finally asked himself that question, too. Prompted by the smell of cut grass in Baton Rouge,

Louisiana; the voices of family and friends; and a pull from his heart that he couldn't explain, Williams decided to try out for Southern's team.

So began a remarkable story that led Williams to be drafted by the Cardinals in the third round in 1991, play 14 years in the NFL, and be inducted into the Pro Football Hall of Fame in 2014. In 10 years with the Cardinals, Williams never missed a game, made eight Pro Bowls, and proved himself as one of the best cornerbacks in history. "While I was playing, I attempted to do the best I could," Williams said. "Everything else, as we say back in Louisiana, is lagniappe."

Lagniappe?

"It means extra," Williams said. "Like if you went to the store and ordered a pound of greens or some other vegetable and they went over that amount and didn't charge you for it, that's lagniappe."

And to think Williams came close to becoming an unhappy accountant. He chose that as a major only because he was following Achilles, who was 18 months older. Aeneas followed Achilles like a needy puppy. Both went to Southern, majored in accounting, and were active in student government. Achilles graduated in the summer of 1989, but he cautioned his brother to get off the fast track occasionally. "Little brother, slow down," said Achilles, who works as a CPA. "You'll be working the rest of your life."

Aeneas Williams was always a talented athlete. As kids he and Achilles played on the same teams and, along with older brother Malcolm, spent hours at a park near their home in New Orleans. Aeneas was always full of energy, and it took a long, full day to deplete it. "They would come home at 2:30 or so, do their homework, then go to the park from 5:00 to 7:00, then come home to eat dinner," said their mother, Lillian Williams. "They were pretty tired by then. Even Aeneas."

When he decided to walk on at Southern, Williams told no one close to him because he was afraid someone might try to talk him out of it. He was due to graduate in just three years, so he wondered how his parents would react. Southern had been practicing for a week or two when Williams walked on, and the only equipment left was raggedy and worn. Williams slipped it on and made an immediate impact. By the second game of the season, he was on the travel squad. It was then that he decided to let his parents, Southern graduates, in on the secret. Williams called home to ask his parents if they were going to make the trip to Houston to watch their alma mater. No, they said. "You might want to come," Williams responded, "because you'll get a chance to see your son play."

By the fifth game, Williams was starting and he led the country in interceptions as a senior. That led him to the Cardinals, who were impressed from the first time Williams stepped on the field as a rookie. Williams, however, took nothing for granted. Near the end of his first training camp, Williams asked secondary coach Jim Johnson to assess Williams' chances of making the team. Johnson smiled. "*Make the team?*" he said. "You're starting."

In 14 NFL seasons, 10 with the Cardinals and four with the St. Louis Rams, Williams finished with 55 interceptions and 23 fumble recoveries. He returned nine interceptions for touchdowns, tied for second most in NFL history. He scored a total of 13 touchdowns, fifth all time among defensive players.

He didn't receive the attention of some of the other great cornerbacks of his time, such as Deion Sanders and Darrell Green, because the Cardinals had just one winning seasons in Williams' 10 years with them. But opponents knew how good he was. "I've had those battles with all those guys you call, 'Hall of Famers,'" said former Dallas Cowboys receiver Michael Irvin, also in the Hall of Fame. "I'm not putting any one of them above Aeneas. Not any one of them above Aeneas. No doubt in my mind."

Williams became the first draft pick in the team's history in Arizona to make the Hall of Fame. Williams remained in St. Louis after retiring and is the pastor of The Spirit Church. He also maintains close ties with the Cardinals, who inducted him into their Ring of Honor. Williams also is part of an NFL program that mentors young players on how to handle business, finances, and relationships.

Williams' message to them is the same one he delivered at his Hall of Fame induction speech: die empty. "I'll tell you where you can find the most wealth," Williams said at his induction. "It's in the cemetery because most people go to the grave full instead of empty."

35 Buddy Ryan

"You've got a winner in town."

Those were Buddy Ryan's first words to the public when he was introduced as the Cardinals coach and general manager in 1994. He hit Arizona like a desert monsoon storm—full of bluster, promise, and bravado. And like a monsoon, Ryan didn't stay long nor accomplish much, other than to rearrange dust. He raised hopes quickly and crushed them just as fast.

Ryan lasted two years with the team, a short tenure that surprised few people in the NFL. Many in the football business questioned why Bill Bidwill, the team's quiet owner, had hired the bombastic Ryan in the first place. "A match made in hell," one NFL coach told *The Arizona Republic*. "Does Bill Bidwill know what he did?" wondered another.

It took Bidwill two years to realize what he had done, but those two years were anything but boring. Ryan was a proven defensive wizard who became famous as a Chicago Bears assistant under Mike Ditka. Ryan's defense led the 1985 Bears to a championship, and that led Ryan to becoming the Philadelphia Eagles head coach.

He lasted five seasons there, winning one division championship but no playoff games. From there, he became the Houston Oilers defensive coordinator, where he infamously punched offensive coordinator Kevin Gilbride during an argument on the sidelines. That was enough to scare many owners from hiring Ryan as head coach. But Bidwill decided he needed that fiery temperament and Ryan's fame on the Cardinals sidelines.

He was the Cardinals' fourth coach since the team moved to Arizona in 1988. He was given primary control over personnel decisions, something Bidwill had never given to a head coach before. As he had done at coaching stops in Chicago, Philadelphia, and Houston, Ryan polarized fans and players. They loved him or hated him. No one was in between.

He called one overweight player "fatso." Asked about another player who had gained weight, Ryan said the tight end was so fat that "he lost his features." Upset with the number of injured players during one training camp, Ryan ordered they spend practice pushing wheelbarrows full of sand. At first, Ryan succeeded. Season-ticket sales doubled. The team went 8–8 his first season, its best record since moving west in 1988.

Ryan polarized the team, too. Early in his tenure, he made a reference to there being a cancer on the roster. "You know what you do with cancer?" Ryan asked. "You cut it out, and I'm the damn doctor." It was a thinly veiled reference to quarterback Steve Beuerlein, who lasted one season under Ryan.

Ryan promised to win early and often, and nobody reined him in. He hired his twin sons, Rex and Rob, as assistant coaches. A third son, Jim, represented an average offensive tackle named Larry Tharpe, whom Ryan signed to an above-average contract worth $1 million, an enormous sum at the time. Tharpe had not played a down of football the season before he signed with Arizona. Bidwill didn't overrule Ryan, saying only that Tharpe "better be able to play."

But Bidwill's eyebrows were raised. As the Cardinals started to lose in 1995, fans and media turned on Ryan. Instead of "Buddyball," the Cardinals were playing "Cruddyball." Season-ticket sales dropped about 7,000 between Ryan's two seasons, and average attendance dropped plummeted by an average of 15,000.

The last game of the 1995 season convinced Bidwill he had to make a change. The Cardinals were 4–11, and the team was in disarray as it prepared to play the Dallas Cowboys on Christmas night in prime time. For the Cardinals the day became a debacle a minute after they opened presents with their families that morning. Two players fought in the locker room before the game, a fracas witnessed by broadcaster Dan Dierdorf, a former Cardinal and a Hall of Famer. Players were divided into pro and anti-Ryan factions, and the whole atmosphere was poisonous. "Only a fool would say it wasn't," said kicker Greg Davis at the time.

The Cardinals fell behind the Cowboys 24–0, and perhaps worse, most of the crowd at Sun Devil Stadium was cheering for Dallas. Ryan watched the final seconds of his final game from the tunnel at Sun Devil Stadium, mistakenly thinking the game was over. That wasn't the reason Bidwill fired Ryan the next day, but it did symbolize Ryan's two years in Arizona. To the end, Bidwill said he could deal with Ryan's personality, just not the losing. "If he was 12–4, I'd be patting him on the back," Bidwill said. "4–12 wasn't good enough."

Bidwill slept on the decision and decided to fire Ryan the next day. The two shook hands, and Ryan cleared out his office.

He made only one brief comment to a reporter, saying the firing surprised him. "You know me," he said. "I always figure I'm going to win."

36 Ernie Nevers

Ernie Nevers played just five seasons of professional football and only three with the Chicago Cardinals. Yet it's easy to see why he's in the Pro Football Hall of Fame and the Cardinals ring of honor. Nevers, who also played professional basketball and baseball, was an All-Pro all five seasons and in 1929 set an NFL record that might never be broken: he scored 40 points in one game.

The game was on Thanksgiving Day and against the cross-town rival Bears. A heavy, wet snow had fallen in Chicago, and only about 8,000 fans attended. They witnessed history. Nevers rushed for six touchdowns and kicked four extra points, scoring every one of the Cardinals' points in the 40–6 victory. Oddly, the teams had played to a scoreless tie in their first meeting of the season, but Nevers and the Cardinals were confident they would whip the Bears in the rematch, according to *When Football Was Football*. "I told my players, next time we meet the Bears, we'll beat the hell out of 'em," Nevers said years later. "I knew we could. I just knew it."

According to Chicago legend, Nevers was calling his shots that day, pointing where he was going to be running. Still, the Bears couldn't stop him. Like any good running back, Nevers always gave his offensive line credit. "They made it all possible," he said.

Nevers led the league in scoring that season despite missing two games because of his baseball commitment. He was one of the greatest athletes of his time. A collegiate star at Stanford, Nevers was compared to Jim Thorpe. After college he signed with the Duluth Eskimos and played a grueling schedule. Nevers was one of the NFL's biggest stars, and the Eskimos' owner agreed to play most of the team's games on the road.

From September of 1926 through February of '27, the Eskimos played 29 games, including 14 against NFL opponents. Nevers played 1,714 of 1,740 possible minutes in that stretch. The Eskimos finished 19–7–3. Years later, Nevers said he made only one mistake in signing with the Eskimos out of college. "I forgot to ask how long the season would be," he said.

Nevers was a player/coach for the Cardinals in 1930 and 1931. After retiring as a player, Nevers continued coaching and returned to head the Cardinals in 1939. It didn't work out. That team was hampered by surprise retirements and numerous injuries. The Cardinals finished 1–10, the worst record in team history to that point.

When World War II started, Nevers was too old to be drafted, so he enlisted in the Marines. While serving in the Pacific, Nevers and his battalion were reported missing for several months. By the time they were found on a deserted island, several had died. Nevers suffered from beriberi and weighed only 110 pounds. Nevers' wife died of pneumonia while he was in the service. He later remarried and returned to California and worked for beverage distributors.

37 Jim Hart

Jim Hart started 180 games over 18 seasons for the Cardinals, which is more than any other quarterback in team history. It was a magnificent feat since the odds were against him ever getting one start. Hart, who played at Southern Illinois, was not drafted in 1966, and the Cardinals signed him as a free agent only because his college coach, Don Shroyer, was an assistant with the Cardinals. "They sent their ticket manager to sign me," Hart said. "Later, I thought, *So that's where I fit in.*"

Hart was sick with tonsillitis when the ticket manager arrived in Carbondale, Illinois, and was unable to meet the man for dinner. Over the phone the man offered Hart $1,000 to sign. Hart asked for a little more, but the ticket manager said he would have to return to St. Louis to ask owner Bill Bidwill. Afraid he'd never hear from the Cardinals again if he allowed the ticket manager to leave, Hart agreed to the $1,000 bonus.

When Hart reported for camp, he discovered he was the sixth of six quarterbacks at camp. But he crept up the depth chart over the next year. By training camp of 1967, Hart was the backup to veteran Charley Johnson. Given that he was being paid far below a backup's salary, Hart asked for a raise. The Cardinals put him off, telling him to wait until they returned to St. Louis. By then, team president Stormy Bidwill said, Hart might be the starter.

Hart returned to his room discouraged and told Johnson about his failed attempt to get a raise. "You haven't read the paper yet, have you?" Johnson said. "You've got to be the last one to know. I've been called into active duty."

Just like that, Johnson was in the service, and Hart, a year out of college, was the Cardinals starter. "You talk about scared?" Hart said. "Holy crap, I was scared to death."

Hart overcame his nerves and remained the Cardinals' starting quarterback in all but a few seasons until 1981. In 18 seasons with the Cardinals, Hart passed for 34,639 yards and 209 touchdowns. More importantly, the Cardinals went 87–88–5 in his starts. That sounds average until you consider that in team history, only two other Cardinals quarterbacks (Johnson and Carson Palmer) with at least 10 starts have a .500 record or better. "Jim Hart had a cannon for an arm," said Dan Dierdorf, the former Cardinals offensive tackle. "He was a gifted thrower of the football and he had tremendous instincts in the pocket and a quick release. Jim Hart was a damn fine football player."

Not everyone saw that.

Bob Hollway, who coached the Cardinals in 1971 and 1972, benched Hart and traded for Minnesota Vikings quarterback Gary Cuozzo. Everyone else knew it was a mistake. By the end of 1972, Hollway admitted his error to Hart. Hollway didn't last, and neither did Cuozzo.

When Don Coryell took over as coach in 1973, he quickly made Hart his starting quarterback. Hart thrived in an offensive system that gave players great freedom. Coryell was one of the game's great innovators, and with Hart at quarterback, the Cardinals developed the game's most exciting offense.

Much of it was built around the pass. When Coryell told players how much he planned to throw, Hart was thrilled while some of the offensive linemen, who preferred run blocking, were dubious. "Dan [Dierdorf] says, 'You've got be happy,'" Hart said. "I said, 'Yeah, I am.' I went from being almost out of the league to starting quarterback again. That was pretty neat."

Hart made the Pro Bowl in four of five seasons under Coryell. If Coryell had stayed longer, Hart may have built statistics that would have put him in the Hall of Fame. "He was the best passer I ever had to face, and I had to do it every day in practice," said cornerback Roger Wehrli. "He made me a better defensive back by challenging me with his best in practices. He was a great quarterback who gets much less credit than he deserves because we didn't make it to the big dance."

38 The 2005 Game in Mexico City

The 2005 season was the Cardinals' last in Sun Devil Stadium, and their new home, University of Phoenix Stadium, was under construction. So there was no better time to take a working vacation to Mexico. On October 2, the Cardinals played the San Francisco 49ers in Mexico City. It was the first NFL regular-season game played outside the U.S., and it drew a crowd of 103,467, an NFL record.

The setting was memorable, but the game itself was not. The Cardinals entered the game with a 0–3 record and looked horrible early, committing turnovers that led to two early touchdowns by the 49ers. The Cardinals settled down and scored the next 31 points to win 31–14. "[We] defensively shut them out and didn't let them in the end zone," Cardinals coach Dennis Green said that night. "Offensively, we made some mistakes early…but never got discouraged."

Watching the crowd was more interesting than watching the game. More fans wore 49ers jerseys than wore Cardinals jerseys, and the crowd was notably partial to the 49ers in the early going. But as the Cardinals started to dominate, fans either started to switch allegiances, or Cardinals supporters just got louder. They liked it when safety Robert Griffith carried the Mexican flag out of the tunnel to open the game.

With less than two minutes to go in the game, Cardinals defensive end Bertrand Berry grabbed the flag and waved it from the sideline. "The fans, like the flag, swayed even more to the Cardinals' favor," according to *The Arizona Republic*. "Even those wearing the 49ers gear were cheering and clapping. Then there was wide receiver Charles Lee after the game, salsa dancing to the music as Mexican girls screamed." Players were amazed at the size of Azteca Stadium. "You can definitely feel the size of this place," Cardinals receiver Larry Fitzgerald said. "It's not like any stadium you see in the states."

The biggest star of the week didn't even play in the game. Cardinals offensive lineman Rolando Cantu was the first player born in Mexico to stick on an NFL roster, though he was on the practice squad and could not play in the game. "Dude is big time," wide receiver Anquan Boldin told the *East Valley Tribune*. "He runs the city, man."

The game was successful in drawing a record crowd, and there was considerable interest in it on both sides of the border. But it's hard to see any long-term benefits. The NFL did not return to Mexico until 2016, partly out of concerns for the safety of its teams. In 2005 players didn't venture far from their hotels. There was little interaction with local citizens.

The game, however, did pay off for the Cardinals. Officially, it was a home game for them, and they won only two others all season. And it often took them three games to draw 100,000 fans to Sun Devil Stadium. They were shaky the rest of the season and finished 5–11.

But the Cardinals drafted quarterback Matt Leinart the next season and moved into their new home, where they've sold out every game.

39 Adrian Wilson

For a dozen years, safety Adrian Wilson was a menacing force on the Cardinals defense. He roamed the secondary and was intimidating enough to shorten the arms of receivers going across the middle. But Wilson was at his most dangerous near the line of scrimmage, where opponents could only guess where he was going to strike.

When Wilson hit receivers and other ball carriers, marks were left. The ferocity with which he played was unusual even by NFL standards. But perhaps more importantly, Wilson made an impact in other ways during his 12 years with the team. He came to the Cardinals in 2001 and lived through terrible seasons that cost coaches their jobs and prompted players to leave for other teams at the first opportunity.

But Wilson stayed and played a pivotal role in the team's reversal of fortunes in the first decade of this century. "If I'm going to be a part of something, I'm going to be a part of something all the way," Wilson said. "I'm not going to be part of something halfway. So, I think what separated me from everybody else is it's not about the money. It's not about the fame. Yeah, you get paid to play, but for me, it's about turning something around. It's about being important and meaning something to the franchise. I think that's what motivated me more than anything."

Wilson, who retired in the spring of 2015, made five Pro Bowls and was a team captain five times. He was inducted into the team's ring of honor in 2015 and now works for the Cardinals as a scout.

Wilson was far from an immediate success when he arrived in Arizona as a third-round pick out of North Carolina State in 2001. Physically, he looked like a statue come to life, but he had

Safety Adrian Wilson celebrates after sacking Philadelphia Eagles quarterback Donovan McNabb during the second half of the 2009 NFC Championship Game.

little clue about how to play football at the NFL level. He never dreamed football could be so complicated. As a rookie he became so frustrated at one practice that he left the field, saying he was done with football.

But Wilson stayed, and veterans such as Pat Tillman and Corey Chavous were willing to teach him until the wee hours of the day. "When he came out, I think he was 6'2", 215 pounds and he ran 4.37 [in the 40-yard dash] for me," said Cardinals general manager Steve Keim. "He jumped 42 inches in the vertical jump. His skillset was off the chains, but he had to hone his skills on the field and had to be a true pro. The minute he walked through the door here, he did that."

Wilson was far from an immediate success. In his early seasons, he sometimes struggled in pass coverage. And like many young players, he could be fooled by savvy quarterbacks. But he improved and became a force that frightened receivers and offensive coordinators. Wilson played in an era of great safeties, and he and others caused the NFL to change rules in order to protect receivers. As the years progressed, coaches played Wilson near the line of scrimmage more often. The result often was havoc. *Would he blitz? Fall into coverage?* And with the body of a linebacker, Wilson was a difficult blocking matchup on running plays, too. Wilson finished his career with 27 interceptions and 25.5 sacks, becoming only the 10th player in history to register at least 20 of each.

It took time for Wilson to develop into a team leader. He could be moody. He had a scowl that kept teammates, especially younger ones, away. He had a smile that invited them to ask him anything. He was always fiercely independent and he had little patience for teammates who didn't take the game as seriously as he did. Wilson gradually came to learn that few others were wired like him. Some teammates needed a pat on the back, some a kick in the rear. All needed someone to turn to when they had questions, someone who was approachable in the locker room.

Wilson became one of those people. "On gameday all 11 guys are in it for one reason, and that's to win and to make that game plan go," Wilson said. "For me, every single teammate that I had, whether I was nice to him or terrible to him, we all had one goal, and that was to win. We didn't do a lot of winning here early on in my career, but that grind and that adversity helped mold a lot of guys. It helped mold Larry Fitzgerald. I know for a fact it helped mold Darnell Dockett, Anquan Boldin. I can keep naming guys that were just top guys, that were winners coming here. But we didn't win early on, so it kind of helped that grind mentality."

For years Wilson's desire was to retire as a Cardinal. He accepted a pay cut before the 2012 season. The Cardinals released him in early 2013. It was Keim's first year as general manager, but he might not make a more difficult decision in his career. His relationship goes back to Wilson's freshman year at North Carolina State. Keim, who played for the Wolfpack, was an assistant strength and conditioning coach there when Wilson showed up as a freshman.

By the time Wilson left college a year early, Keim was an area scout, and he pushed the Cardinals to draft Wilson. Wilson and Keim remained good friends through the years even after Keim cut Wilson. "He set the bar for this organization," Keim said. "When we send our scouts on the road, we truly tell them, 'Let's find the next Adrian Wilson.' It's not just the player on the field; it's the person, it's the character, it's the intangibles that made him special."

As much as the sacks, the interceptions, and memorable hits, those are the reasons Wilson is in the team's ring of honor. "My whole life, all I ever wanted to do was matter, to be a part of a change, to be a part of a centerpiece, and to turn a team around," Wilson said. "I poured my heart and soul into this organization and led with a quiet storm mentality. When I walked through the doors April 22, 2001, I knew I was an alpha. It didn't matter win, lose, or draw, I had a responsibility to that locker room and every single teammate."

40 Participate in Pat's Run

In the summer of 2004, three friends met in a Phoenix suburb to brainstorm ideas of how to honor Pat Tillman, the former Cardinals safety turned Army Ranger who was killed a few months before in Afghanistan. Three of Tillman's favorite things were present at the table: beer, friends, and planning a new experience. Someone mentioned a golf tournament, and beer was almost spewed. That didn't fit Tillman, who as a student at Arizona State climbed light towers to contemplate life, and completed a marathon and triathlon during the offseasons as an NFL player.

Then Perry Edinger, the head athletic trainer at Arizona State when Tillman played there, came up with the idea of a run. It was simple, and the community could participate. "I just started thinking of as many ideas as possible about how we could honor Pat and make it fun for people," Edinger said.

Edinger wanted to make the race accessible to everyone. After all, everyone had identified with Tillman, who left a football career that would have paid him millions to become an Army Ranger.

The run would be something an entire community could do, maybe, say, 4.2 miles, in honor of the No. 42, which Tillman wore at Arizona State. And, hey, someone suggested why not have runners finish at the 42-yard line of Sun Devil Stadium, where Tillman played both in college and for the Cardinals. The idea quickly grew legs. "I thought it would be great if a thousand people showed up," said Doug Tammaro, one of the three people at the initial meeting.

The first Pat's Run in April of 2005 drew 5,500 runners to a course on and near the Arizona State campus. Over the next 11 years, it grew exponentially to the point where the Arizona race is capped at 35,000 or so participants. Money raised from the event goes to the Pat Tillman Foundation, which provides scholarships to military veterans and their spouses. With the races as its main fund-raiser, the foundation has been able to donate more than $10 million.

Pat's Run has become one of the state of Arizona's biggest celebrations, and for one April morning each year, one of the country's biggest metropolitan areas is transformed into a small town. People smile at each other. Families run and walk together. It's not unusual to see fathers running with sons, mothers with daughters. Many people volunteer to push the disabled in wheelchairs. Entire military units sometimes run with full gear on their backs.

Celebrities participate—usually with little fanfare. Wide receiver Larry Fitzgerald is one of many Cardinals who are regular participants. Pat's widow, Marie Tillman, is usually on the course as are several members of his immediate family. Tammaro watches the start of every race from the top of Sun Devil Stadium. From there he can see thousands gather in corrals near the starting line. Every year he is amazed. "Our state's greatest day never fails to deliver," he said.

Pat's Run is not just an Arizona phenomenon. From the beginning it's been held in Pat's hometown of San Jose, California, too. And over the past few years, it's spread across the country. In 2015 more than 40 "shadow runs" were held from Seattle to Albuquerque to Oklahoma City to New York. Runners no longer have to live near a race site to participate. They can register as "virtual runners" and travel the 4.2 miles in their own neighborhoods. So, check it out. You don't have to be a runner to participate. You can be as competitive or non-competitive as you want.

If you are able to participate in the one in Arizona, you might want to head over to Rula Bula, a Tempe, Arizona, bar just a few blocks away from the course. Tillman was known to knock back a Guinness or two there. Hoist one with friends, laugh, and make plans for other challenges. That's part of Tillman's legacy, too.

"People ask how the foundation was started—if Marie started it, or if a group of friends started it," said Alex Garwood, Pat's brother-in-law and one of the three friends who met over beer that summer day in 2004. "I would tell you, Pat started it."

41 A Comeback for the Ages

There were six seconds left when Cardinals quarterback Neil Lomax jogged to the sidelines at Sun Devil Stadium on November 6, 1988, to discuss strategy with coach Gene Stallings and his staff. The Cardinals had come back from a 23–0 deficit to close to within a touchdown of the San Francisco 49ers. It was second and goal at the 9-yard line, and Stallings emphasized to Lomax that he needed to make sure he left time for a second play. "We only need one," Lomax responded.

And he was right. Lomax called the play, "89-69 seam," which meant all receivers go to the back of the end zone. "I was hoping they would blitz, and we could get one-on-one coverage on Roy Green," Lomax said. "I'll go to Roy every time he gets one-on-one coverage."

That's exactly what happened. The 49ers rushed seven, leaving cornerback Darryl Pollard on Green, who faked outside then went in, and Lomax hit him perfectly with three seconds remaining. Al Del Greco's extra point gave the Cardinals the improbable 24–23 victory against the 49ers, who had had won two Super Bowls earlier in the decade. "It's brutal, it's awful," 49ers coach Bill Walsh said after the game.

Few people expected the Cardinals to make a game of it. It was their first year in Arizona, and they had muddled around through the first nine games of the season. They desperately needed a victory to remain in playoff contention. For much of that Sunday afternoon, it appeared the Cardinals would go back into irrelevancy. The 49ers led 16–0 at halftime and 23–0 midway through the third quarter. Then Lomax and the Cardinals offense got hot. Lomax threw a 35-yard touchdown pass to Green in the third quarter, and Del Greco added a field goal early in the fourth. "At that point an electrical, magical current started flowing through everybody on the sidelines," fullback Ron Wolfley said that day. "We started to believe."

Suddenly, the Cardinals were within two touchdowns. The defense stiffened, and Lomax couldn't miss. He completed 16-of-25 passes for 182 yards and two touchdowns in the fourth quarter. In the final 1:27, he drove the Cardinals 66 yards in seven plays with no timeouts

Wide receiver J.T. Smith, who had two catches for 17 yards in the winning drive, described the huddle during those moments to *The Arizona Republic*. "You got a couple guys looking around, a few guys holding and wringing their hands," Smith said. "It's kind of quiet. A few guys are talking. The receivers are always talking. Everybody is kind of boosting each other up. It all starts with the line. We're always saying, 'Come on, baby, just give me a little more time.'"

Lomax had been sacked seven times in the game but not on the Cardinals' final two possessions, both of which ended in touchdowns. A religious man, Lomax said a little prayer before the final drive. "I just said, 'Jesus, it's up to you, man,'" Lomax said later.

It was a huge victory for the Cardinals. Local fans had yet to warm up to them, or to the team's ticket prices, the highest in the

NFL. The players hoped for a sellout the following week against the New York Giants. "There are no excuses for it not being a sellout," tight end Rob Awalt told reporters. "They want a good product, and we've given 'em one. They've shown good support so far, but now we have to rise to the occasion, and they have to rise to the occasion."

The Cardinals beat the Giants to improve to 7–4, their best record after 11 games in a dozen years. They were tied for first in the NFC East. But the magical, electrical current that flowed during the 49ers game disappeared over the final five weeks of the season. Lomax suffered ankle and hip injuries, which contributed to the team losing its last five games and finishing 7–9 and out of the playoffs.

By the end of the season, it was the five-game losing streak— not the miracle over the 49ers—that was on the Cardinals' minds. "To live with what happened for the next six months is something I'd just as soon not think about," defensive lineman Bob Clasby told *The Republic*.

42 "Night Train" Lane

Not many people alive today know much about Dick "Night Train" Lane—other than he might have possessed the coolest nickname in sports history. How Lane, the Hall of Fame cornerback for the Chicago Cardinals, Los Angeles Rams, and Detroit Lions, obtained that nickname is not quite clear. According to one story, it was because Lane loved the song "Night Train" by Buddy Morrow and played it often during a training camp with the Rams. The other version is that Lane was given the nickname because he hated flying and often took trains to games.

However Lane obtained the name, it stuck. But he's remembered for far more than just a cool moniker. Lane was one of the most physical cornerbacks in history and made seven Pro Bowls and six All-NFL teams. In 1969 he was chosen as one of the best cornerbacks of the league's first 50 years. "I played with him and against him, and he was the best I've ever seen," former New York Giants kicker and broadcaster Pat Summerall once said.

The son of a prostitute and a pimp, Lane was placed in a dumpster as a baby. He was rescued by Ella Lane and raised in Austin, Texas. Lane played just one year of football in junior college and then spent four years in the Army. Afterward he took a job with an aircraft company but hated it.

He received a tryout with the Rams, and they signed him. As a rookie in 1954, Lane intercepted 14 passes. That remains an NFL record, even though the NFL has since expanded its schedule to 14 games and then to 16. After two years the Rams traded him to the Cardinals. Lane continued to be a force for Chicago, making the Pro Bowl four times in six seasons. The Cardinals then traded him to the Lions, where he played six seasons. He was a vicious hitter, who often liked to bring receivers down by the neck. Dubbed the "Night-Train Necktie," the move was later outlawed by the NFL.

In his later years, Lane attributed part of his success to knowing which angles to take to make plays on receivers and the football. Lane spent his last two NFL seasons with Lions. In his book *Paper Lion*, George Plimpton mentions Lane and teammate Dick LeBeau, a fellow cornerback. In the book LeBeau said Lane talked about angles in such a way that others didn't comprehend. "When the offense comes out of its huddle and takes up a formation, often Train calls out, 'What sort of set-up we got heah?' reflecting on it, like he had something spread out on a newspaper to look at. Then his mind begins to go to work, and that's when you can get into trouble if you listen. One time he calls across to me: 'Dickie-bird, on this play fuss with a zone defense over theah, and over heah I'll play a man-to-man.' I yell at him he's crazy, plumb crazy, and he calls back: 'Mix 'em up, Dickie-bird, confuse 'em.'"

Lane is in the Cardinals' ring of honor and was inducted into the Pro Football Hall of Fame in 1974, becoming the second defensive back to earn induction. He died of a heart attack in 2002 at the age of 73. "He played the game with a ferocity that's seldom been equaled," *Los Angeles Times* columnist Jim Murray once said. "Quarterbacks avoided Night Train's part of the field as a hunter would avoid a rattlesnake nest. There were games in which Night Train had more receptions than the receivers he was covering."

43 "Gateway" Joe Willie Namath?

The best quarterback ever drafted by the Cardinals never played a down for the franchise.

How that happened is a tale that includes a famous college coach, an entertainment executive, and a contract that signaled the dawn of football as a big-money sport. In 1964 the NFL and AFL were bitter rivals for the best football talent in the country. With a new $36 million television contract, the AFL was a force with which to be reckoned, as the Cardinals and the rest of the NFL soon found out.

The leagues both held the 1965 draft on November 28, 1964. That led to all kinds of shenanigans as some teams hid prospects and tried to sign them right after their final bowl games. The owner of the New York Jets, Sonny Werblin, made a fortune in the entertainment industry and he knew what a star looked like. That's why the Jets drafted Alabama quarterback Joe Namath with first overall pick that day.

The Cardinals took Namath with the 12th pick, and a bidding war of sorts was on.

Namath couldn't sign a contract until after Alabama played in the Orange Bowl, but he could talk to representatives for both teams. He went to Alabama coach Paul "Bear" Bryant for advice.

According to the book *Rising Tide*, Bryant asked Namath if the quarterback had a price in mind for his services. For Namath that amount was $100,000. In that case Bear advised, "You go ahead and ask them for $200,000." Namath was shocked by the amount. "Well, hell," Bear reasoned, "you may not get it, but it's a good place to start. You may only get $150."

When the Cardinals' representatives visited Namath in Tuscaloosa, Alabama, the quarterback mentioned that $200,000 and a new car would be nice. The Cardinals reportedly were taken aback and left. But a few days later, they told Namath they would agree to the amount, provided he signed immediately. Namath was smart enough to have an agent, a lawyer and friend named Mike Bite, at the time. "I wasn't bringing you a jock," Bite said, describing his philosophy to NFL Films. "I was bringing you a star."

Cardinals owner Bill Bidwill, though, was balking at the increasingly high contract demands. Bite tried to sell Bidwill on Namath's star power, but Bidwill wasn't buying. St Louis had a new iconic structure, the Gateway Arch, but even a good quarterback wasn't going to capture a country's imagination playing in St. Louis. There were rumors the Cardinals were going to trade Namath's rights to the New York Giants, but it probably wouldn't have mattered.

Werblin wasn't going to let Namath sign with the other team in town. The Jets' opening offer was $300,000. By the time the three-year deal was done, it was worth $427,000, which included a $7,000 Lincoln Continental and hiring two of Namath's brothers and a brother-in-law as scouts. Namath signed the day after Alabama won the Orange Bowl.

Football fans are well aware of what happened next at least with the Jets. Namath became "Broadway Joe," a star on the field and on the streets of New York City. He dated actresses, threw the ball with abandon, and guaranteed the Jets were going to beat the Baltimore Colts in Super Bowl III. Despite not signing Namath, the Cardinals were decent for the rest of the 1960s. Charley Johnson was a solid quarterback, and in 1966 the team added Jim Hart. Besides, "Gateway Joe," doesn't exactly have the same ring to it.

44 "Paddy" Driscoll

John "Paddy" Driscoll was just 5'8" and 160 pounds and played football in an era in which players wore little padding, but he was among the biggest attractions in professional football. And in 1920 Chicago Cardinals owner Chris O'Brien needed a gate attraction. So he signed Driscoll, a triple-threat quarterback, to a contract worth the unheard-of amount of $300 a game with a guarantee of 10 games.

Driscoll, who played at Northwestern University in Evanston, Illinois, was incredibly skilled at all phases of the game. He could defend. He could drop-kick and still holds several NFL records in that department. He could throw and, boy, could he run. According to the *Chicago Tribune*, Driscoll was the first runner to "use the pivot in dodging and he ran with his knees kicking nearly as high as his chest." The pivot move, we assume, is what we call a spin move today.

In one game he drop-kicked four field goals, an NFL record. In 1924 he drop-kicked a 50-yard field goal. Driscoll led the Cardinals to the 1925 championship, but it was to be his last season with the club. The title did not bring great financial rewards to the Cardinals. O'Brien continued to have problems securing a decent venue in which to play, which sounds familiar to modern-day Cardinals fans. In 1926 O'Brien felt he had one move left to keep the Cardinals financially viable. So he traded Driscoll to the Chicago Bears, the Cardinals' cross-town rival, for $3,500. "His financial outlook was dismal," Bears owner George Halas said of O'Brien, according to the book *When Football Was Football*. "He had to cut expenses. The most expensive player was Paddy Driscoll, and common sense told Chris that Paddy deserved a raise, not a cut."

But the deal was far more complicated than a simple trade transaction. Other professional football leagues had popped up, and Driscoll had leverage. A football club named the Chicago Bulls reportedly offered Driscoll $5,000. Driscoll eventually signed with the Bears for $10,000.

It had been a disastrous offseason for the Cardinals. O'Brien had been fined $1,000 by the NFL for using high school players in a game the year before. Now he had lost his lease and, finally, his best player. After winning the NFL title in 1925, the Cardinals didn't have a winning record again until 1931 and they were only 5–4 that year.

Driscoll played for the Bears through the 1929 season and then retired. He remained in football, coaching at a high school in

Chicago and then at Marquette University. In 1941 he became the Bears' backfield coach and was the head coach in 1956–57, compiling a 14–9–1 record. When Halas returned as coach, Driscoll moved into the front office. Driscoll is in the Cardinals' ring of honor and was inducted into the Pro Football Hall of Fame in 1965.

45 Matt Leinart

The Cardinals didn't try to contain their glee or temper fans' expectations when they drafted quarterback Matt Leinart with the 10th overall pick in 2006. They thought the star from the University of Southern California would be taken well before they had a chance. When he fell to them, the Cardinals rushed to turn in Leinart's name as their pick. "It took us about two minutes," general manager Rod Graves said that day. Coach Dennis Green was thrilled. "A huge pick," he said.

In a telephone conversation with Leinart that day, Green was even more effusive. "Coach Green was fired up," Leinart said. "He said it was a gift from heaven." That proved to be hyperbole. In four years as a Cardinal, Leinart played in only 29 games with 17 starts.

In 2010 Cardinals coach Ken Whisenhunt benched Leinart in favor of Derek Anderson. After Leinart voiced his unhappiness with the move, the Cardinals cut the "gift from heaven."

Leinart's years with the Cardinals were filled with disappointment. He was the victim of injuries, bad coaching, poor personal decisions, and a lack of arm strength.

Leinart went on to play a season in Houston and one in Oakland. By 2013 he was out of the NFL. His career started with some promise. As the 10th overall pick, he started 11 games as a rookie. The highlight was nearly pulling off an upset of the powerful Chicago Bears in the opening season at University of Phoenix Stadium.

That 2006 team, however, was poorly coached, and Green was fired at the end of the year. His replacement, Whisenhunt, hadn't drafted Leinart, and the relationship didn't start well. The two first met on the streets of Miami's South Beach at the Super Bowl. Later that spring Whisenhunt criticized Leinart's work ethic, but the quarterback opened that season as the starter.

A fractured collarbone ended his season prematurely, and in 2008 Whisenhunt opened the job to competition between Leinart and Kurt Warner.

Leinart's cause wasn't helped when photos of him partying in a hot tub with girls hit the Internet. "We talked about the level of scrutiny, not only at that position, but who he is just because of having played at a high-profile college team and having been a Heisman Trophy winner," Whisenhunt said at the time. "You would be naïve if you didn't think those things would be of interest. We obviously reinforced there's a standard we hold all our players to that we expect them to keep. I'm obviously disappointed that those pictures showed up."

Leinart's tense relationship with Whisenhunt, however, went beyond the photos. Whisenhunt believed in competition at every position—even quarterback. As a result Leinart never felt the coach had any confidence in him. The situation boiled over in August of 2010. Warner retired after the 2009 season, and Leinart was the heir apparent.

But Whisenhunt became increasingly disenchanted with Leinart as the preseason progressed. So in late August, he announced that

Anderson, signed that spring, would start over Leinart. Incensed, Leinart came off the practice field one day and held an impromptu press conference just behind Whisenhunt's usual spot. "I feel like I've outplayed the competition—training camp, preseason," he said. "My play speaks about that. For me this goes beyond the football field. The philosophy is you want the best 11 guys to play. I feel like I've proved that with my performance. I don't really know what else I could possibly do, so it probably goes beyond football. For me, I just really want an explanation and I haven't been given one."

Leinart had applied both gasoline and the match to his bridge with the team. The situation was poisonous, and Whisenhunt had little choice but to release Leinart. Both the Cardinals and Leinart were relieved, but neither party prospered. After two more seasons, Leinart was out of the NFL. Whisenhunt lasted two more years as Cardinals coach. In that time he went through six starting quarterbacks and was fired after the 2012 season.

46 Whiz

In six years as head coach, Ken Whisenhunt guided the Cardinals to unprecedented heights and to all-too-familiar lows. His tenure ended with him being fired, just as it did for the six head coaches who preceded him in Arizona. Because of that there's a tendency to view Whisenhunt as just another head coach who couldn't win in the desert. That's not fair because in his first three years Whisenhunt was more successful than any Cardinals coach since Don Coryell in the 1970s.

Before Whisenhunt arrived in 2007, the Cardinals had lost at least 10 games for five consecutive seasons, including their first in University of Phoenix Stadium. So it was quite an accomplishment when they went 8–8 in Whisenhunt's first season, 9–7 in 2008, and 10–6 in his third. That second season ended with a heartbreaking loss to the Pittsburgh Steelers in Super Bowl XLIII. "That team was a very average team—strictly from a talent standpoint—top to bottom," said former quarterback Kurt Warner. "It was a team that wasn't going to be able to go out and dominate its opponent week in and week out but had enough difference-making players to beat anyone on any given Sunday."

An argument can be made that Warner was the difference between Whisenhunt's first three years and his last three. With Warner the Cardinals were 27–21. After Warner retired, the Cardinals went 18–30. But that argument fails to give the proper credit Whisenhunt and his staff are due. Warner was on the scrap heap when Whisenhunt arrived in Arizona. From 2002 through 2006, Warner's record as a starting quarterback was 8–23.

Part of the reason for that was poor coaching, sure, but Warner was also struggling. He had a tendency to hold the ball too long, fumble too much, and take too many sacks. Whisenhunt, a former offensive coordinator with the Steelers, emphasized to Warner the importance of ball security. The veteran quarterback worked tirelessly on drills to improve his mobility within in the pocket. That Warner resurrected his career is not only a credit to him, but also to Whisenhunt's coaching. Even though Warner retired after the 2009 season, the Cardinals felt comfortable they were in good shape in Whisenhunt's hands.

Team president Michael Bidwill signed Whisenhunt to a new contract, representing the first time since Coryell that a Cardinals coach was given an extension. For the next three years, Whisenhunt was a victim of bad luck and his own poor decisions. Warner retired a year before the Cardinals expected, leaving the team in a dicey situation at quarterback. Matt Leinart had been drafted 10th overall the year before Whisenhunt arrived, and the coach was never in Leinart's corner.

In 2010 Whisenhunt benched Leinart shortly before the season, opting to go with Derek Anderson instead. Anderson flopped, as did John Skelton and Max Hall, who also started games that year. In 2011 the Cardinals traded for Kevin Kolb, who missed half the season because of injuries. In 2012 Whisenhunt changed quarterbacks again, opting to start Skelton over Kolb to start the season.

An injury to Skelton in Week 1 changed that, and the Cardinals won their first four games by playing conservatively on offense, relying on the defense to carry them. But then Kolb went down with injury again, and the Cardinals finished 5–11 for the second time in three years.

Whisenhunt was fired. "I was very grateful to have had an opportunity there," Whisenhunt said a year after being fired. "The fans were fantastic with me. Michael [Bidwill] gave me the opportunity in this league as a head coach, and I'm very grateful for that. We did a lot of good things there and obviously—as happens in this league—if you lose your job, it's because things didn't go as well."

47 Marshall Goldberg

By today's standards what Marshall Goldberg did after the Chicago Cardinals won the NFL championship in 1947 would be stunning. Even back then, it was surprising. Goldberg, the sensational halfback/defensive back, announced his retirement. He was only

30 and he was playing for a team that looked like it could be a contender for years.

Why retire?

Well, Goldberg had suffered a knee injury that limited his effectiveness in 1947 and already had a successful business career, running a tool machinery company. The Cardinals desperately wanted him back and struck a deal with Goldberg. If he returned, he could concentrate on just playing defense, a rarity at the time.

Goldberg retired for good in 1948. He helped revolutionize the defensive back position and was excellent on offense, too. At the time of his retirement, Goldberg held team records for yards gained, attempts, touchdowns, and interceptions. He is one of five Cardinals to have his number (99) retired and he's in the team's ring of honor. The senior committee of the Pro Football Hall of Fame has recommended him twice for induction. "He might well have been the first defensive specialist in pro football," former Cardinals coach Jimmy Conzelman said, according to the book *Pro Football's Rag Days*. "Marshall Goldberg may be one of the most underrated players ever to play in the pros. At one time in a season, he led the league in five different departments. Imagine what a player with those statistics could command in today's market!"

Goldberg was born in Elkins, West Virginia. As a sophomore in high school, he weighed only 110 pounds, which earned him the nickname "Biggie." By the time he became a star running back/defensive back/returner at the University of Pittsburgh, he was 195 pounds and he became a two-time All-American there.

The Cardinals drafted him in the second round in 1939, and historians point to that move as the first step toward the team's improvement in the late 1940s. "The class of '39 didn't have many business opportunities," Goldberg told Joe Ziemba, author of *When Football Was Football*. "For the first time, some of the better players looked at professional football as a chance to make some money and perhaps use it as a way to get into the business world."

That's what Goldberg did. He was a standout player for the next four seasons before World War II interrupted his career. Goldberg joined the Navy in 1943 and spent two years in the Pacific, rising to the rank of lieutenant. Goldberg mustered out of the service in 1946 and boarded a train in San Diego to return to Chicago. It should have been a joyous trip, but it wasn't.

Before the trip he had noticed he had been losing weight. And he was so ill on the train that he rarely left his lower bunk. As soon as he arrived in Chicago, Goldberg saw a doctor.

The diagnosis was testicular cancer. "I had an operation in March of 1946," Goldberg told Ziemba. "And after the operation, I bought an exercycle and stayed on that to get in shape. The Cardinals were scared to death and they kept the whole thing out of the papers, but I was able to play in August. The doctors said if I lived seven years, I'd be okay."

Goldberg lived until age 88, passing away in 2006. He enjoyed a successful business career in Chicago, but his later years were spent in a nursing home. He battled the effects of several concussions suffered in his career, according to his family.

Goldberg was inducted into the National College Football Hall of Fame, and many people believe he has a strong case to be in the Pro Football Hall of Fame. He once was asked if it bothered him not to have a bust in Canton. "I haven't thought much about it," he said. "I know a lot of great football players who aren't in there. I don't worry about that. There's an old Italian proverb that says, 'Life begins tomorrow.' I can't worry about those things. I worry more about the stock market than I do about getting into the Hall of Fame."

48 Neil Lomax

There are pivotal points in the history of every long-standing organization, times people later can readily identify when things went north or south. For the Cardinals August 29, 1989, was such a point. That's the day quarterback Neil Lomax was placed on injured reserve because of degenerative arthritis in his left hip. Lomax, 30 at the time, never played again. And the Cardinals fell into a deep morass, losing at least 11 games in each of the next four seasons.

Poor quarterback play wasn't the only reason, but it was the primary one. The season before had contained such promise. In their first season in Arizona, the Cardinals started 7–4 and were tied with the New York Giants for first place in the NFC East. "We had some guys who were pretty good," said former running back Stump Mitchell, "and we were moving in the right direction."

But Lomax suffered a torn knee ligament in the 11th game and missed two games. He returned for the last three but wasn't himself. The Cardinals lost their last five games. All the while, Lomax also was dealing with the hip ailment. That led to the Cardinals placing him on injured reserve for all of the 1989 season. Lomax spent the season watching practice and working with a therapist.

Entering the 1989 season, the Cardinals seemed to expect the worst. Coach Gene Stallings chuckled when someone suggested a week before the season opener that the Cardinals were healthier than at the start of previous years. "Sure, if you're counting the quarterback as just another man," Stallings said. "I doubt if you take [John] Elway out of Denver's team, they'd say they're healthy."

That's how much Lomax meant to the Cardinals and why everyone hoped for a miracle and that a season off might make the

St. Louis Cardinals quarterback Neil Lomax is considered one of the best passers in franchise history, even though a hip injury ended his playing career prematurely. (USA TODAY Sports Images)

difference for Lomax. "We all hoped for the best but expected the worst," tight end Rob Awalt said in 1989. "I watched him trying so very hard to come back and I saw all the pain he went through and the anger at not being able to do what he used to do."

The condition never improved, and in January of 1990, Lomax announced his retirement. "I can go ahead and retire and get on with life," Lomax said at the time. "The Cardinals can get on with the quarterback they have now and not be wondering about, 'What's Neil Lomax's situation?'" Lomax, wife Laurie, and his kids moved back to the Portland area, where Lomax has worked in private business and as a high school coach.

The Cardinals drafted Lomax out of Portland State in the second round in 1981, figuring he could be Jim Hart's eventual replacement. By his second season, Lomax was the regular starter. And by the end of his career, Lomax had set a handful of franchise records, including passing yards in a season (4,614 in 1984) and in a game (468 in 1984). He made two Pro Bowls.

Lomax finished his career with more than 22,000 passing yards, 136 touchdowns, and 90 interceptions. If Lomax's career had not been cut short, he would have been the best quarterback in Cardinals history, said receiver Roy Green, one of his favorite targets. "His numbers would be staggering, and I'm guessing he threw about a third less than they do now," Green said. "We threw it maybe 25 times a game, not 35 to 40. As far as accuracy, nobody was as good. I had the opportunity to play in a couple Pro Bowls with guys like Joe Montana and Joe Theismann. I saw [Dan] Marino play. Neil was more accurate. He was just amazing."

49 Jackie Smith

The best tight end in Cardinals history was a 10ᵗʰ round pick in 1963, and Jackie Smith was shocked he was taken that high. He wasn't used much as a receiver in four seasons at Northwestern State (Louisiana), so playing in the NFL wasn't something he even dreamed about.

But Cardinals athletic trainer Jack Rockwell, who also scouted some, had noticed Smith in a spring game. He told the team's scouts about the big, fast redhead at the small school in Natchitoches, Louisiana, so the St. Louis Cardinals took a flyer on Smith. "Getting drafted? I didn't even consider it a possibility," Smith told *Sports Illustrated.* "Somebody was looking out for my sorry ass, or the Gods were on my side, or [the Cardinals coaches] all just got drunk that day and didn't make good decisions."

As it turned out, somebody was looking out for the Cardinals' sorry asses that day, or the Gods were the team's side, and if the coaches were drunk when they picked Smith, they should have drank heavily on every draft day thereafter. Smith played 16 seasons, including 15 for the Cardinals. When he retired he was the game's all-time leading receiving tight end with 480 catches, 7,918 yards, and 40 touchdowns. He played in 210 games, made five Pro Bowls, and was all-NFL twice. He was inducted into the Pro Football Hall of Fame in 1994, one of only a dozen Cardinals so honored.

Smith didn't think he would make it through one training camp with the Cardinals, much less 15. But he became a starter in Week 5 at Pittsburgh because of an injury to starter Taz Anderson. In that game against the Steelers, Smith caught nine passes for 212 yards and two touchdowns. He helped the Cardinals overcome a 13-point, fourth-quarter deficit to win 24–23.

It was years before Smith came out of the starting lineup. He played in 121 consecutive games before missing his first one in his ninth season. Smith was different than most other tight ends of his day. Back then, a tight end was mainly a blocker, and Smith excelled at that.

But what set Smith apart were his speed and receiving ability. In 1967 he finished third in the NFL with 56 receptions and averaged an astounding 21.5 yards a catch.

Throughout his sterling career, Smith never let himself dream of making the Hall of Fame. He described his philosophy to *The Dallas Morning News* in 1994. "I never would give myself the luxury of thinking how good it would be if I made it," he said. "I kept my head down and butt up and worked as hard as I could. I never gave myself the luxury of longing for it, so I wouldn't be disappointed. This is similar to making the team as a rookie. I looked around the huddle at guys like Bobby Joe Conrad and John David Crow. I thought, *What am I doing here?*"

Smith's time with the Cardinals franchise did not end well. He retired in 1977, but Cardinals coach Bud Wilkinson wanted him back in 1978. Smith was willing, but team management, namely owner Bill Bidwill, rejected the idea. "I talked to Bud later on that day," quarterback Jim Hart recalled, "and he said, 'You're not going to believe this. Billy won't let me pick him up.' That's when Jackie went to Dallas." Smith played one year for the Cowboys, infamously dropping a sure touchdown pass in Super Bowl XIII. It's sad that some fans remember him more for that drop than the incredible career he had in St. Louis.

Raw feelings between the Cardinals and Smith apparently remain. He is the only Hall of Famer in team history who is not in the franchise's ring of honor. Smith thinks Bidwill was upset with comments Smith made about the Bidwill family as Smith was leaving for Dallas. "I don't need to be revered or anything," Smith told *Sports Illustrated*, "but to not acknowledge that I even played? It's embarrassing."

The Cardinals do have two large photos of Smith at University of Phoenix Stadium, and Smith, who lives in St. Louis, has been invited to alumni events.

50 Larry Centers

Nothing was going right for the Cardinals that Christmas night in 1995, which wasn't a surprise since little had gone right for them that whole season. Here they were 4–11, entering the final game of the season, on Christmas, on Monday night, against the Dallas Cowboys, the best team in the NFL. The Cardinals were in disarray. Two players fought in the locker room before the game. Everyone knew coach and general manager Buddy Ryan was going to be fired the next day. There was little incentive for a Cardinal to do anything extraordinary, but that's exactly what fullback Larry Centers did.

Centers already was a fan favorite for the way he played the game: all-out and full speed, no matter what the digits on the scoreboard read. Often, he was the only reason to watch the Cardinals, as he was that Christmas night. Centers took a short pass, ran down a sideline, and hurdled Cowboys cornerback Larry Brown. Fans at Sun Devil Stadium and viewers at home turned to friends to confirm what they just saw. When Centers returned to the huddle, he asked his teammates, "How did that look?"

"Larry," center Ed Cunningham replied, "you are a bad dude."

When people recognize or meet Centers, many bring up the famous hurdle on Christmas Night, which was shown in the movie *Jerry Maguire.* Centers remembers it well. "Somebody at *The Arizona Republic* caught me at the highest of my flight and took that picture," he said. "I've got a painting based off of it hanging in my office."

A fifth-round pick out of Stephen F. Austin in 1990, Centers spent nine seasons with Cardinals. He made two Pro Bowls with Arizona, including 1995, when he set an NFL record for running backs with 101 catches, also a franchise record.

While he is remembered most for his receiving ability, Centers could do other things, too. He was a good runner, especially in goal-line and other short-yardage situations, and he could block. "Over the years, I've read things about myself that weren't necessarily true," Centers said. "Some people don't think I was that good of a blocker. I wasn't a bruiser, but I think I got the job done. I just didn't bruise a lot of people getting it done."

When Centers left the Cardinals after 1998 via free agency, he held the franchise record for career receptions and receptions in a season. They were remarkable accomplishments, especially since Centers played a total of 15 games in his first two seasons. Going from Stephen F. Austin, a Division I-AA school, to the NFL was a big leap, and Centers needed the time to make it. As Centers showed later in his career, he was good at clearing hurdles.

It was good for him to watch and learn those first two seasons, he said. "I was fortunate," Centers said. "We hired a running backs coach named Bobby Jackson. Bobby came to the Cardinals at the right time for me in my development and my growth as a player. He taught me the meaning of a professional football player."

Being a professional meant putting in a full-day's work, no matter the circumstances. And that's what fans appreciated about

Centers. The Cardinals could be down by three scores in the fourth quarter—and they often were—and Centers would make astounding catches and then bounce off defenders like he was in a video game. "I'm most proud of how I was able to find a way to continue to play hard, even though things didn't look great week to week, especially late down the stretch," Centers said. "I'm proud that I never threw any of my teammates under the bus. There were times when I could have and maybe should have in retrospect."

The struggles Centers endured during his first eight NFL seasons are what made the 1998 season so sweet. The Cardinals finally made the playoffs, winning their last three games to qualify. "Oh, man, I was able to exhale," Centers said. "I didn't know how to feel. I had been busting my butt for a long time. I wasn't being utilized that much. That was a concern of mine, but at the same time, as long as we were winning, I'm good to go."

The Cardinals couldn't sustain success. Management let three key players—Centers, left tackle Lomas Brown, and outside linebacker Jamir Miller—leave in free agency. A lot of ability and leadership walked out the door. Centers spent two years in Washington and two more with the Buffalo Bills before finishing his career with the New England Patriots in 2003. He earned a Super Bowl ring in that final year. While he wears the ring often, Centers considers himself a Cardinal, first and foremost.

Centers' love for the game was obvious when he played, but off the field, he didn't take himself too seriously. During one season, he called a reporter over to his locker to let him in on a secret. "I've come up with my own marketing slogan," Centers said. "Want to hear it?"

"Sure," the reporter replied.

"Larry runs, Larry blocks, Larry catches—Larry Centers."

51 Tour University of Phoenix Stadium

Not every Cardinals fan can break away on a fall weekend to see a game or can escape in the summer to watch a training camp practice. And many simply view games as too expensive. That doesn't mean University of Phoenix Stadium is inaccessible. All true Cardinals fans should take the time to visit the stadium, and they don't have to wait until there is an event there.

Tours are conducted throughout the year, and the charge is reasonable: $9 for adults and $7 for kids ages 4-12, members of the military, and anyone 65 or older. For tour dates and times, go to universityofphoenixstadium.com. Tours are scheduled to last 75 minutes, include a mile or so of walking, and are completely handicapped accessible. It's fun to wander the stadium on your own and visit the team shop there. During football season and other big events, the outside of the stadium is lit and is worthy of at least a drive-by look.

A tour provides additional behind-the-scenes knowledge of the unique multipurpose facility. You can find out how the first fully retractable field in America slides in and out on an 18.9 million-pound tray and a roof made of translucent fabric opens and closes. The outside of the stadium is unique. It's meant to resemble a barrel cactus. Shimmering metal panels reflect the desert light, and there are 21 vertical glass slots on the exterior of the stadium, allowing light inside and a view of the horizon.

You can see the four columns inside that contain hieroglyphics of the team's records and history. At the north entrance, there is a 60-foot logo and a wall honoring some of the great men and women in team history. There are six levels in the stadium, and a

Press Box

Steve Schoenfeld arrived in Arizona shortly after the Cardinals did, and from 1988 until his death in 2000, no one covered the team or the NFL better. The press box at University of Phoenix Stadium is named in honor of Schoenfeld, who was killed by a hit-and-run driver in October of 2000.

A huge picture of Schoenfeld and an impressive display of his work greet visitors as they exit the elevator in the press box. Schoenfeld worked in Tulsa and Dallas before coming to Arizona to cover the NFL and the Cardinals for *The Arizona Republic*. He spent the last few months of his life covering the NFL for CBS Sportsline.

In the team's media guide, Schoenfeld is described as "a tough but fair reporter and an eloquent writer." Steve left behind a wife, Robin. She remains a passionate Cardinals fan and season-ticket holder.

large mural on each represents Arizona's natural attractions. The one on the 400 level, the highest in the stadium, replicates the night sky and has the names of state observatories on it. Others highlight state rivers, canyons, deserts, and mountain ranges.

After the tour there is plenty to do in the area surrounding the stadium. There are shops and restaurants at the Westgate Entertainment District nearby. In downtown Glendale there are numerous antique shops and excellent non-chain restaurants. And downtown Phoenix is 20 minutes away if there isn't traffic.

52 Packers-Cardinals Wild-Card Game

On January 10, 2010, two of the greatest quarterbacks of their generation met at University of Phoenix Stadium for a little post-holiday backyard football. At least, that's how easy the Cardinals' Kurt Warner and the Green Bay Packers' Aaron Rodgers made their jobs look that day in the wild-card round of the playoffs.

The Cardinals won 51–45 in overtime in the highest scoring game in NFL playoff history. Combined, the teams gained 1,024 yards. There were 13 touchdowns by 11 different players, and each team punted only once. Warner had more touchdown passes (five) than incompletions (four). Rodgers passed for 423 yards and four touchdowns. "Whew," Warner said minutes after the game. "Anyone else tired?"

Not just tired. Exhausted. Spent.

Receiver Larry Fitzgerald had a dentist appointment the next day at 8:00 AM. He slept instead and later called the game "one of those classics, one of the best games probably ever played in the playoffs."

Warner was the star, completing 29-of-33 passes for 379 yards and no interceptions. The Packers were helpless in trying to stop him. "I'm glad he's on my squad," linebacker Karlos Dansby said.

The Cardinals started fast, scoring 17 points in the first quarter. By early in the third quarter, they led 31–10. Then Rodgers got hot, throwing all four of his touchdown passes in the second half, including one to tie the game with 1:52 left. That allowed plenty of time for Warner and the Cardinals to operate. Four consecutive completions brought the Cardinals to the Packers' 16-yard line with 14 seconds and one timeout remaining.

It was first down, and Cardinals coach Ken Whisenhunt elected to try the field goal. The plan was to let the clock run down to seven seconds and then take the final timeout. But Fitzgerald became excited and mistakenly called timeout. Whisenhunt was not happy. "He said I was an idiot and he's probably going to release me at the end of the game," Fitzgerald said afterward.

With no timeouts remaining, Whisenhunt decided to try the field goal. But kicker Neil Rackers was still warming up, thinking

During a 2010 wild-card game, cornerback Michael Adams strips Green Bay Packers quarterback Aaron Rodgers, and linebacker Karlos Dansby returns the fumble 17 yards for an overtime touchdown to win the highest scoring playoff contest in NFL history.

more time would be run off the clock. Holder Ben Graham yelled at Rackers to get his helmet and get on the field. Rackers missed from 34 yards. "He rushed it, and that's why I think he missed the kick," Whisenhunt said. "I'll take the blame for that because I should have communicated better to Neil during the timeout."

For 60 minutes neither offense had been slowed down, so winning the coin toss for sudden death overtime seemed vital. The Packers won it. "It was almost like we'll just flip the coin, and whoever wins the toss, wins the game," Whisenhunt said. "We don't even have to play it. I'm glad we did." The Cardinals players were having the same thoughts as most of the 61,296 in attendance. Game over. "My reaction was like, 'Damn! Everything is bouncing their way right now,'" Dansby said after the game. "I was like, 'Shit, we've got to do something.'"

Then Rodgers did something uncharacteristic. On the first play of overtime, receiver Greg Jennings maneuvered behind the Cardinals secondary. He was wide open, but Rodgers overthrew him. Two plays later the Packers faced third and 6 from their own 24. Rodgers dropped back and was hit by cornerback Michael Adams, who was blitzing off the Packers' right side. One of Adams' hands seemed to briefly grab Rodgers' facemask, but no penalty was called. The ball popped loose, bounced off Rodgers' foot and into Dansby's hands. He returned it 17 yards for the victory.

An awesome display of offensive firepower ended in a defensive touchdown. Oh, the irony. Packers coach Mike McCarthy couldn't believe it and fell to his knees on the sideline.

Packers fans were upset no facemask penalty was called, but Rodgers refused to blame the officials. Instead, he kicked himself for missing Jennings on the first play of overtime.

It turned out to be Warner's last Cardinals home game. He had yet to announce his retirement, but he made no secret that he was considering it. After the game he took a victory lap and marveled at what he had just been a part of. "From a fan's perspective, it was a fabulous game," Whisenhunt said. "From my perspective, it was a gut-wrenching game."

53 Dennis Green

The question was coming. Everyone in the press conference knew it. It was asked every time the Cardinals hired a new coach, which was often during their first 20 years or so in Arizona. "What makes you think you can win here when no one else has?" In 2004 Dennis Green had a unique answer. He said nothing, which was unusual for Green, and just pointed to a chart that showed his winning percentage as NFL coach: .610

He likened his offense to a "high-performance helicopter" and his disciplinary philosophy to his child's kindergarten teacher. People heard that and left bewildered. That reaction also describes Green's failure in three years as a Cardinals coach. How did someone who built great offenses and won 61 percent of his games with the Minnesota Vikings go 16–32 (.333) with the Cardinals?

Well, it took some work. And many, many bad decisions.

First, Green had trouble putting a coaching staff together because many of his top choices were under contract elsewhere. Then he changed assistants like he changed socks. In 2004 he fired an offensive line coach the day the team left to play the Buffalo Bills in the eighth week of the season. Three weeks later he benched quarterback Josh McCown the night before playing the Carolina Panthers. In 2006 Green melted down in a press conference after losing to the Chicago Bears on Monday night. The next day he demoted his offensive coordinator, Keith Rowen, even though it was Green's decision to play conservatively in the second half against the Bears. In three years Green fired seven assistant coaches and started five different quarterbacks. General manager Rod Graves and others were criticized for not stopping some of those moves. "We knew he would be making bold moves as he came in," Michael Bidwill, a team vice president, said the day Green was fired. "As Rod said, he supported many of those moves because we saw Coach Green as somebody who was very innovative and bold in terms of how he would mold a team. I think in some areas we've made a lot of progress. Unfortunately, we didn't have enough wins."

Green wasn't a complete failure in his tenure. His press conferences could be wildly entertaining and bewildering. He once responded to a question by saying: "That's awfully philosophical for a Wednesday." And, of course, there was the famous Monday Night Meltdown after the Bears loss, when he barked: "The Bears are who we thought they were!" Coors Light even featured that in a commercial.

Green helped the team redevelop the way it drafted, ranking the top 120 prospects regardless of position and then sticking with that order during the draft. It paid off immediately. In 2004 the Cardinals selected perhaps their best class ever, taking receiver Larry Fitzgerald, inside linebacker Karlos Dansby, and defensive lineman Darnell Dockett with the first three picks. Defensive lineman Antonio Smith was selected in the fifth round. All played integral roles in the team advancing to its first Super Bowl, and each played in the NFL 11 or more seasons.

Overall, however, Green's penchant for bold moves did far more harm than good. With the Vikings, Green had a history of making audacious moves, but they worked. Minnesota went to the playoffs eight times in his 10 seasons. Under Green, however, the Cardinals stayed well below .500. Part of the reason was that Green could never build the quality of coaching staff he had with the Vikings, where Brian Billick and Tony Dungy served as coordinators.

The Cardinals went 6–10, 5–11, and 5–11 under Green. In 2006 they won their opener and then lost eight consecutive games. Among their 11 losses were three close ones at home. The Bidwill family had seen enough. "In the final analysis, when you look at the three years, we didn't win enough games," Michael Bidwill said. "Dennis Green understands that in this league you've got to win games. We're all sorry it didn't turn out."

54 The Car-Pitts

The Chicago Cardinals struggled during the early years of World War II, but hopes were high for the 1944 season. It wasn't because of an infusion of talent but because the Cardinals were merging with the Steelers for one season. While NFL teams were struggling to find enough decent players to field one team, the Cardinals and Pittsburgh Steelers had the advantage of combining two rosters and two coaching staffs.

Or so they thought.

What resulted was a team so bad that a fan suggested to a newspaper columnist the club be called the Car-Pitts (read as carpets). "I think it's very appropriate as every team in the league walks over them," the fan said.

He was right. The Card-Pitts finished 0–10 and were a dysfunctional mess from the start of training camp through the end of the season. Forty-five players reported for training camp in Waukesha, Wisconsin. Six of them couldn't make it through the first practice because of heat exhaustion.

The team had a decent quarterback, Coley McDonough, to start the season. But after one game, he was re-called into military service because the country was so desperate for soldiers. The Card-Pitts tried various replacements, but every one of them stunk. Opponents intercepted 41 passes, and the Card-Pitts threw for only eight touchdowns.

The coaching staff didn't help much. Separately, Cardinals coach Phil Handler and assistant Buddy Parker, and Steelers coach Walt Kiesling and assistant Jimmy Leonard, weren't bad at their jobs. Together, they were a disaster. Steelers owner Dan Rooney was 12 at the time and he remembered the dysfunction. "You know that old saying that too many chefs will spoil the soup? Well, we had too many chefs," Rooney told the *Pittsburgh Post-Gazette* in 2009.

In the season opener, the Card-Pitts actually had a 28–23 lead late in the game against Cleveland. (The team had the lead only one other time the whole season.) The Card-Pitts intercepted a pass and took over at the 1-yard line. They had two viable options to close out the victory: try to run out the clock or take a safety and play defense. Apparently, the coaching conglomerate decided there was a third option: punting on first down. The kick went 10 yards, and Cleveland scored three plays later to win the game.

The situation never improved. After the first game against the Chicago Bears that season, three players, including star runner Johnny Grigas, were fined $200 apiece for "indifferent play." Their teammates were upset and refused to practice until the situation was addressed. Owner Art Rooney rescinded two of the fines and waived the third player.

Against Washington there were two fights among players in the first half and a bench-clearing brawl. Later in the season, Grigas quit the team rather than try to win the NFL's rushing title against the Bears on frozen turf at Pittsburgh's Forbes Field. According to the *Post-Gazette*, Frigas left a note explaining his decision. "When your mind is changed because of the physical beating week in and week out, your soul isn't in the game."

Not a bad decision, Dan Rooney said: "The field was frozen solid. He may have been the smartest guy on the team." The Bears won 49–7, handing the Card-Pitts their worst defeat of the season.

Thankfully, it was the last game of the season. The Card-Pitts disbanded after the 1944 season with both franchises going to their respective corners, the Cardinals back to Chicago, the Steelers to Pittsburgh. No one shed tears. "We were the worst team of all time," Art Rooney said.

55 The Stadium Vote

For NFL coaches and players, Saturday afternoons are usually reserved for relaxing and mentally preparing for the game the next day. That wasn't the case for all of the Cardinals on November 4, 2000. Dave McGinnis, the interim coach, and two of his stars, quarterback Jake Plummer and wide receiver Rob Moore, spent part of that Saturday afternoon knocking on doors to tout the benefits of a proposition that would build the team a new stadium in Glendale. "It's not my strong suit," McGinnis said then of campaigning, "but I jumped in there and tried like hell anyway."

What the Cardinals did the next day might have made more of a difference. They beat Washington 16–15 with the help of a 103-yard fumble return by cornerback Aeneas Williams, which tied an NFL record. "When I took this job, I said I wanted us to transfer the feeling of heart and passion from the field to the stands and back to the field," McGinnis said after the victory. "Now, we need our fans one more time on Tuesday."

The fans delivered, passing the proposition that funded much of the cost of University of Phoenix Stadium, which opened in 2006. It was a controversial proposal, and many taxpayers in Maricopa County questioned the wisdom of building a stadium for a franchise that had delivered one winning season in its previous 12 in the desert. The 2000 team was not good either.

Coach Vince Tobin was fired after a 48–7 loss to the Dallas Cowboys in late October. McGinnis, the defensive coordinator, was promoted to interim coach and lost his first game to the New Orleans Saints at Sun Devil Stadium the week before the vote.

The vote was going to be close, so the Cardinals could ill afford anything to go wrong in the days before the vote. So players knocked on doors and conducted interviews wearing hats that promoted the proposition. "If it does end up being a win, it's definitely a relief in two ways," Plummer said at the time. "A win makes us all happy, knowing what the future holds for us. And now we can focus on just playing football. There's no vote, no stadium hanging over how we perform."

Most people were receptive when they found Cardinals on their doorsteps that Saturday afternoon. And a handful were not. "Some of the looks on the people coming up there, I was on my heels ready to get out of there," Plummer said that weekend. "They come off a hard day's work, they're ready to go vote, and the last thing they want is someone to throw a bunch of paper in their faces and confuse them even more."

No one was more nervous about the vote than owner Bill Bidwill and his son, Michael, a team vice president who led the effort to build a new stadium. "I don't think he wants to see me walk through his office door again," Michael said then, referring to his father. "Sometimes I deliver good news and sometimes we're back on the roller coaster heading downhill again. He's like a rock sometimes. He'd say, 'Just do your best. Just keep going after it.' He's given me a lot of support that way—not only as a father but as an employer." As Michael Bidwill talked to reporters, his father walked in the room, observed the scene and smiled. "For those of you who don't know," he said, "children are highly overrated."

The Bidwills promised a new stadium would help the Cardinals field a more competitive team. It did. In their first 10 years at University of Phoenix Stadium, the Cardinals had five winning seasons. That's not great, but it was a vast improvement. In the previous 20 years, the Cardinals had just one winning season. "Everyone sees the possibility of what it does for an organization," said wide receiver Frank Sanders. "I think the stadium will help draw [free agents], but also you have to look at the management saying, 'This is where this team is going.' [The players] have to see other benefits here besides playing golf in the offseason."

56 The Stan Mauldin Tragedy

Minutes before the first game of the 1948 regular season, Chicago Cardinals tackle Stan Mauldin complained about a headache to teammates in the locker room. No one thought much about it because, as halfback Marshall Goldberg explained later, tension is common before games, especially one like this: a rematch of the 1947 NFL title game, which the Cardinals won. So Goldberg rubbed Mauldin's neck to help him relax.

Later, everyone would realize something was wrong. Mauldin wasn't a complainer. He had been an All-American tackle at the University of Texas and had flown 35 bombing missions during World War II. When the war ended, he joined the Cardinals and by the end of 1947 had become one of the game's fiercest offensive linemen.

On that Friday night, Mauldin played the entire way in the 21–14 victory against the Philadelphia Eagles in Chicago. In the locker room afterward, Mauldin told line coach Phil Handler, "I feel dizzy" and collapsed into the coach's arms.

Mauldin was unconscious, and the winning locker room became quiet. In those days a pulmotor squad was used to try and resuscitate patients. In Mauldin's case it was of no use. He was pronounced dead at 1:00 AM on September 25. He was 27 and left behind a wife and a son.

A story in the *Chicago Tribune* described the awful scene in the Cardinals locker room: "Teammates of Mauldin knelt in prayer while Dr. Samuel Goldberg and Dr. Sidney Portis bent over the body as the pulmotor squad worked in shifts. There wasn't a person in the dressing room who wasn't crying when the end came. Athletes who would battle until they no longer could stand before giving a football player an inch cried unashamedly as their teammate passed into the shadow of death."

All signs pointed to a natural death, mostly likely a heart attack. Only a handful of the 25,875 fans in attendance that night at Comiskey Park had any idea of the tragedy in the locker room. Those who did waited on the stairs to the locker room for word about Mauldin. The city of Chicago, the Cardinals, and the rest of the NFL mourned. Eagles coach Earle "Greasy" Neale called Mauldin the best tackle in the league, and the Eagles players voted to give Mauldin's widow a share of money if they won the 1948 championship. (The Eagles did, beating the Cardinals 7–0 on December 19.) "Mauldin is irreplaceable as both a great football player and as a man," Cardinals coach Jimmy Conzelman said.

Two days after Mauldin's death, the Cardinals players met at the Dearborn Street Train Station in Chicago to say good-bye to their teammate, who was taken home to Texas for burial.

It was perhaps fitting that the farewell happened at the train station. Most road trips in those days were taken by train, which fostered a family atmosphere among players.

The Cardinals elected to practice on Monday morning, perhaps recalling what Mauldin had said the year before after punter Jeff Burkett was killed in a plane crash in Bryce Canyon, Utah. "Fellows, there's a show that's got to go on."

The Cardinals' 1948 show went on. Their only regular-season loss came the following week to the Chicago Bears. The Cardinals won their final 10 regular season games before losing to the Eagles in the NFL championship. "It was tragic," running back Charley Trippi said of Mauldin's death. "When you play football like we did, it was like a family. If you lost a ballplayer like we did, it was just a tragic event. We kind of lived with that for a long time."

57 J.V. Cain

565 Stop

Jim Hart remembers the play call clearly, even though it came in a training camp practice decades ago. The two outside receivers were to run deep out routes, and tight end J.V. Cain would go down the middle 12 to 15 yards and then turn inside or out, depending on what the defense did. It was just another play at training camp. Everyone did what they were supposed to, and Hart ended up throwing it to the flanker to the right. It was no big deal to the players or the hundreds of spectators watching practice that Saturday evening, July 22, 1979, at Lindenwood College in St. Charles, Missouri. "Everyone was headed back to the huddle, including J.V.," Hart said. "And then we heard this big thump.

Everyone turned around real quick, and there was J.V. out on the turf."

The team's athletic trainers and doctor were immediately at Cain's side. But resuscitation efforts were futile. Cain had died on the field. It was his 28th birthday. "I don't have the words to describe what a great guy J.V. was," said former teammate Dan Dierdorf. "I'm stumbling to portray just how popular he was. He was a hell of a man, a great guy, a wonderful teammate. We were devastated."

The St. Louis Cardinals selected Cain with the seventh overall pick of the 1974 draft. He was not as talented as the Cardinals' starting tight end at the time, Hall of Famer Jackie Smith, but Cain had excellent speed and hands. An All-American at Colorado, Cain had a breakout season in his third year in 1976. He caught 26 passes for 400 yards and five touchdowns.

After Cain collapsed, coach Bud Wilkinson ended practice, of course, and the players returned to their dormitories. But no one could sleep. "At three in the morning, we were all walking around the campus at training camp," Dierdorf said. "Some guys were by themselves, and some were in groups."

They were young men. Many, like Dierdorf, had thought of little else but football. They thought they were invincible. And they had been so excited to see Cain running so well after missing the previous season with a torn Achilles tendon. "He was running around like a 10-year-old," Dierdorf said.

For Dierdorf and others, it was a life-changing moment. "I was a player who went through my 20s with blinders on," Dierdorf said. "I focused on nothing but trying to be the best football player I could be. I was a driven man. When you're young, you can afford to do that.

I had never seen someone die in front of me, 20 feet from me. I started thinking, *Oh, God. Look at how you've looked at hardly anything else other than playing football.* That cloak of invincibility you draped around yourself, in an instant it's gone. For the first time in my life, I realized it wasn't the most important thing in the world. It was a life-changing experience for me. It made me a better person."

An autopsy revealed that Cain died from a congenital heart defect. He left behind his wife of six months and broken-hearted teammates. "He was a great talent who was ready to become a force in the NFL," said teammate Roger Wehrli. "I'm not sure we as a team ever quite got over his death that year."

58 Michael Bidwill

A day or two after voters approved funding in 2000 to build the Cardinals a new stadium, owner Bill Bidwill visited the team's media relations office and saw his son, Michael, talking with reporters. "For those of you who don't know," he said with a slight smile to reporters, "children are highly overrated."

And then he left.

Michael laughed because he and everyone else knew father and son valued each other's opinions over anyone else's. Yet, the two couldn't be more different, and it's those differences that have helped lift the Cardinals from perennial losers to championship contenders. Bill Bidwill is quiet and introverted. He was not good at glad-handing, back-slapping, making deals, and interacting with fans and business partners.

Those are some of Michael Bidwill's strengths, and his father was smart enough to know that. After serving as a federal prosecutor from 1990 to 1996, Michael joined the Cardinals as vice president and general counsel. In 2007 he was promoted to team president and has handled most of the day-to-day operations of the team since that point. However, it's not as if Michael flipped a switch that improved the organization.

In his early years with the team, he had a reputation among some employees as a stubborn micromanager. He butted heads with some of the largest and most important entities in the greater Phoenix area: Arizona State and the Fiesta Bowl. Critics said his main goal in negotiations was to win by a large margin. "I never meant to offend anybody," Michael said. "Sometimes when I make a case, I get passionate about it. And if you're on the other side of the table, you might see that as a fault."

Michael's crowning achievement was the building of University of Phoenix Stadium. Its construction meant the Cardinals had a home of their own for the first time in franchise history. Michael worked tirelessly to obtain funding for the stadium—even if it meant alienating some people along the way. "He's the one primarily responsible for getting that done," Bill said several years ago.

A new stadium was the key to the Cardinals' reversal of fortunes. It opened in 2006, a year before Michael became president. The change has been drastic. From 1949 through 2007, the Cardinals made the playoffs in non-strike seasons just three times. From 2007 through 2015, they did it four times. Although his father had a reputation for being cheap, Michael has been willing to spend millions. In 2013 new general manager Steve Keim asked for money to expand a woefully understaffed scouting department. Michael approved it. In 2013 coach Bruce Arians asked for money to hire additional coaches. Michael approved it.

And the Cardinals recently spent millions on upgrades to their headquarters in Tempe, including the construction of an indoor practice facility, a new dining area, and an expanded weight room. There is even a rest and recovery room, where players can enjoy quiet when not in meetings or at practice. "He has made our facility first-rate," wide receiver Larry Fitzgerald told azcentralsports.com.

"For free agents and for our guys, it's a destination. He has instilled a winning culture."

Ex-Cardinals from decades ago marvel at the improvements. Many of them had to beg Bill for raises, and the team's facilities usually were second class—mostly because they were tenants in someone else's building. Under Michael's leadership many of those former players have been welcomed back to the team.

It's cool to be a Cardinal now.

Michael grew up in St. Louis around those players. He began visiting training camps when he was four or five and started working as a ballboy when he was about nine. Dan Dierdorf, a Hall of Fame tackle, developed a special relationship with Michael back then. They teased each other constantly, and Dierdorf could tell then there was something special about the kid. "He's whipsaw smart and he always was," Dierdorf said. "Michael's a pisser. He's always had that spark. I'm not the least bit surprised how successful he is in running the team. He inherited from his father that deep love of the NFL and the game of football. There is a respect for the game and a respect for the guys that play it."

59 Rolle's Returns

Safety Antrel Rolle didn't know he had tied an NFL record when he did a cartwheel and a backflip to celebrate his second interception return for a touchdown against the Cincinnati Bengals in 2007. All Rolle knew is that he had returned two interceptions for touchdowns, and it was a pretty big deal. The gymnastics judge on the Cardinals' sideline, coach Ken Whisenhunt, gave the performance low marks and was ready to lecture Rolle.

Other players suggested Whisenhunt reconsider. "A number of other players said, 'Coach, that's his second touchdown. You can't say anything,'" Whisenhunt said that day. "I said, 'Well, yeah, you're right.' So for the record, I'll make the special exception that on your second interception return for a touchdown, I'll forgive you for a celebration."

Rolle was the 23rd player in the NFL to return two interceptions for touchdowns. He is most likely the first to celebrate with a cartwheel, a backflip, and a fall into the end zone. "I was caught up in the moment," said Rolle, who became the fifth Cardinals player to return two interceptions in a game. "It wasn't much of a backflip."

Rolle's touchdowns were from 55 and 54 yards out. He still shares the NFL record, but it really should be his alone. He returned a third interception 71 yards for a touchdown in that game—only to have an official throw a flag on defensive end Antonio Smith for hitting Bengals quarterback Carson Palmer. *Yes, that same Palmer who came to the Cardinals in 2013.*

A few days later, the NFL admitted the penalty should not have been called. "It will be tough to forget this one," said Palmer after the game. "When you throw four [interceptions] and don't give your team a chance to win, it just feels horrible. I feel like I let our team down—our coaches, the organization, and our fans."

Eight years later Palmer was asked what he remembered about the interceptions. A lot, as it turned out. "I know he jumped a route," Palmer said of Rolle. "I know he took the ball out of T.J. [Houshmandzadeh's] hands on another one. And I threw him an easy one on the other."

Replays showed that the hit on Palmer after the third interception was legal, and Whisenhunt lobbied referee Ron Winter to pick up the flag. "The kid should have the NFL record," Whisenhunt said he told Winter. Winter and his crew, however, stuck with the call.

That interception came late in the game, and after Rolle had traveled 71 yards to the end, he just fell chest first. He was too tired to celebrate. Rolle wasn't too upset at the penalty that cost him the record. "That's last week," Rolle said at the time. "I've gone past that point already. I've never been too fond of accolades anyway. If I get it, I get it. If I don't, we live to play another day."

The Cardinals didn't make a big deal out of the mistake because they were giddy about beating the Bengals 35–27. It was Whisenhunt's first season, and the victory was the second one in a row for the Cardinals. It evened their record at 5–5, the Cardinals' best mark after 10 games since 1998.

60 Simeon Rice and His Contract Dispute

Contract squabbles are common in professional sports, but rarely are they as bizarre, contentious, and comical as the one defensive end Simeon Rice had with the Cardinals in 2000.

Rice was the team's third overall pick in 1996 and he produced right away. Despite missing training camp because he didn't have a contract, Rice set a team record and tied an NFL rookie record with 12.5 sacks. By 2000 Rice had played out his rookie contract and he was tired of Arizona.

While weary of Rice's theatrics, the Cardinals weren't willing to let an elite pass rusher walk out the door, at least not without being compensated. So they placed the franchise tag on Rice, meaning if another team signed Rice, it would have to give the Cardinals two first-round picks. Rice was not happy. He ripped the Cardinals, owner Bill Bidwill, teammates, fans, and the Phoenix area. "The armpit of the NFL," he called it.

By September, Rice figured it was better to make $4.25 million, the salary for a franchised defensive end, than $0. So he surprised the Cardinals by appearing on their doorstep one Wednesday morning. The coaches were relieved, but general manager Bob Ferguson vented, telling Rice that he had bridges to repair because many people in the organization didn't want him back. Rice left to take his physical and the more he thought about Ferguson's lecture, the more it irritated him. He did not return to sign his contract.

Now, it was Ferguson's turn to be incensed. His face turning an interesting shade of purple, Ferguson pounded a table during a news conference and ranted against selfish athletes who allowed greed to get in the way of others to make a living. By Thursday, Rice was back. This time he met with Rod Graves, an assistant to owner Bill Bidwill who was far less volatile than Ferguson. Rice signed the contract and met with reporters after practice.

Asked about his "armpit" comment, Rice replied, "Personally, I feel like I am the deodorant, the spray. It's funny. It's a game. That's all it is. I hope people can put it in the past and forget it. I am. At the same time, I can't regret it. That was the situation at the time. If I offended anybody by it, so be it."

Rice lasted one more season in Arizona, recording 7.5 sacks on the season and 51.5 in five years. That ranks second to Freddie Joe Nunn on the team's all-time list. Rice moved on to the Tampa Bay Buccaneers, where he continued spraying criticism at his former employer. Here's how he described his time in Arizona to the *Chicago Tribune* in 2001: "You have a player who is really at the top of the league at what he does, and I'm aided with a bunch of nobodies, a bunch of guys that were really lackluster and all the attention fell toward me."

Vince Tobin, who coached Rice for most of "the Deodorant's" tenure in Arizona, disputed Rice's view of history. In Tobin's opinion missing that first training camp impacted Rice. "Now he decides you don't have to go to camp," Tobin told the *Tribune*.

"In fact he got worse because he didn't know what it takes to be successful."

There is no question, however, that Rice brought two things to the Cardinals: the ability to sack the quarterback and drama. The team needed the one and could have done without the other.

61 2004 Draft Class

The days leading up to the NFL draft are usually exciting ones, but the 2004 draft was different for the Cardinals and their fans. On Friday, April 23, the day before draft weekend, news broke that Army ranger Pat Tillman, a former Cardinals safety, had been killed in Afghanistan. There was a pall over the team's facility in Tempe the next day as the Cardinals held their first draft under the leadership of coach Dennis Green.

That draft became memorable in another ways. It turned out to be the best one in the team's history in Arizona. With their first three picks, the Cardinals selected receiver Larry Fitzgerald, linebacker Karlos Dansby, and defensive end Darnell Dockett. On the next day, they selected defensive end Antonio Smith in the fifth round. All four of those players ended up spending at least 11 seasons in the NFL.

Fitzgerald, drafted third overall out of Pittsburgh, holds almost every Cardinals receiving record. He has been chosen to eight Pro Bowls (and counting), and one day likely will be in the Pro Football Hall of Fame. Dansby, from Auburn, had two different stints with the Cardinals and is considered one of the game's best inside linebackers. Dockett, from Florida State, started 10 seasons for the

Cardinals, making three Pro Bowls. And Smith, from Oklahoma State, started 133 games over his first 12 seasons, a remarkable feat for a fifth-round selection.

Dockett has always credited Green for the group's success. "We always talk about that," he said in 2013. "Even to this day, we're thankful to him to come get us and giving us the opportunity to play early. A lot of teams would get young guys, and they'd have to sit on the bench for two, three years. But he put us right in and let us play."

Green didn't have much choice. He inherited a team that won nine games the previous two seasons. Before that draft the Cardinals streamlined the way they selected players. They built a draft board of the top 120 players and vowed to stick by those rankings when making selections. No last-minute waffling. No drafting a player only because he played a position where the Cardinals needed help.

Early on, mock drafts had Fitzgerald going to the Cardinals because of his ties to Green.

Green was close with Fitzgerald's father, Larry Sr., a journalist in Minneapolis who also hosted Green's radio show. Green met Fitzgerald Jr. when the receiver was eight and hired him four years later as the Vikings' ballboy. Green never concealed that Fitzgerald was No. 1 on the Cardinals' draft board. "A lot of people across the country thought it was a smokescreen," Green said after drafting Fitzgerald. Green turned to Rod Graves, the team's vice president of football operations, and added, "Unfortunately, Rod, I've been known to be a little bit of a big mouth."

It wasn't a controversial pick, but some observers thought the Cardinals would have been better served by taking a quarterback. Philip Rivers was available. So was Ben Roethlisberger.

Green and the Cardinals never wavered. "I felt a lot of conversations along the way between he [Green] and myself caused us to focus a lot harder and to really be prepared in ways that maybe we haven't been prepared in the past," Graves said at the time. "When you're prepared, things seem to just fall right for you."

Things continued to fall right in the second round. The Cardinals selected Dansby and followed that by picking Dockett. All three became Cardinals on the same day and played together over the course of the next 11 seasons. "That's strong man, that's strong," Dansby said in 2013. "We've all had a lot of success. That's a good thing. It's a real good thing."

62 1984 Finale

The disappointment in former Cardinals receiver Roy Green's voice was real, even though more than three decades had passed since the event happened. It was December 16, 1984. The Cardinals were playing Washington at RFK Stadium. The NFC East was at stake, and the Cardinals needed a victory to make the playoffs for the first time in a non-strike season since 1975.

They lost. "Ooooooh," Green said. "I ain't been able to shake that."

That's how crushing the Cardinals' 29–27 loss was. The Cardinals had won the three previous games to improve to 9–6 and put themselves in contention for the division title.

It appeared Washington had dashed those hopes quickly, taking a 23–7 lead into halftime.

At halftime Green couldn't believe what he was hearing. Coaches were talking about sticking with the run game, even though it hadn't worked in the first half. The Cardinals' only score had come on a 1-yard "drive," set up by an interception. "I was really cursing out the whole thought," Green said.

Luckily, the Cardinals reconsidered and came out throwing in the second half. Quarterback Neil Lomax caught fire, completing 25-of-28 passes for 314 yards and two touchdowns in the second half. He finished 37-of-46 for 468 yards—the most yards and completions in Cardinals history at that point.

Gradually, the Cardinals crept back into the game. Neil O'Donoghue made two field goals for the Cardinals. Lomax hit Green for two touchdowns. "We came out in the second half expecting to pound and pound away," Washington tackle Mark May told *The Washington Post*. "But they came out and scored twice quick, and we had to change."

Lomax and the Cardinals weren't greedy. They moved the ball via short passes until Lomax found Green behind the secondary for the 75-yard score. Washington led 26–20 and drove to the Cardinals 34 with eight minutes left. Coach Joe Gibbs decided against a 51-yard field goal attempt and opted to punt.

It looked like a good strategy when the Cardinals took over at their 6-yard line. But the Cardinals weren't done. Lomax drove them 94 yards in six plays: a 21-yard completion to Danny Pittman, a 28-yarder to Green, and then an 18-yard touchdown pass to Green, who had beaten Hall of Fame cornerback Darrell Green. "I was the only guy in the league who could run with him," Roy Green said.

That touchdown gave the Cardinals their first lead—27–26—with 6:15 left to play.

Washington drove 53 yards, and a field goal by Mark Moseley put the home team back ahead 29–27. The Cardinals had one last chance. They took over at their 20 with 1:27 to play and no timeouts. Content to let the Cardinals complete short passes, Washington rushed only three and had six defensive backs in the game. "It seemed like that they had 13 defensive backs," Lomax said afterward.

It didn't matter much. Lomax completed five of six passes. The last one came on a play that started with 25 seconds remaining.

Instead of throwing to the sideline, Lomax hit Pittman for five yards over the middle. With no timeouts the Cardinals field goal team rushed on the field. With just a second left on the clock, O'Donoghue attempted a 50-yard field goal. It went wide left. The Cardinals' season was over, and Washington was relieved. "I'm almost too tired to have a cocktail," Washington running back John Riggins told reporters.

Trading Places in the 1998 NFL Draft

In the 1998 NFL Draft, the Cardinals and San Diego Chargers pulled off a blockbuster trade that both teams hoped would set them on a course for success. The Chargers obtained the franchise quarterback they needed, and the Cardinals added an elite player to a formidable defensive line.

Or so both teams thought.

The two centerpieces never panned out. The Cardinals pick, defensive end Andre Wadsworth, also didn't produce, though it wasn't his fault. He had numerous knee problems and underwent four surgeries in his first three years in the NFL. Both players lasted just three seasons with the teams that drafted them. Quarterback Ryan Leaf was petulant, pouty, and lazy and is recognized as one of the biggest busts in draft history. He wore out his welcome in San Diego not long after he said hello. "I have never seen a player that had so much talent do so little with it," general manager Bobby Beathard told beat reporters at the time. "He always blamed everybody else. He was never to blame for anything. You can't live your life that way. It's kind of sad."

On draft day the Cardinals were thrilled at the deal they made. They had drafted Jake Plummer in the second round the year before, so they had minimal interest in selecting a quarterback high in the 1998 draft. With the second overall pick, they were in a position of power because a number of teams were interested in trading up to get a quarterback.

A debate raged in the weeks leading up the draft: which quarterback was better, Peyton Manning or Leaf? The Indianapolis Colts wisely picked Manning with the No. 1 selection.

Where Leaf ended up depended upon what kind of deal the Cardinals could pull off to move out of the No. 2 slot. The Cardinals demanded—and received—a ransom from the Chargers. In exchange for moving down one spot from the second overall pick to the third, the Cardinals received a second-round pick in 1998, a first rounder in 1999, and two players—kick returner/receiver Eric Metcalf and outside linebacker Patrick Sapp.

The Cardinals were excited to take Wadsworth, whom experts compared to Buffalo Bills great Bruce Smith. At Wadsworth's introductory press conference, Cardinals general manager Bob Ferguson got teary when asked about the youngster from Florida State and where the Cardinals franchise was headed. Ferguson said he would be delighted if one of his daughters brought someone like Wadsworth home. As for the franchise, Ferguson sensed things were looking up. "Maybe I don't know it, but I sense it," he said then. "It's like falling in love. When it happens once, you know what it feels like. How's that for an analogy?"

Wadsworth, however, played in just 36 games in three years and was out of the league after the 2000 season. Even considering that, the Cardinals got the best of the Chargers in the trade, though no one from Arizona bragged about it. Wadsworth missed training camp in 1998 because of a contract dispute. The Cardinals had a well-earned reputation for being cheap then, and the team seemed willing to stand firm. With criticism mounting, Michael Bidwill, a team vice president, entered negotiations and quickly got a deal done. But it was a bad one. Three years later the Cardinals exercised an option to void the contract.

With the Chargers' pick in the second round, the Cardinals drafted defensive back Corey Chavous, a steady player for many seasons. They took receiver David Boston with the Chargers' pick the following year. He had some good seasons for the Cardinals, but the immature player didn't last long.

The men who made the deal paid a price, too. Beathard has the credentials to become a Hall of Famer, but the Leaf trade was a huge black mark on his stellar career. He retired in 2000, knowing his last major deal was also his worst. It hurt Ferguson, too. If Wadsworth had been a perennial Pro Bowler, Ferguson would have been lauded as a genius.

The Cardinals did go to the playoffs in 1998, but they couldn't hold it together. Wadsworth had knee problems, and key veterans were allowed to leave via free agency. The dramatic turnaround Ferguson envisioned for the Cardinals never happened under his watch. By 2001 he was stripped of power and eventually replaced by Rod Graves. General managers like to say the best trades are the ones that benefit both teams. The value of the 1998 trade between the Chargers and Cardinals, however, can be judged by which side was hurt the least.

64 Dress Up as Bruce Arians for Halloween

By his second season as Cardinals coach, Bruce Arians had noticed that Bruce Arians was pretty popular in the Phoenix area, especially around Halloween. The coach already was a favorite with fans,

Head coach Bruce Arians has a patented style that has become a Halloween staple in the Phoenix area. To truly capture the look, he says bring plenty of "attitude and a cocktail."

having won 10 games in his first year. By his second season, folks apparently recognized that looking like Bruce Arians made for an excellent Halloween costume.

Arians has a distinctive look that makes imitating him fairly easy. Off the field, his shaved head is usually topped by a Gatsby-esque driver's cap. He wears designer black-rimmed glasses and he sometimes is a bit hefty, especially during the season when he doesn't make time to work out. Throw in a headset and a large, laminated card that resembles his play-call sheet, and the average Jill or Joe can easily go as Arians for Halloween.

Or so it would seem.

All of the above items are essential, Arians acknowledged, but it takes a little more than that to get the whole look right. "You've got to have the attitude," he said, pausing before adding, "and a cocktail."

Attempting to look like Arians can benefit a good cause, too. His distinctive driver's caps, made by New Era, are available through the Cardinals team shop. A portion of the proceeds are donated to the Arians' favorite charity, CASA (court-appointed special advocates), which helps children in the court system receive the help they need.

65 Waving Bye to "Flag"

For their first quarter century in Arizona, the Cardinals had at least one thing in common with most people in metropolitan Phoenix: they made sure to head for the mountains in the summer. The Cardinals held summer training camp in Flagstaff for most of their first 25 years in Arizona, and by most accounts, it was popular among players, coaches, and fans.

At 7,000 feet elevation, Flagstaff's high temperatures often are 30 degrees lower than in Phoenix. The smell of pine trees is heavy in the air, and many fans built part of their summers around catching a practice or two during the Cardinals' four-to-six week training camps. The experience was charming, romantic, and nostalgic.

The memories are vivid: quarterback Kurt Warner signing autographs until the sun set. Injured players pushing wheelbarrows of sand during Buddy Ryan's tenure as coach. Skunks terrorizing the old dorms where the players used to stay. Bumping into receiver Larry Fitzgerald at the Sizzler near the Northern Arizona University campus. "They treated us like family," Fitzgerald said of Flagstaff residents. "Hopefully, we can get back up there."

Don't count on it.

In 2013 the Cardinals and NAU officials couldn't agree on a new lease, and the Cardinals moved training camp to University of Phoenix Stadium in Glendale. They stay in a posh hotel—instead of college dormitories—and all of their practices are held indoors in air conditioning.

As far as preparing a team for the season, the new setup works. And fans in the Phoenix area don't have to make the two-hour drive north to watch their team.

But the charm has gone.

The Cardinals reported to camp in Flagstaff for the first time on July 20, 1988, and players had to drive through a storm to get there. "It was like, 'Auntie Em, Auntie Em,'" fullback Ron Wolfley told reporters upon arrival on that day. "The clouds were four feet off the ground. You could see where the lightning bolts were going through the clouds. I had my head between the steering wheel. One lightning bolt had my name on it. I almost got in three accidents. I almost hit a biker, whose beard was down to his gut. It was raining so hard, it was like being in an aquarium. I was waiting for a big fish to come after me."

Veteran reporters and longtime fans have many memories of having camp in "Flag." In 1994 Ryan became irritated at the growing number of injured missing practice. So he ordered a strength coach to come up with something rigorous for the players to do during practice. Wheelbarrows filled with sand were the answer. The players pushed wheelbarrows up and down the field. As Ryan expected, the ranks of the injured dwindled. Ryan said then that center Ed Cunningham has the best line about it. "He said that was career-planning day," Ryan said. "If you can't [play football], then that's your career."

In 2003 wide receiver Bryant Johnson, one of the team's first-round picks, was taken to the hospital one Sunday morning after apparently celebrating too much the night before. Coach Dave McGinnis addressed the issue during a team meeting, telling other players that one of their teammates had gotten into some trouble. Wide receiver Anquan Boldin had left Flagstaff that weekend to attend to a family matter and was sitting next to Johnson in the team meeting. Boldin leaned over to Johnson and asked: "Who is [McGinnis] talking about?"

"I don't know," Johnson replied.

66 Running to Retirement Plan

Arizona is a haven for retirees for several reasons:

- Great weather
- Plenty of golf courses
- Communities designed specifically for those in their golden years
- A football team willing to give running backs lucrative deals just before they put away their cleats for good

At least the latter point described the Cardinals in the first decade of the 21st century.

In 2003 they signed 34-year-old Emmitt Smith to a two-year, $7.5 million deal. All that was expected of him was to gain 1,200 yards or so, sell thousands of tickets, and lend credibility to what, at the time, was one of the least successful professional sports franchises. "That was the whole focus," general manager Rod Graves said. "Let's try and change the attitude of our team."

Three years later the same was expected of Edgerrin James when he signed a four-year, $30 million deal, about half of which was guaranteed. "It's a great situation. All they really need is a back," James said at an introductory news conference. "They've got an MVP quarterback [Kurt Warner], they've got two Pro Bowl receivers. They got a back and they're going to shore up the offensive line."

Neither signing worked as the Cardinals hoped, though that was more the fault of the organization than the player. Smith's signing did not cause disgruntled fans to suddenly become gruntled

Hall of Fame running back Emmitt Smith runs through a hole against the New Orleans Saints during a 2004 victory in which he posted his 77th career 100-yard game.

and head to the ticket office. It also did not help the team win. Smith was past his prime. Over his two seasons in Arizona, he averaged just 3.3 yards a carry, though he did score nine touchdowns in 2004, his final NFL season.

Smith came to the desert at one of the franchise's lowest points in its history in Arizona. The Cardinals were coming off painful seasons. They endured salary cap hits as they cleared the roster of expensive players no longer producing. Smith's signing was supposed to be an indication that the franchise was bouncing back. "If I were a player on this team, I would be embarrassed if any little tweak was keeping me out," coach Dave McGinnis said, "and there's a first-ballot Hall of Famer who is out there every practice."

Smith wasn't the only reason the Cardinals won only 10 games in his two seasons. He suffered a fractured scapula in his first season, missed six games, and finished with 256 yards, a career low. "They doubted me when I came in [the NFL]," Smith said in 2003, "and they're doubting me on my way out."

Smith returned to play that season. McGinnis was fired the day after the last game and he appreciated what Smith contributed. "You have a first-ballot Hall of Famer on the youngest football team in the National Football League," McGinnis said, "and he busted his ass to rehabilitate himself and come back to play. Think about that a minute."

James was only 27 when he signed with Arizona and had rushed for more than 1,500 yards the two previous seasons with the Indianapolis Colts. But there were similarities between his situation and Smith's. In both cases there was only one team pursuing the backs: the Cardinals. Both running backs saw opportunity in Arizona, where other players saw only dysfunction and desolation. And both players made contributions to the Cardinals, just not at the level expected.

James rushed for more than 1,000 yards in his first two seasons with the Cardinals and added a sense of professionalism to the organization. He also was fun to have around. After photos emerged of quarterback Matt Leinart in a hot tub with girls, a reporter asked James if he allowed friends to use cell phone cameras while out with him. "Where I go it's too dark to take pictures," he said, laughing.

In 2008, his third and last season, he emerged as a force late in the year and played a big role in the team making it to its first Super Bowl. The Cardinals released James in the spring of 2009 after drafting running back Beanie Wells in the first round. James knew his release was coming and he welcomed it. "I can't go through this again," James said after the 2008 season. "I think the feeling is mutual. It's not something I'm going to contest."

James played briefly with the Seattle Seahawks the next year before retiring. Like Smith, he never came close to regaining the greatness he displayed with his original team.

67 Inglorious Endings

Thousands of people migrate to Arizona once their careers are over. But for three Hall of Fame players, Arizona is where their careers ended. Quarterback Steve Young, wide receiver Jerry Rice, and running back Emmitt Smith all played their last games either for or against the Cardinals at Sun Devil Stadium.

Young's inglorious ending came on a Monday night in September of 1999. He led the San Francisco 49ers against the Cardinals that day but was knocked out of the game in the second quarter. Cardinals cornerback Aeneas Williams blitzed off the right side of the 49ers line. Williams hit Young in the chest, and as Young fell, his head hit a teammate's knee. He was out cold. "I was just saying, 'Get up, get up, get up,'" 49ers coach Steve Mariucci said after the game.

Young suffered a concussion on the play, but the injury didn't seem severe at the time. At halftime he lobbied to return, but Mariucci held firm that Jeff Garcia would play the second half. Young talked to reporters after the game and was coherent. There was talk of him playing the following week, but symptoms persisted, and it's the last down of professional football Young played.

No one saw that coming on that Monday night. Young thought he would resume his career in a week or two, but after the game even he acknowledged the seriousness of the injury. "I am much more sober about it than ever before," he said, "and I'll deal with it as realistically as I possibly can. In the past I was not as conscious of my future. And now I'm very, very conscious about my future."

Smith, in contrast, knew when he took the field on January 2, 2005, that it could be his last NFL season. The NFL's all-time leading rusher, Smith was productive for the Cardinals that season, gaining 937 yards and rushing for nine touchdowns for a team that finished 6–10.

But it was clear the Cardinals didn't want Smith back for 2005, and chances seemed remote of any other team being interested in a running back who would be 35 when the following season started. In what turned out to be his final game, Smith rushed 23 times for 69 yards against the Tampa Bay Buccaneers. "It's not in my hands any longer," he said after that game. "I can make a decision based upon whether I want to continue or not, but still somebody has to make a decision on whether or not they want me to continue. That part is out of my hands."

A month later, Smith announced his retirement. "Emmitt Smith is NFL royalty," former Cardinals coach Dave McGinnis said at the time.

Nine months later, another legend played his last down of football at Sun Devil Stadium.

It was odd seeing Rice in a Denver Broncos uniform in 2005, but the 42-year-old receiver was confident he could still play. The Broncos came to town for the final game of the preseason against the Cardinals. Rice, who held 38 NFL receiving records, caught two passes for 10 yards on that Friday night. Upon returning to Denver, coach Mike Shanahan told Rice he would be no better than fourth on the depth chart. On that Monday, Rice announced his retirement. "I never thought this day would come," he said.

68 Ottis Anderson

The Cardinals were notorious for making bad draft picks over their final decade in St. Louis. But from the beginning, everyone knew they got their first-round pick in 1979 right. Running back Ottis Anderson, the eighth overall pick, rushed for 193 yards in his NFL debut, at Dallas. "You just didn't see the big back, 225 pounds with feet like Barry Sanders," said former Cardinals receiver Roy Green. "And he had speed, power, and later movement. There's game tape of him out there where he literally made a Giants safety take a knee. Put three moves on him, and the safety dropped to a knee."

Anderson, from the University of Miami, rushed for 1,605 yards, setting an NFL record for rookies, and scored 10 touchdowns. He went on to gain at least 1,000 yards in each of the next five full NFL seasons. Nearly 30 years later, he still holds most of the franchise rushing records, including career yards (7,999), attempts (1,858), touchdowns (46), and rushing yards in a season (1,605). "Ottis was a big back, very physical," said former teammate Stump Mitchell. "He loved pass blocking. I've been around two people, Ottis and Clinton Portis, who just tried to take the head off the guy when they went to protect. And Ottis had to go against Lawrence Taylor, Hugh Green, guys of that nature. And he did a good job."

Anderson also was an accomplished receiver, averaging just more than 40 receptions a year in his seven seasons with the Cardinals. That happened despite the fact that the Cardinals rarely, if ever, had a pass play designed to go to Anderson other than the occasional screen.

Players joking referred to it as a "whoo, whoo," play. "He would block for a while, and if the quarterback hadn't thrown it yet, O.J. would flare out and go, 'Whoo, whoo,'" Green said, laughing.

As good as Anderson was in his prime with the Cardinals, he's better known for what he did later in his career. In 1986 Anderson and new coach Gene Stallings weren't seeing eye to eye. Stallings liked Mitchell, who was beginning to emerge, so the Cardinals felt Anderson was expendable. Still, their decision to trade him to the New York Giants, a division foe, shocked everyone, including Anderson.

At the time of the trade, Anderson said he was called off the practice field by Larry Wilson, the Cardinals' director of pro personnel. "Around here, anything is possible," Anderson said, according to wire services. "You just never know what will happen. We had just finished up with the offensive period, and I was going for a water break. Larry walked over and said to come, that I've just been traded. I thought maybe it was a joke, but when Larry Wilson comes by to talk to you, basically there's no jokes involved."

Anderson was 29 at the time. He didn't have immediate success with the Giants. In fact he later said he was afraid he was going to be cut. But Giants coach Bill Parcells loved him, and Anderson emerged as a physical, short-yardage back who would gain the tough yards. He was named Super Bowl XXV's Most Valuable Player after gaining 102 yards on 21 carries in the victory against the Buffalo Bills. "Ottis is one of the few backs that I ever saw who was able to change his running style through his career and still be effective at the end," Giants offensive line coach Fred Hoaglin told Bob McGinn, author of *The Ultimate Super Bowl Book*. "When he came to New York, he knew he was losing speed, so he went in the weight room and got stronger and bigger."

69 Jetstream Green

In the late 1970s and early '80s, it wasn't unusual for defensive back Roy Green and a few other young Cardinals players to fool around a bit before or after practice. Green and running backs Ottis Anderson and Theotis Brown used to run pass routes against each other just because it was fun and it took the drudgery out of conditioning.

Early in the 1981 season, however, running routes became more than a hobby to Green. The Cardinals had injuries at receiver, and Green's extracurricular activities caught the eye of coach Jim Hanifan. "You know what?" Hanifan said to Green. "You might be our best receiver."

Strictly a defensive back his first two years in the NFL, Green became a two-way player in 1981, the first "authentic" one in the

NFL in more than two decades, according to the team's media guide. "I was so excited," Green said. "We had injuries at receiver, and back then you only carried four on your roster—not like today when there are six or so."

Green's career as a wide receiver began in Week 2 against the Cowboys in Dallas. He had one reception that day, but it went for 60 yards. The Cardinals were on to something.

Green continued to play both ways through 1982. After that he was a full-time receiver and one of the NFL's best. By the time he left the Cardinals after the 1990 season, he held team career records for receptions, receiving yards, and touchdowns. That's remarkable considering he caught one pass—off a fake punt—in his first two NFL seasons. "To this day a lot of people around the country just assume I was always a receiver," Green said. "Even looking at my sports cards, they only show I was a receiver. But if you add up all of my 14 years, which included the strike in 1982, I was a full-time receiver for only a little over 10 years."

In his two years going both ways, Green said he probably played an average of 60 snaps a game. Occasionally, there was heavier duty. At New England in 1981, the Cardinals lost a safety to injury, so Green played that spot for the entire game in addition to his duties on offense. He estimated that he participated in about 110 snaps that day. It didn't seem to affect him. All three of his receptions came in the fourth quarter, including the game-winning 33-yard touchdown with 33 seconds remaining.

In 1983 coaches scaled back Green's duties and had him concentrate on offense only. "What stopped me is I pulled a hamstring," Green said. "It was difficult going both ways because of the demands on your body, running forwards, then backpedaling. It was very, very taxing."

If Green had played in today's NFL, he probably could have gone both ways for a few more years, but when he played there were no restrictions on practice time, padded practices, and days off. Training camps lasted six weeks and players wore pads in nearly every practice. Coaches tended to overwork players. "It was just a different era," Green said. "It was very taxful on the body."

Cutting Green's workload provided immediate dividends for the Cardinals. Green produced his two finest seasons in 1983–84, catching 156 passes for 2,782 yards and 26 touchdowns. He made the Pro Bowl both years as well as an All-Pro team.

Green had great speed, which earned him the nickname "Jetstream Green," and he was smart, too. He knew a lot about offensive schemes. At Henderson State in Arkansas, he played several positions, including defensive back, receiver, running back, and a little quarterback. In his junior year, he played all of those spots in one game. The Cardinals drafted him as a defensive back and returner in the fourth round in 1979. He made immediate contributions in both those roles.

Playing defensive back greatly aided Green's transition to receiver because he understood what defenses were trying to do to him. "There are so many route adjustments to make, depending on what the defense is doing," Green said. "I had a good indication of what they were going to do to me. It was definitely an advantage."

Green finished his career as a part-time player for the Philadelphia Eagles and then retired to the Phoenix area. He spends part of the year preparing receivers for the draft and other NFL opportunities. He calls upon his experience both as a receiver and defensive back. "When I work with receivers today, I tell them to pay attention to the other side of the ball," Green said. "After running a route, if the defensive backs coach is saying something to the cornerback, stop and listen."

Green has maintained close ties with the Cardinals organization, occasionally working on their broadcasts. Twenty-three years after his final game with the team, he visited team headquarters in Tempe and bumped into receiver Larry Fitzgerald, who now holds all of Green's old records. "Hey, Roy," Fitzgerald teased, "are you the second or third best receiver in franchise history?" Green just smiled—content that he had done pretty well for a converted defensive back.

70 Oh, No, Bono

Steve Bono might not be the slowest quarterback to ever play in the NFL. He might not even be the slowest quarterback to ever score a touchdown in the NFL. But odds are that he is the slowest quarterback to run 76 yards for a touchdown in NFL history.

As a member of the Kansas City Chiefs, Bono did that in 1995 against the Cardinals in Sun Devil Stadium. At the time it was the longest scoring run by a quarterback in league history.

Bono's run was the ultimate indignity for Cardinals coach and general manager Buddy Ryan, one of the NFL's greatest defensive innovators.

He was also one of the NFL's most boastful coaches and he constantly bragged about his defense. But the Cardinals were 1–3 entering the game with the Chiefs that October day, and fans were angry that the Cardinals were getting worse, not better, under Ryan. So letting a slow quarterback run 76 yards for a touchdown triggered showers of boos from fans in attendance at Sun Devil Stadium. "If I would have thought I was capable of tackling him, I might have," Cardinals defensive coordinator Ronnie Jones said at the time. "But I didn't want to look any worse than anyone else, so I just stood on the sideline."

The play was a great call by the Chiefs, who took advantage of the Cardinals' aggressiveness. Through tape study the Chiefs noticed the Cardinals sold out in short-yardage situations and that outside linebacker Seth Joyner had been successful crashing down the line of scrimmage. The first play of the second quarter was the ideal time to call the Bono bootleg. On third and 1, Bono faked a handoff to running back Marcus Allen. All 11 Cardinals plunged to stop him, and Bono was 30 yards downfield before anyone noticed he had the ball.

Chiefs lineman Joe Valerio (who later caught a touchdown pass on a tackle-eligible play) was Bono's escort down the field—just in case there was someone to block. There wasn't. And Valerio waved Bono through. "The first person I saw was the ref," Valerio said. "And I was hoping he didn't make the tackle."

According to the game clock, it took 13 seconds for Bono to cover the 76 yards, but to most everyone else, it seemed to take an hour and a half. "As slow as I was running, I didn't want to let any defensive backs catch me from behind," Bono said.

Afterward Bono's teammates and coaches teased him, saying they could have used an hourglass to time him. Allen said the television network "could have called two TV timeouts" in the time it took Bono to cover the distance. "I did say to Bono on the sidelines, 'Don't pull a hamstring,'" said Chiefs coach Marty Schottenheimer. "At the rate of speed he was running, I didn't think there was any danger of it."

The Cardinals were shocked. And embarrassed. "In four previous games, they hadn't shown a bootleg," Joyner said. "My job is to contain the quarterback on that play, keep the ball inside of me, and I was blocked in on the dive play and I went for the play."

The Chiefs won 24–3, and Schottenheimer pointed to his team's goal-line stand as the turning point. He's the only one who saw it that way. Everyone else pointed to Bono's run.

Late in the game, some fans behind the Cardinals bench chanted "Buddy must go!" And someone threw a cup of beer at him as Ryan walked to the locker room. Afterward Ryan took responsibility—sort of—for Bono's run and the 1–4 start. "It's all my fault. These are my players, my guys. I brought them here or kept them here. I'm the No. 1 guy you can point the finger at as being responsible. But I'm also going to be responsible when they do good. Don't forget that."

Ryan, though, kept his sense of humor despite the embarrassment that day. "As general manager," he said, "I think the coach is doing a hell of a job."

How the Cardinals Got Their Name and Colors

The Cardinals are the oldest professional football franchise in existence, so it figures their history is long and, literally, colorful. The Cardinals were founded in 1898, primarily by Chris O'Brien, a member of the Morgan Athletic Club. The club gathered to play football in the predominantly Irish area on the South Side of Chicago.

For a short time, the Cardinals played as the Normals, a name derived from its playing site, Normal Field. The Cardinals name first appeared in 1901 when O'Brien and others left the Morgan Athletic Club and formed the Cardinals Social and Athletic Club. Around that time O'Brien bought used jerseys from the University of Chicago, which called its team the "Maroons." Their jerseys were maroon, or at least were supposed to be. According to Cardinals lore, O'Brien, who apparently took uniform colors very seriously, looked at the faded jerseys he had acquired and declared, "That's not maroon; it's Cardinals red!"

With the new-old jerseys and a new home field near 61st and Racine, the team became known as the Racine Cardinals. Around that same time, O'Brien and directors from other athletic clubs organized to help protect the game in the city of Chicago, according to *When Football Was Football*, a history of the team's early years. Football was not a popular sport at the time, and many influential people thought it was too dangerous. Opponents became hard to find, and the Cardinals disbanded in 1906, according to the franchise's media guide.

In 1913 O'Brien reformed the team again, and by 1917 the team was able to buy new uniforms and hire a coach, Marshall Smith. The Cardinals lost two games that season and won the Chicago Football League Championship. Operations were suspended again in 1918, but O'Brien reorganized the Cardinals later that year when World War I ended. The Cardinals have operated every year since.

In 1922 a team from Racine, Wisconsin, joined the NFL, and the Cardinals changed their name to the Chicago Cardinals. That same year, they moved into Comiskey Park, which they would share with White Sox baseball team for 37 years. The Cardinals and Bears are the only two of the 11 charter members of the NFL still in operation.

The Bears have an interesting history, too. They were originally based in Decatur, Illinois, and called the Decatur Staleys after their sponsor, the Staley Starch Company. The team moved to Chicago in 1921 and changed their name to the Bears the following year. The Bears became the No. 1 football team in Chicago and became the only team when the Cardinals moved to St. Louis in 1960.

72 Conrad Dobler

Conrad Dobler was a mainstay on the Cardinals' great offensive lines of the mid-1970s, and the guard was selected to three Pro Bowls. That's quite an accomplishment for a fifth-round pick out of Wyoming who was cut before his rookie season and re-signed a few weeks later when the St. Louis Cardinals suffered several injuries.

But hardly anyone remembers Dobler for that. He became famous—or infamous—for doing whatever it took to block the guy in front of him. That included holding, leg-whipping, biting, and a handful of other transgressions. Dobler earned a reputation for being one of the game's dirtiest players. He neither embraced the moniker, nor ran from it. "What you need when you play against Dobler," one opponent told *Sports Illustrated*, "is a string of garlic buds around your neck and a wooden stake. If they played every game under a full moon, Dobler would make All-Pro. He must be the only guy in the league who sleeps in a casket."

That magazine article from 1977, which dubbed him "Pro Football's Dirtiest Player," helped Dobler emerge from anonymity. Football fans everywhere now knew his name. Players, however, knew of Dobler many years before that. And many opponents detested him.

Former Cardinals quarterback Jim Hart remembered one game in particular. It was against the Rams at the Coliseum in Los Angeles. Rams defensive tackle Merlin Olsen was facing Dobler that day, and it wasn't long before Olsen grew frustrated with Dobler's leg-whipping. Olsen and Hart were friends, so during a timeout Olsen approached the Cardinals quarterback. "Jim, you and I've been friends for a while. You can't condone what Dobler is doing," Olsen said.

"First of all, Merlin," Hart responded, "I don't know what he's doing. I'm not watching the linemen."

"Well, you have a feel for what he's doing," Olsen said.

"Yeah," Hart admitted. "What do you want me to do?"

"Well, you guys have got to stop that."

"Merlin," Hart said, "his job is to keep you away from me, and as far as I know, he's doing that. You haven't touched me yet, have you, Merlin?"

"No."

"Then he's doing his job. Am I going to tell him, 'Don't do that anymore, Conrad?'"

Olsen just shook his head and walked away.

Hart also confirmed that there was at least one biting incident involving Dobler. "I remember the excruciating scream," Hart said. "We get in the huddle and he's giggling."

In the huddle a teammate asked Dobler what he had done. "I bit him on the finger," Dobler said. "He has his hand under my facemask. He's trying to rip the lips off my face. You're damn right I bit him, and I'll do it again if he puts his hand in there."

Dobler played for the Cardinals from 1972 through 1977 and didn't miss a start his last four seasons. He retired after the 1981 season, and the years of playing football have taken a toll on him. In 2010 Dobler told the *Los Angeles Times* he had undergone around 30 knee operations. Dobler has always maintained that his reputation as a dirty player was exaggerated, but it did pay off for him. He appeared in beer commercials and has written books. But he told the *Times*, "My reputation probably did more damage to me than help me. I kind of lived in a fishbowl."

73 The Big Swap

In 1951 Ollie Matson was a big deal at the University of San Francisco; Pete Rozelle was not. But the connection the two men made there played a role eight years later when Matson, a running back, was the centerpiece of the biggest trade in the first three decades of NFL history.

In the early 1950s, Matson was one of the best athletes in the country. He helped San Francisco to an undefeated season in 1951, won silver and bronze medals in track at the 1952 Olympics in Helsinki, and was the first player drafted by the Chicago Cardinals in 1952. Matson was an immediate success in the NFL, too. In six seasons with the Cardinals, he only missed two games and became one of the best all-around backs in league history.

As a Cardinal, Matson rushed for 3,331 yards and 24 touchdowns, caught 130 passes for 2,150 yards and 16 touchdowns, and scored nine touchdowns on kick returns. He did that despite missing the 1953 season while in the Army. "Speed and quickness, that's what you need to return kicks," he said. "I was big, but I was swift for that size. I could either run around you, over you, or through you. I didn't do a lot of hard cutting like Gale Sayers did. But we both had that peripheral vision to know where guys were going to be and we had that speed to get there."

With the Cardinals, Matson was a star player on bad teams. Only once did the Cardinals have a winning record with Matson on the roster. That led to Matson crossing paths again with Rozelle. When Matson was at San Francisco, Rozelle was the school's sports information director. Rozelle later joined the Los Angeles Rams and eventually became general manager.

It was in that role that Rozelle and the Cardinals pulled off the huge trade. On February 29, 1959, Rozelle swapped nine players—seven on the current roster, one draft pick, and a player to be named later—to the Cardinals for Matson. Four starting linemen and three backs were included in that trade. The Pro Football Hall of Fame has the telegram that announced the stunning deal. Matson reportedly was not thrilled. "I wanted to finish my career with the Cardinals," he said.

The Cardinals, though, opted for quantity over quality. They had won a total of five games over the previous two seasons and figured they needed major changes. With an almost completely new roster in 1959, the Cardinals opened in promising fashion, beating Washington in the opener. But that team won just one more game all season. Matson went on to star with the Rams and also played for the Detroit Lions and Philadelphia Eagles. Rozelle, on the 23rd ballot, became NFL commissioner in 1960.

Matson, who played on just two winning teams in 14 years, was inducted into the Pro Football Hall of Fame in 1972 and is also in the Cardinals ring of honor. "The things I cherish most are the Olympic medals and the Hall of Fame," Matson once said. "In the Olympics you're competing against the best there are. It's isn't the Iowa State Fair. It's the world championship. The Hall of Fame is the same."

74 Darnell Dockett

Darnell Dockett shared many things with the public during his 11 years as a defensive end with the Cardinals. He had a crush on Oprah, an affinity for small people, a deep, abiding love for wild animals, and the ability to play defensive end at the game's highest level.

Drafted in the third round in 2004, Dockett missed only two games over the next decade. You could count the number of practices he missed on your fingers. A fan favorite, "Nine-Oh" was full of a lot of things: energy, passion, life, and, of course, himself. He made the Pro Bowl three times and set an NFL record with three sacks in Super Bowl XLIII. He loved to be in the center ring of the circus. One year he claimed the Cardinals thwarted his efforts to bring an alligator to training camp. Another year, it was a tiger. Neither claim was true, of course, but for some reason, a good number of people, including the media, took Dockett seriously, making his pranks big news.

Dockett, however, was not a full-time clown. Many people didn't think he would be mature enough to last in the NFL, misjudging his character and commitment to the game.

Both were the result of hard times as a kid. Dockett's mother was murdered when he was 13. His father died of cancer shortly later, and he was raised in Maryland by his uncle Kevin. "He was a troubled kid, as you would expect," Kevin Dockett said in 2004. "He really didn't have respect for others. He was bad. He was just bad." Dockett never was in serious trouble, but he tended to talk back to adults, and Kevin was a regular visitor to Darnell's schools. "I stayed on his ass like white on rice," Kevin said. "I would take him to the garage and beat his ass."

By high school Dockett was a man playing among boys and he became a prime recruit. He signed with Florida State. Again, he didn't get in serious trouble there, but there were allegations that he tried to hurt opponents during games, and a theft charge caused him to be suspended for a bowl game. That charge stemmed from a cheap discount given to him by a store clerk. Those incidents probably caused him to drop to the third round, and that snub motivated Dockett throughout his career.

Dockett was a model citizen throughout his NFL career, though he did like to stir things up. "I let people do their thing," he once said. "I'm not here to make anybody happy or anybody like me." Twitter was made for Dockett, who never held back on his opinions or cared that his words might not be politically correct. His tweets ran the gamut—from pretending he wanted to bring a tiger and an alligator to training camp to live-tweeting a time he was pulled over by a police officer in Maryland.

Most of what Dockett said and did was harmless. But he occasionally crossed the line.

In 2012 he and Cardinals safety Kerry Rhodes had a heated disagreement late in a game against the New York Jets. Trailing 7–6 the Cardinals coaches wanted to allow the Jets to score because it was the only way Arizona was going to get the ball back. Dockett didn't follow instructions, and he and Rhodes exchanged words. It appeared Dockett spit in Rhodes' direction, but both players denied that happened. "It was something I don't believe in. I didn't understand," Dockett said at the time of the strategy. "I am never, never going to lay down and quit. I've been playing football for over 20 years. I've given this organization, I've given Florida State, I've given my high school everything I've got. I play with passion and I'll never quit. I play it to the whistle and I play it until the clock reaches zero."

Coach Ken Whisenhunt was not amused. He fined Dockett between $100,000 and $200,000, though it's questionable if

Dockett ever had to pay. Dockett lasted two more seasons with the Cardinals, spending the last one on injured reserve due to a knee injury. He still traveled with the team and occasionally made news. Like the time in Oakland when he made a sign to remind Raiders fans that their team had not won a game that year.

In the spring of 2015, the Cardinals asked Dockett to take a pay cut. He refused, was released, and then signed with the 49ers. They cut him before the 2015 season began, even though he was healthy. No one else picked him up. It marked the likely end to a remarkable and interesting career. Receiver Anquan Boldin, a teammate of Dockett's at Florida State and with the Cardinals,

Defensive lineman Darnell Dockett, who played 11 years for the Cardinals, readies to explode out of his three-point stance. (USA TODAY Sports Images)

probably best summed up Dockett soon after the defensive lineman was drafted. "Darnell is a guy who you love to play with and hate to play against," he said. "If he's on your team, you love him because he makes a lot of plays. If he's on the opposite team, you hate him because he makes plays and he lets you know he's going to be there on every down."

75 Keim Time

As a boy growing up near Harrisburg, Pennsylvania, Steve Keim was smart, devoted, and passionate—just not to schoolwork. Keim loved playing football and studying it. He pored over magazines, draft previews, and anything that had to do with evaluating players. His mom laughed to herself when her young son said he wanted to be the general manager of an NFL team one day. "She said, 'If you only worked on your math and your science as hard you did on knowing these players, you may end up being successful,'" Keim said.

Turns out, the kid did all right for himself. After spending 15 seasons working his way up in the Cardinals organization, Keim was named general manager on January 8, 2013. "There are two things in my Cardinal career that give me that passion," Keim said on the day he was hired. "One is the day I stood on the field in 2008 and we won the NFC Championship, and all that confetti was sticking to my sweaty head. That thought drives me. The other thought that drives me is when I was sitting at our game in Seattle [in 2012] and lost 58–0 and making a pact with myself that that will never happen again."

The years of preparation produced results immediately. Along with team president Michael Bidwill, Keim hired Bruce Arians as coach. Together, that management team put together a roster that brought the Cardinals unprecedented success. The team won at least 10 games in each of the next three seasons on the job, something it hadn't accomplished since the mid-1970s. Following the 2014 season, Keim was named the NFL Executive of the Year by *The Sporting News*.

Keim quickly proved to be a bold decision maker. He made 193 roster moves in his first season on the job, helping to execute one of the best turnarounds in league history. In his second year, the Cardinals roster was decimated with injuries with 21 different players missing 109 games, but Keim and the Cardinals front office made 217 roster moves as the team won 11 games and made the playoffs for the first time in five years. Just two years into their jobs, Keim and Arians were signed to contract extensions by Bidwill. It's not an exaggeration to say they have formed the best coaching and management structure in franchise history.

Keim remains consumed with player evaluations, just as he was as a boy. "To this day I don't have hobbies," Keim said. "I don't have the patience for golf. With having four children, it's a situation where I feel like I would be cheating them and my wife if, after the long hours I put in here, I went off to the golf course or off to go hunting or fishing."

Keim was an excellent guard at North Carolina State, but a knee injury late in his career hurt his chances of playing professionally. He joined the North Carolina State staff as a strength and conditioning coach, but his eyes were on becoming an NFL scout. So when scouts came to campus, Keim made sure to introduce himself. Rod Graves, who ran the Cardinals football operations, was impressed and hired him in 1999 as a college scout in the East. He was promoted to director of college scouting in 2006, director

Fergie

The Cardinals didn't win much in their first two decades in Arizona, but that doesn't mean they lacked personality in some of those years. That was due in part to Bob Ferguson, a member of the team's front office from 1996 to 2003. "Fergie" held various job titles—from temporary personnel assistant all the way up to general manager.

Highly respected within the NFL, Ferguson was an open-collar guy working for a buttoned-down team. He cried at press conferences, pounded tables when he was mad, fought hard for his beliefs, and never hid his emotions. Asked if he thought he hurt the feelings of Simeon Rice when Ferguson criticized the defensive end for holding out, he replied, "Toughski shitski."

Ferguson was a football man through and through. He's from Seattle, and his first job in the NFL was with the Seahawks. It's also where he met his wife, Colleen. She was managing a men's clothing store that Ferguson visited. "I thought I was pretty hot stuff," he said. "I went in and bought three pairs of slacks and made her measure my pants."

Ferguson was a visionary at a time when the Cardinals needed one. He had helped Bill Polian revitalize the Buffalo Bills, and Ferguson was confident the same thing could be done in Arizona. "We will build a stadium in this valley," he said in 1998. "When? Hopefully, soon. We have to win. And if they give me the chance, I know what we can do to get there."

Ferguson didn't get much of a chance. When he was with the Cardinals, there was no clear delineation of power in the front office. That, more than anything, kept the team from building upon a playoff berth in 1998. Ferguson lasted five more seasons in Arizona. By the end he held a title but little power. "I haven't been in charge of anything around here in a long time," he said near the end of his time in Arizona.

Ferguson was fired in January of 2003 and was hired as the Seahawks' general manager about a month later. When the Seahawks announced that move, Ferguson was relieved the lengthy interview process was over. "I'm running out of ties," he said.

of player personnel in 2008, vice president of player personnel in 2012, and general manager a year later.

Keim had firm ideas about how the Cardinals could improve. First the college and pro scouting departments had to be bolstered. There were too few people, and they were spread too thin. Bidwill agreed, and the investment has paid off. In three years Keim has been successful in identifying and acquiring veteran talent for minimal financial risk.

He's also encouraged his scouts to voice their opinions—even if they run counter to his own—and to evaluate mistakes in order to improve. After all, that method worked for him. "Maybe it's because I'm not smart enough, but I've always thought one of the reasons I've ascended to the position I have now is that I wasn't scared to voice my opinion," he said. "I'm very confident in my ability."

76 Mr. Reliable

From 1962 through 1978, the Cardinals had more than their share of concerns. Finding a kicker, however, was rarely among them. That's because they had Jim Bakken, who was among the best in the game. Bakken played 17 seasons with the Cardinals—second most in team history to quarterback Jim Hart. His 234 consecutive games remains a team record.

For a kicker to remain steadily employed that long is astounding. But then Bakken was an astounding kicker. He made the NFL's All-Decade Team for the 1960s and was second team on the '70s squad. Bakken still holds eight franchise records. "In athletics it seemed like I was able to come through in tight situations," said Bakken, who also played defensive back and backup quarterback in college at Wisconsin, "whether it's adrenaline or focus or whatever."

Oddly, Bakken's NFL career could not have started worse. The Los Angeles Rams drafted him in the seventh round in 1962, but he performed so badly in preseason that he was cut. "I might have been intimidated," Bakken said. "I just didn't perform well."

The St. Louis Cardinals and Green Bay Packers claimed Bakken on waivers, and he was awarded to the Cardinals, who had a worse record than the Packers. Bakken arrived in St. Louis and stayed through the 1978 season. He led the NFL in field goals in 1964 and 1967 and was selected to four Pro Bowls, the last in 1976. "He was a tremendous athlete," former Cardinals coach Jim Hanifan told the *St. Louis Post-Dispatch* in 2007. "When he was playing here, he won two or three state championships in handball. And I remember he'd go down to Busch Stadium and take some batting practice, and he'd put the ball out of the park."

Bakken never set out to be a kicker. Growing up in Madison, Wisconsin, he was a big Packers fan. He listened to the games on the radio and liked their kicker, Fred Cone. The Bakkens had a large yard on the side of their house, and young Jim would make a divot with his heel and then kick the ball with his toe. Bakken's high school coach, Fred Jacoby, emphasized the kicking game, believing at least one contest a year would be decided by an extra point. So Bakken took kicking seriously.

With the Cardinals he set a NFL record by making seven field goals in one game. During that game at Pittsburgh, his kicks were all short, but five were into the wind, and most came after Bakken's regular holder, safety Larry Wilson, left the game with an injury. "I've seen a picture of the last one I made, and it's probably the worst technique I've ever had," Bakken said.

It was 40 years before Rob Bironas of the Tennessee Titans broke it by making eight field goals. Bakken was informed of the news when his grandson, John, who was 11 at the time, called him. "Don't worry, Grandpa," John said. "He's really good!"

"Well, John, 40 years is a pretty long time to hold a record," Grandpa replied.

What Bakken is most proud of in his NFL career, he said, is that he played for five different head coaches. "A kicker having an off year can be replaced," Bakken said. "I was able to fool five different head coaches for a number of years."

Bakken was famous for making kicks in pressure situations, especially for the "Cardiac Cardinals" of the mid-1970s, who seemed to take every game down to the final seconds.

Never did he feel more pressure than an extra point against Washington in 1975. Receiver Mel Gray had just scored on the "phantom catch" to bring the Cardinals to within one point with 25 seconds left. As officials huddled to decide if Gray had caught the ball or not, Bakken waited on the sideline. "One of our rookies, I don't remember which one, said to me, 'I'm sure glad I don't have to kick this one,'" Bakken said.

That made Bakken even more nervous. But he made the extra point and converted a field goal in overtime to give the Cardinals the victory. "That's the hardest extra point I've ever made," Bakken said.

77 Passing on A.P.

In hindsight drafting running back Adrian Peterson with the fifth overall pick in 2007 should have been a no-brainer for the Cardinals. And in hindsight, we all should have invested in Google and Facebook when they were start-ups. In the moment, though, the right decision isn't always clear.

It wasn't in 2007, when the Cardinals passed on taking Peterson in favor of selecting offensive tackle Levi Brown out of Penn State. It's a move that's caused many Cardinals fans to slap their foreheads with their palms. Peterson, of course, went on to become the best running back of his generation. And Brown went on to become a pedestrian offensive lineman who will always be an answer to a trivia question: who did the Cardinals draft instead of Adrian Peterson?

Oh, what could've been. "Could you imagine?" receiver Larry Fitzgerald said in 2015. "I always mess with [general manager] Steve [Keim]. I'm like, 'Steve, we should have just took him with the fifth pick a couple years back. We might have a couple of Super Bowls right now.'" Keim wasn't the Cardinals' general manager in 2007; Rod Graves was. The team had a new coach, Ken Whisenhunt, who wanted to bolster the offensive and defensive lines.

And besides, one year before the Cardinals had signed free agent running back Edgerrin James to a four-year deal, paying him $11.5 million in bonuses. So the Cardinals drafted Brown, whom they envisioned playing left tackle for many, many years. The Minnesota Vikings took Peterson two picks later. The folly of the Cardinals' decision was apparent right away. In his first two seasons, Peterson rushed for 3,101 yards and 22 touchdowns.

That draft day decision was a hot issue when the Cardinals played the Vikings in 2008, the second season for Peterson and Brown and a year in which the Cardinals won the NFC West. "If you told me we could take Levi Brown and be division champions in our second year, I'd say, 'Sign me up,'" Whisenhunt said at the time. "I think [Levi] has done a good job. Our sack totals in terms of protecting the quarterback have been very good. Obviously we haven't run the ball as well as we wanted to, but we are doing a number of good things offensively. That starts up front."

The Cardinals obviously loved Brown when he came out of Penn State. He had a reputation for toughness and he was smart, having earned two college degrees. But he was an average NFL player and a much better right tackle than left tackle. He made 79 starts over seven years in Arizona. Four games into the 2013 season, the Cardinals traded Brown to the Pittsburgh Steelers for a conditional pick. Brown played in one game for the Steelers, was injured, and never played another down in the NFL.

Peterson, meanwhile, proved to be a freak of nature. From 2007 through 2015, the Cardinals had to face Peterson six times. Each time questions from reporters forced them to revisit the 2007 draft. Even Peterson has had daydreams of himself in a Cardinals uniform. "Yes, I think about that sometimes," he said before the Cardinals played the Vikings in 2015. "My uncle, Ivory Lee Brown, played for the Cardinals for about three or four years. [It was actually one.] I was like, 'It'd be pretty cool to go down there and play for the same team my uncle played for.'"

78 Luis Sharpe

Rarely has a player seemed better prepared for life after football than former Cardinals left tackle Luis Sharpe. He was smart, happily married with five children, and spoke two languages fluently. When he retired in 1994, Sharpe seemed destined for success in broadcasting, business, and anything else that might interest him. Instead an addiction to crack cocaine caused his life to spiral out of control. From 1996 to 2013, Sharpe was in and out of prison. "Longer than I played football," Sharpe told *The Arizona Republic* in 2011.

He was convicted of nine felonies and shot twice during that time. Sharpe lost his marriage, a lot of money, and his family—at least for a time—because of his addiction. "If he isn't a case study of what drugs can do to somebody's life, I don't know what is," former Cardinals public relations director Paul Jensen told *The Republic*.

Sharpe has always been open about his addiction. He's discussed it with reporters from various publications and after his release from prison he participated in a documentary about his life called *Mountain Highs and Valley Lows*. "I had my struggles and I was not the man I should have been," Sharpe said in the film. "I spent many nights out doing things in the streets that if I had the knowledge and wisdom then that I have now, I would not have done. I paid some tremendous consequences, had some tremendous losses because of my negative choices."

For much of his young life, Sharpe was an amazing American success story. Born in Havana, Cuba, he immigrated at age six with his parents to Detroit, where he grew into an outstanding athlete.

He played college football at UCLA, and the Cardinals drafted him 16th overall in 1982. Sharpe became a starter immediately and was chosen to the Pro Bowl three times—from 1987 through 1989.

By the time the team moved from St. Louis to Arizona in 1988, Sharpe had developed into one of the game's best left tackles. A captain, he was admired by other players for his willingness to speak out on significant issues, including the Cardinals' questionable commitment to winning.

There were signs, however, that Sharpe was struggling with demons off the field. In 1992 the *Mesa Tribune* reported that Sharpe had been seen at a known crack house in Glendale, according to police reports. Sharpe denied the report at the time, but it was true.

When a knee injury forced him to retire in 1994, Sharpe couldn't cope. He turned to drugs, mainly crack cocaine. Friends tried to help. In 1995 two friends, former Cardinals receiver Roy Green and Larry Little, drove Sharpe to the Betty Ford Clinic in California. Sharpe stayed a day or two and then spent $550 for a taxi ride back to Arizona.

Sharpe was released from an Arizona prison in 2013, completed terms of his probation, and moved back to Michigan in 2016. He's heavily involved in his church and wants to mentor young people. "I feel I have something to share," he said.

When asked what that is, Sharpe replied, "Oh, my goodness, do you have two hours? Just the fact there are consequences for the choices we make. There are only two outcomes when you involve yourself with drugs: jail or death. I'm glad I went through the things I went through. I made it through and I'm a much stronger person now."

79 The Post-Warner QB Debacle

For Cardinals fans the only thing more depressing than quarterback Kurt Warner announcing his retirement in early 2010 was watching what came after. It was far uglier than anyone imagined. Over the course of three years, the failure to adequately replace Warner cost general manager Rod Graves and coach Ken Whisenhunt their jobs. After Warner retired, six different quarterbacks started over the next three seasons.

Warner led the team to consecutive playoff appearances in 2008–09, and since he had a year left on his contract, everyone hoped he would return for one last season. He didn't and the position became a turnstile. Matt Leinart, the 10th overall pick in 2006, was the starter until late August, when Whisenhunt replaced him with Derek Anderson. Anderson was horrible, completing just 51.7 percent of his passes. So Whisenhunt replaced him with rookie John Skelton, who completed just 47.6 percent of his throws. That led to rookie Max Hall starting, but he had six interceptions and one touchdown pass.

It was the first time in the NFL since 1994 that a team had two rookie quarterbacks start games in a single season. Everyone knew something had to be done in 2011, but for months nothing could be accomplished. NFL owners locked out the players as the two sides worked out a collective bargaining agreement. When that agreement was reached in July, the Cardinals quickly acquired Philadelphia Eagles quarterback Kevin Kolb by trading cornerback Dominique Rodgers-Cromartie and a second-round pick in 2012. That didn't work either. Kolb showed promise at times, but he couldn't stay healthy.

The Cardinals won seven of their final nine games to finish 8–8 in 2011. Skelton started those games, so Whisenhunt stuck with him at the beginning of 2012. That didn't last long. Skelton suffered an injury in the first game, and Kolb led the Cardinals on the game-winning scoring drive. The Cardinals won their first four games, and it appeared Whisenhunt had finally found a capable replacement for Warner. But against the Buffalo Bills, Kolb suffered dislocated ribs and he never played another game for the Cardinals. They released him the spring of 2013. Kolb was picked up by the Bills but suffered a severe concussion in the preseason. He never played football again.

After Kolb went down, Whisenhunt and the Cardinals were scrambling to find anyone who could complete a pass. Skelton went 1–5 as the starter. Rookie Ryan Lindley went 1–3, and Brian Hoyer, signed late in the year, started the final game of the year, which the Cardinals also lost.

When Hardy Threw Eight Interceptions in a Game

The 1950 season could not have started worse for Chicago Cardinals quarterback Jim Hardy. He was driving four teammates to the game at Comiskey Park against the Philadelphia Eagles and was involved in an auto accident. The other players took a cab to the park, while Hardy had to wait while the accident report was taken. "I arrived at the field just in time for the kickoff and entered the game without a warm-up," Hardy told Stan Grosshandler of *Football Digest*. "That day started out bad, and then it got progressively worse."

A lot worse.

The Eagles, the defending NFL champions, intercepted eight of Hardy's passes in their 45–7 victory. It still stands as the NFL record for most interceptions thrown in a single game. "I felt so bad that day," Hardy said years later, "that after the game I was wishing I was a mole so that I might burrow my way out of the place under the grass."

Hardy was an average player who had an awful day. But after the season opener, there was nowhere to go but up. He showed his wherewithal the following week, throwing for six touchdowns against the Indianapolis Colts.

In an interview with Grosshandler, Hardy recalled how the Eagles game started for the Cardinals. "On the first series, Bob Shaw came into the huddle and told me he could get clear on a post pattern, so I called one," Hardy said. "I hit him right on the money, but he dropped the ball. He came back and said, 'Jim, I can still get clear,' so I called the same play again. This time I got hit just as I threw, and as the ball fell short, Joe Sutton of the Eagles intercepted it."

Hardy had three passes intercepted in the first half, and the Cardinals trailed 31–0. "I really felt low at halftime," Hardy said. "I can still remember sitting on a bench in the dressing room with my head in my hands, thinking that nothing could be worse than three interceptions in one half. Just three years before with the Rams, I had been the No. 2 quarterback in the league and only thrown seven interceptions all year. Little did I know I was to have five more."

By the second half, Hardy recalled, his pass protection had broken down, and he was throwing in desperation. Coach Earl "Curly" Lambeau took pity on Hardy, replacing him with Frank Tripucka. But even that didn't work. Tripucka was injured on the third play, and back came Hardy.

He did complete a 54-yard pass to Mal Kutner and a touchdown pass to Fran Polsfoot for the Cardinals' only score. Hardy and the Cardinals did exact some revenge, beating the Eagles, 14–10 later in the year. Hardy passed to halfback Elmer Angsman for a touchdown in the third quarter.

Over the next seven decades, Hardy's record has been threatened but never broken. On seven other occasions, quarterbacks have had seven passes intercepted, and on 32 occasions, passers have had six attempts intercepted (including Joe Namath three times). "You know," Hardy told *Football Digest* "people will still call me today if a game is on TV and a quarterback has thrown several interceptions and say, 'Hey Jim, he only needs two or three more to beat your record.'"

81 Duke Slater

When his father finally relented and granted him permission to play football at Clinton (Iowa) High, Fred "Duke" Slater faced a difficult decision: shoes or a helmet? It was 1913. Players furnished their own uniforms, and his family couldn't afford both. Slater chose shoes, though his feet were so big the cleats had to be special ordered.

By the time he joined the Chicago Cardinals in 1926, Slater was the proud owner of a helmet and already had a lengthy resume as one of the NFL's finest linemen. He was a trailblazer in other ways, too. For much of the 1920s, Slater was one of only a handful of African American players in professional football. In 1927 and 1929, he was the only one. Slater never made any All-NFL squads, a reflection of the racial climate at the time rather than his abilities. He made the second team almost every year of his career. For some reason Slater is not in the Pro Football Hall of Fame, but he should be.

His story is a Hollywood script with a cool little coincidence: Slater and Cardinals running back David Johnson are products of Clinton High, having graduated nearly 100 years apart. Slater spent his younger years in Chicago and he spent time playing football at a vacant lot on Racine Avenue, which later become home to the Cardinals, according to Dan Daly, former *Washington Times* columnist and a pro football historian.

When he was 13, Slater's father, a minister, moved the family to Clinton. Duke loved football, but his father didn't. It was too dangerous, George Slater said. Duke was not deterred. Without his father's knowledge or consent, Duke joined the football team. His father eventually found out when he saw his wife repairing tears in his son's uniform.

George Slater demanded his son quit. Duke refused and went on a hunger strike for a few days in protest. George Slater relented, and Duke (sans helmet) quickly became a star. He went from Clinton High to the University of Iowa. By his sophomore season at Iowa, he had been named first team All-Big Ten and second-team All-American. Slater became a professional in 1922, joining the Rock Island Independents.

Unlike Major League Baseball, the NFL had not banned African Americans from playing, and Slater was among a handful of men of color to play in the era. When the Independents folded after the 1925 season, Slater joined the Cardinals the following year and was a mainstay through 1931. In all, he played 10 professional seasons, an astounding achievement in that era.

Slater was 6'1" and 215 pounds. He was a devastating blocker and dominant on defense. *Chicago Tribune* sportswriter Wilfrid

Smith described him as "one of the best tackles who ever donned a suit. His phenomenal strength and quickness of charge make it almost impossible for his opponents to put him out of any play directed at his side of the line."

While still playing football, Slater studied law and became a practicing attorney. After his playing career ended, Slater lived in Chicago and served as an assistant district attorney and then a municipal court judge. Slater died in 1966 from stomach cancer.

82 Coach Mac

On Dave McGinnis' last day as Cardinals head coach, a beat writer covering the team called the coach looking for comment. In the background there was noise from packing tape being ripped off a dispenser. "Hear that?" McGinnis said in good humor. "This is what it sounds like when a coach gets fired."

McGinnis had been on the job just three and a half seasons, but it felt like far longer because of everything that happened under his tenure. McGinnis was named interim coach in late October of 2000 after Vince Tobin was fired after a 2–5 start. There was considerable pressure on everyone in the organization. In early November of that year, Maricopa County residents were scheduled to vote on a proposition that would fund a new stadium for the Cardinals.

A week into his tenure as interim coach, McGinnis was not only working as a coach, but he was also a campaign volunteer. He and a handful of players spent part of a day knocking on doors, urging voters to approve funding. It didn't hurt that McGinnis' only victory that year came two days before the election. The proposition barely passed, so it's possible the win was the deciding factor.

In mid-December, McGinnis was named permanent head coach—if there is such a thing in the NFL. The Cardinals were much better in 2001, finishing 7–9. Hopes were high as the Cardinals prepared for the 2002 season.

On May 23 three beat reporters received phone calls from the team's public relations department asking them to come to team headquarters for an announcement from Coach Mac. "Pat Tillman is joining the Army," McGinnis said. He let the words hang there and then described his meeting with Tillman. The coach did not try to talk Tillman out of it. "I honor that, the integrity of that," McGinnis said. "This is not a snap decision he just made yesterday. He feels very strongly about it, deeply convicted about it."

McGinnis was close to Tillman, as he was with most of those who played for him. McGinnis loved people and he had a knack for relating to everyone in the organization—whether it be the millionaire quarterback or the custodian whose wife was undergoing cancer treatment. McGinnis not only knew employees' names, but he also knew the names of their kids. All the corny stuff he preached to players—about having one heartbeat—was not just some act. McGinnis believed in that.

The problem was that he never stood much of a chance as a head coach. The Cardinals got off to a 4–2 start in 2002 before getting decimated by injuries and finishing 5–11.

Everyone knew if the Cardinals didn't turn things around quickly, 2003 would be McGinnis' last season as head coach. But circumstances made winning difficult. The Cardinals cut salaries and took hits against the salary cap in the process.

The team let quarterback Jake Plummer and wide receiver David Boston go via free agency. It drafted poorly. The Cardinals finished 4–12 in 2003, and McGinnis was fired the day after the season. He became the fifth head coach to move out of that office in the team's Tempe headquarters.

McGinnis, as usual, refused to feel sorry for himself on the day he was fired. Instead he reflected on the previous day, when the Cardinals beat the Minnesota Vikings on the last play of the game. "Where is a grown man going to have as much fun as I did when Nate Poole caught that pass in the end zone?" McGinnis asked. "I mean, legally, where is he going to have that much fun?"

83 Eric Swann

Eric Swann did not take a normal career path to the NFL, to say the least. He spent his first year out of high of high school working as a maintenance man at the North Carolina state fairgrounds while he tried to meet college entrance requirements. He failed the test eight times and earned $6 an hour. Swann spent his second year out of high school playing defensive line for the Bay State Titans. It was a semipro team in Massachusetts—with the emphasis on "semi." Players weren't paid unless fans made donations. In 1991, his third year out of high school, Swann was drafted sixth overall by the Cardinals, signed a five-year deal worth nearly $4 million, and played in the NFL.

He was 21. It sure beat mowing grass at the fairgrounds in Raleigh, North Carolina. "I'm still floating on Cloud No. 9," Swann said after being drafted. "I can't even explain the feeling that went through my heart." Some draft experts, such as Mel Kiper Jr., thought the Cardinals had made a bold and smart move in drafting Swann. Others, however, criticized the team for taking too big of a risk on someone who hadn't played college football. "We feel very comfortable that he is a safe pick," general manager Larry Wilson said on draft day.

Swann was the first non-college player to be drafted by the NFL since Emil Sitko was drafted by the Los Angeles Rams in 1946. Sitko, however, never played for the Rams. Instead, he went to Notre Dame and played with the San Francisco 49ers in 1950 and the Chicago Cardinals in 1951–52.

Swann arrived in the NFL, thanks to a chance meeting with a scout who put him in touch with Dick Bell, a sports agent who also was the Bay State Titans' general manager. After Swann's one season with Bay State, Bell sent video of Swann to every NFL team. Bell became Swann's agent and let it be known that the team drafting Swann would have no trouble signing him. "I'm here to play football, not count money," Swann promised.

At 6'4" inches and 311 pounds, Swann possessed a rare blend of size, speed, and power. When the Cardinals watched tape of Swann playing for Bay State, they couldn't believe his athleticism. "The first thing that hit my mind was here's a 311-pound lineman making plays 40 yards downfield," said Carl Hairston, a former NFL defensive lineman who worked as an administrative assistant for the Cardinals when Swann was drafted. "That's something you can't teach. That's the kind of instincts and ability he has."

Swann's career did not start smoothly. He suffered a knee injury in minicamp and underwent two surgeries before playing in a game. During that rookie season, the kid who vowed to not count money complained about his contract, saying the Cardinals "got a Rolls-Royce for the price of a Cadillac." That didn't endear Swann to management or to fans, but Swann started to grow up in the latter half of his rookie year.

The Cardinals had an excellent defensive coaching staff then led by coordinator Fritz Shurmur. Defensive line coach Ted Cottrell mentored Swann, and the defensive tackle began to blossom. "Eric has matured a lot as a football player," Shurmur said at the time. "A lot of lights have turned on. Things are starting to make sense to him. It's all new from the standpoint of having [teammates] on him, coaches on him, all that pressure. He's probably experiencing the same things that college freshmen are now in terms of adjustment, but he's going through it at an even higher level."

Swann never fulfilled his potential, but he wasn't a bust either. He played 10 seasons in the NFL, including nine with the Cardinals. He made the Pro Bowl twice. In 1997 the team signed him to a five-year, $10 million deal that included a $7.5 million bonus. It was the richest contract in team history. The Cardinals, however, never got a return on that hefty investment. Swann suffered from chronic knee problems and played in just 16 games over the next two years. The Cardinals released Swann in 2000. He lasted one more year in the NFL, finishing his career with the Carolina Panthers.

84 Passing on a Local Pass Rusher

After a disastrous 2002 season in which they went 5–11, there was no doubt what the Cardinals needed to address in the offseason— everything. But finding a pass rusher was near the top of the list, and there was a great one practically just up the street, who was anxious to stay home and play for the Cardinals. Terrell Suggs played high school football in the Phoenix suburb of Chandler and played at Arizona State. He wanted nothing more than to don a

Cardinals uniform, a desire not shared by many top prospects at that time.

The Cardinals had only 21 sacks in 2002. That same year Suggs set an NCAA record with 24. They seemed like the perfect match. The Cardinals, however, passed on the chance to take Suggs, a decision that still rankles their fans. The decision to trade the sixth overall pick to the New Orleans Saints for the 17th and 18th overall picks was so puzzling that Rod Graves, the vice president of football operations, was bombarded with questions about the team's thinking. Critics opined that the Cardinals traded out of the top 10 because they didn't want to pay the money required to sign the player. Not true, Graves said. "I welcome anybody to come out next weekend [at the minicamp] and take a look at the players from this draft," Graves said. "I trust our information a lot better than some of the people who have had comments regarding the quality of our picks."

Time proved that those commenters were right, and the Cardinals were wrong. The Baltimore Ravens took Suggs, and all he did in his first 12 years was produce 106.5 sacks and make six Pro Bowls. One day he will receive serious consideration for the Pro Football Hall of Fame. The players the Cardinals ended up drafting in the first round—wide receiver Bryant Johnson and defensive end Calvin Pace—enjoyed nice careers. But they weren't close to the level of Suggs, taken by the Ravens with the 10th pick. "I believe Terrell Suggs will be an outstanding football player," Graves said. "But I also believe Terrell Suggs went in the area we thought he would go [10th to Baltimore]. For us the question was not going to be Terrell Suggs at No. 6."

Suggs' stock supposedly fell after he worked out poorly for pro scouts that spring. But nobody in college or pro football ever had 24 sacks in a season before Suggs did it. "I was hoping that's what they'd look at," Suggs told *The Arizona Republic*. "Don't look at T-shirt and shorts. Look at me for what you want me to do. You don't look at a doctor for his lawyer skills. Everybody had an opinion. They don't all know the sacrifices I made. I'm not going to let anybody ruin the best day of my life."

The Cardinals were sensitive to the draft-day criticism. They had made several controversial moves in the offseason, including not placing the franchise tag on either quarterback Jake Plummer or receiver David Boston, allowing them to depart in free agency.

After the team drafted Suggs, scout Steve Keim was dispatched to the press room to say nice things about Johnson and Pace.

When the Cardinals were on the clock, Suggs chewed gum and waited nervously. The Cardinals used 13 of the 15 minutes before announcing their decision. "I thought for sure if the Cardinals had a chance they were going to lock me up," Suggs told *The Republic*. "It doesn't always work that way. I knew they had lost some people and needed more picks."

The Cardinals didn't come up empty in the draft. They selected receiver Anquan Boldin in the second round, and he quickly became a star. Linebacker Gerald Hayes, taken in the third, was a steady player for years. But without a player such as Suggs, the pass rush remained anemic. That played a factor in the Cardinals going 4–12 in 2003 and coach Dave McGinnis being fired.

85 Boomer's Big Day

Quarterback Boomer Esiason's stint as a Cardinal was as short (one season) as it was disappointing (he was benched twice). But for part of one glorious Sunday afternoon in the nation's capital in 1996, Esiason and the Cardinals passing offense were unstoppable. Esiason passed for 522 yards, the third most in NFL history, to help bring the Cardinals back from a 14-point deficit to a 37–34 overtime victory against Washington.

It was clear and cold on that November 10th, and at 3–6 the Cardinals were on their way to another disappointing season. Benched in mid-September after the team started 0–3, Esiason was back in the lineup because Kent Graham had suffered a knee injury. It was Washington's last season in RFK Stadium. Washington was 7–2 and big favorites over the 3–6 Cardinals.

That seemed particularly justified after Esiason had two passes intercepted in the first three-and-a-half minutes. If the Cardinals had another healthy backup besides Stoney Case, who was in his second year, coach Vince Tobin might have benched Esiason again. "I was just trying to stay away from Vince, so he wouldn't bench me," Esiason said. "He let me play into it. Then after I had taken some shots and guys were making plays, things starting coming around.

"Early on, I was so excited about getting back on the field that the ball was sailing on me. And when you get into that zone and you throw the ball and they catch it and they run with it, it's a thing of beauty."

The Cardinals trailed 27–13 early in the fourth quarter, and offensive coordinator Jim Fassel knew he had to put the game in Esiason's hands. Those hands became hot. Esiason passed for 252

Quarterback Boomer Esiason scrambles during the 1996 game in which he threw for 522 yards, which ranks as the third most in NFL history.

yards and two touchdowns in the fourth quarter alone. Both teams missed field goals in the fourth quarter, and it looked like the game would end in a tie when Cardinals kicker Kevin Butler missed another one with 37 seconds left. But Washington was called for offside, and Butler made a 32-yarder for the victory. "This one comes under the general heading of 'laugher,'" Cardinals owner Bill Bidwill said.

Esiason completed 35-of-59 passes for 522 yards that day. Only Norm Van Brocklin (554 yards in 1951) and Warren Moon (527 in 1990) had passed for more yards in a game. "I'm grateful Vince didn't bench me after the first quarter," Esiason joked. "He has a habit of hooking me out of games, you know."

A month later, Tobin reminded everyone, in case they had forgotten. After watching Esiason and his offense struggle again, he benched Esiason, who believed the team had an ulterior motive: on the bench Esiason could not earn the $350,000 in bonuses he was on target to achieve. So in the same season in which he set a team record for yards in a game, Esiason quit the team, walking out on a Wednesday. He returned on Friday, but it was clear his time in Arizona was done.

But at age 35, Esiason fully appreciated what had been accomplished on November 10, 1996. "In this stadium, on this grass, an overcast day, in November, this is what the NFL is all about," he said that day. "These things don't come along very often. Just to let it all sink in and realize what we accomplished today and the way we accomplished it, it was really an amazing thing."

86 Q's Debut

The Cardinals knew they had something special in Anquan Boldin before the receiver ever played an NFL game. A second-round pick out of Florida State in 2003, Boldin excited everyone in the offseason with his strong hands, quick feet, and sharp mind. The Cardinals didn't want the rest of the NFL to know it just yet, so in the preseason they played Boldin just enough to prove the kid was alive. In four exhibition games, he caught only four passes for 44 yards. He looked pedestrian and far from special.

That flipped against the Detroit Lions in the opener of the regular season. Boldin caught 10 passes for 217 yards and two touchdowns. It was the most receiving yards ever by a player in his first NFL game and the second most in franchise history. "I've been around long enough to know what's good and what's bad," Cardinals quarterback Jeff Blake said after that game, the first of Blake's 12th NFL season. "I've seen a lot of guys play, and this guy is special."

The Cardinals lost to the Lions 42–24 that day, but it was a coming-out party for Boldin, one of the few bright spots in what turned into a 4–12 season. Boldin caught 101 passes for 1,377 yards and eight touchdowns as a rookie. He went on to play six more seasons with the Cardinals and was an integral reason for the franchise's improvement over the first decade of this century.

As good as the Cardinals thought Boldin was in 2003, no one expected a debut like the one he had in Detroit. The only way the Lions stopped Boldin is when he stopped himself by fumbling away a punt that led to a touchdown. In Boldin's mind that mistake, as well as the loss, took the thrill out of his receiving statistics. "I would give those stats back for a win," he said after the game.

Boldin wasn't even the first receiver the team drafted in 2003. First round pick Bryant Johnson had a decent NFL career, but he was no Boldin. It's just one more example of the imperfection of scouting. Boldin dropped in the draft because he was timed in the 40-yard dash at around 4.7 seconds, which is slow for a receiver. But he was a football player. He was tough, could run after the catch, and had a great understanding of defensive schemes.

That was a product of playing quarterback in high school and some at Florida State. "In high school my coach did a great job of teaching me football, not just letting me go out and play," Boldin said. "He walked me through coverages, what defenses do in this coverage, what they do in that coverage."

On draft day Cardinals offensive coordinator Jerry Sullivan lobbied hard for the team to take Boldin. "What you love about him is that he wasn't awed by it," Sullivan said after Boldin's debut. "He wasn't one of those guys who was trying to get the last word in. He just kind of went out there and did it with his actions, which says a lot for him."

Boldin didn't explode immediately that day against the Lions. In the first half he caught four passes for 54 yards and a touchdown. But on the third play of the second half, he caught a 71-yard touchdown pass from Blake and gained 91 more yards in the half. Offensive tackle L.J. Shelton found himself near Boldin as they walked off the field after the game. Shelton pointed to Boldin and said, "Better get him on your fantasy team."

87 Palmer Tears His ACL

Carson Palmer propped his crutches against the wall, walked a couple of steps to the small podium, and began a news conference he never wanted to hold. It was November 10, 2014, and Palmer's season ended the day before when he suffered a torn ACL in his left knee. The Cardinals went on to beat the St. Louis Rams that day to improve to 9–1, but Palmer was in anguish that he no longer would be part of one of the franchise's best seasons. "I'm not going to lie. I cried like a baby last night," Palmer said. "I'm not an emotional guy. I don't cry. The last time I cried like that was when I lost my friend and teammate, Chris Henry, back in '09. It's obviously not ideal and not something anybody wants to go through, especially with all the positive and the good going on, but I fully expect the good and the wins to continue to come because we've got a great group of guys in that locker room, very resilient, and guys that are going to show up every week like they have all season long."

It was the second major injury Palmer had suffered to the left knee. In a 2005 playoff game, Palmer, the Cincinnati Bengals starter, suffered two torn ligaments and other damage but returned to start all 16 games in 2006. The injury in 2014 was not as severe, though it was devastating nonetheless. The Cardinals were the best team Palmer had played for, and there was considerable optimism they could contend for the championship.

Palmer was so distraught that he thought it was a possibility the Cardinals would release him, even though he had signed a contract extension two days before the injury. That new deal included $20.5 million guaranteed. "There's millions of unknown questions and I hope, I hope that…I'm going to play football again and I hope it's here," Palmer said. "I know there are a lot of unknowns in the future, and this organization, just seeing what I've seen the last two years, they're going to do what's best for our organization. I know it, I understand it, and I agree with it. I hope I'm a part of that equation, and nobody really knows that right now. All I can do is take it one day at a time and get back as quickly as possible and prove that I'll be ready to go."

The Cardinals never considered moving on from Palmer. Not only had they committed a lot of money to him, but they also thought he was a good fit for the organization. In the short term, Drew Stanton took over as the starting quarterback, and the Cardinals remained competitive, going 3–2 over his next five starts. But then Stanton went down with a knee injury in the 14th game, and the Cardinals lost their next three games, including a wild-card playoff contest against the Carolina Panthers.

Palmer, meanwhile, worked like he never had before. And that's saying something because he was never one to slack off. In addition to rehabbing the injured knee, Palmer worked hard to strengthen his right shoulder. By summer time—just seven months after surgery—Palmer was ready to practice. He started all 16 games in 2015 and set team records for passing yards, touchdown passes, and passer rating.

The Cardinals finished 13–3 and advanced to the NFC Championship Game, where they were beaten by the Panthers. The Cardinals—and Palmer—had come a long way since he arrived via a trade with the Oakland Raiders in the spring of 2013. "It has been crazy and it has been an absolute blast," Palmer said. "I have learned a ton, I have experienced a ton, and I wouldn't trade it for anything."

88 Arians' Wit and Wisdom

In his first three seasons in Arizona, Bruce Arians filled the win column unlike any Cardinals coach before him. He also filled reporters' notebooks with more great quotes than any other coach in the NFL. The filter between Arians' brain and tongue isn't very thick, and that's a good thing for everyone. Unlike most NFL coaches, Arians isn't afraid to say what is on his mind. And he often does so in very colorful ways.

Here's a sampling of his best quotes over his first three years as coach:

Asked why the Cardinals don't have organized stretching at the start of practices; players are expected to do it on their own and be ready to go when the horn blows: "If a Doberman jumped out of a car with a gun, you wouldn't be stretching. When the horn blows, we're practicing."

Asked why he hates fights between players at practice: "The first thing you do is break your hand, might as well punch the wall. If you want to break your hand, break your hand. If you want to fight, I'll put boxing gloves on you and you can fight your ass off. That's what Coach [Bear] Bryant used to do. Want to fight? Wear 18-pound gloves. And they were not allowed to stop swinging...They both passed out. It only happened once."

On his penchant for yelling at players during practices: "I was taught a long time ago: coach 'em hard and hug 'em later…Rip a guy's ass out there and go in, [tell him], 'It's just football, nothing personal. Your football stinks, you're a pretty good guy.'"

On the idea that players view him as a father figure: "I don't like that. I'm the cool uncle you like to have a drink with. Everybody had that uncle. You just loved that uncle, you know? He might call you a little shit or something, but you really liked him. That's me."

On how he tells players to conduct themselves during a bye week: "Too many times when a guy gets days off, he gets tasered in Miami at South Beach or something. We don't want any of that stuff."

On how he tells players to handle praise from fans and media during good times: "Don't believe it. It's a short elevator ride back to the shithouse. All of a sudden, I'm the greatest damn coach in the world. I've been a sorry son-of-a-bitch for 17, 18 years now. That ain't changed just because we won a couple of games. When they're patting you on the back, they're looking for a soft spot where to stick the knife."

Asked if he had a "gut feeling" that an injured Carson Palmer might play that week: "I quit trusting my gut a long time ago. That sumbitch has been lying to me forever."

On the possibility of Oakland Raiders fans throwing eggs at the Cardinals team bus: "Hopefully we've got windows on that sumbitch."

On becoming the head coach at Temple at age 30: "Oh, God, I love Philadelphia. I was 30 and thought I knew everything. About five years later, I finally get out of the hospital and said 'I don't know shit.' It was a great time, gained about 30 pounds eating pretzels and drinking beer."

Upon being informed that people were dressing up as him on Halloween, Arians said it takes more than a hat and glasses to pull off the look: "Yeah, you've got to have the attitude—and a cocktail."

To an out-of-breath writer arriving at a post-practice press conference: "Easy, brother, you ain't getting no mouth-to-mouth around here."

On hiring a female, Jen Welter, as a coaching intern during the 2015 training camp: "Coaching is nothing more than teaching. One thing I have learned from players is: 'How are you going to make me better? If you can make me better, I don't care if you're the Green Hornet. I'll listen.'"

On how first-round pick D.J. Humphries earned the nickname "Knee-Deep" during his first training camp: "A knee in his ass every day. A foot wasn't going to do it, so I nicknamed him 'Knee-Deep.'"

On why he's not one for delivering fiery, emotional pregame speeches: "Snot bubbles and tears don't win shit."

89 Gramatica's Bad Leap

There are several famous leaps in NFL history: San Francisco's Dwight Clark's touchdown catch in the NFC Championship Game in 1982, Denver quarterback John Elway's helicopter-like spin in Super Bowl XXXII, and, of course, the Lambeau Leap, the Packers' traditional touchdown celebration. But there are none as embarrassing as the one made by Cardinals kicker Bill Gramatica in 2001.

A rookie, Gramatica leaped in celebration when he made a 42-yard field goal against the New York Giants in the first quarter at the Meadowlands. There wasn't much to celebrate. It was mid-December, and neither the Cardinals nor the Giants were very good that season. The field goal was the first score of the game. But Gramatica celebrated after every made attempt—even back in college.

This one, however, was different.

He landed awkwardly on his right leg, his plant leg, and wobbled off the field. A few days later, the injury would be diagnosed as a torn ACL. It was another embarrassment to a franchise that had suffered plenty of them since moving to Arizona in 1988. "It's incredible," coach David McGinnis said the day after. "How many times do you figure he's jumped in his life?"

The leap might have cost the Cardinals a .500 season. That's no small thing for a franchise that had accomplished that just twice in its previous 13 seasons in Arizona. They finished 7–9, and Gramatica's leap changed the complexion of the Giants game, which the Cardinals lost 17–13.

After the injury Gramatica was able to make a 23-yard field goal and an extra point, but he had to adjust his approach because his plant leg was unstable. Gramatica attempted place-kicks straight-on instead of soccer style and he couldn't kick off. To say the least, McGinnis was not pleased that the injury was self-inflicted. Asked after the game if Gramatica would temper future celebrations, McGinnis looked at reporters for a long time and said finally: "He'll never do that again."

Those involved now look back at the incident with humor and nostalgia. McGinnis recalled a conversation with safety Pat Tillman, who approached the coach on the sideline after Gramatica limped off the field. "You know who your backup kicker is, don't you?" Tillman asked.

"You?" McGinnis said.

"Fucking A," Tillman replied.

Tillman did a decent job. He did not attempt a field goal or extra point but kicked off twice for 40 and 48 yards. The Giants returned each for 8 yards, so the Cardinals didn't suffer when it came to field position. After the game Tillman was asked if he was nervous about kicking for the first time since high school. "No," he said, "I was stoked, man."

Gramatica was not. He avoided reporters after the game, but he did speak a few days later after finding out the severity of his injury. He defended his celebration. "The feelings I have after I make a kick are not for show," said Gramatica, taken in the fourth round that year. "When you ask me what I do after a kick, I can't tell you sometimes. Nothing is planned. What hurts the most is I came here to help the team, and if I'm on the sideline, that's not possible."

To replace Gramatica, the Cardinals signed Cedric Oglesby, who was working as a substitute teacher in Atlanta. McGinnis' first piece of advice to his new kicker was simple: "If you make one, don't jump in the air."

The Cardinals and McGinnis, though, were forgiving, and Gramatica stayed with the team for two more seasons.

90 George Boone

The Cardinals struggled during most of the last quarter of the 20th century and earned a reputation for being an organization mired in the past—blind to the way the game and league were changing. Other than owner Bill Bidwill, no man was blamed more for that than George Boone, who worked 24 years in the team's personnel department, including the last 19 as player personnel director. In that role Boone ran the team's drafts, which were, for the most part, horrible.

The Cardinals ran drafts the old-school way. Coaches had little input and were not allowed in the draft room on draft weekend. Boone did not believe in interviewing draft prospects either. "I'm not much into personal interviews," he once said. "Some of these personal interviews can turn you off."

That contributed to the Cardinals making some of the biggest draft blunders of the era.

In 1977 they took quarterback Steve Pisarkiewicz in the first round, even though the team had just enjoyed three successful seasons with Jim Hart starting. Coach Don Coryell blew his top and left after that season.

In 1978 the Cardinals drafted Steve Little, a punter and kicker, in the first round. In 1984 it was receiver Clyde Duncan and in 1987 it was quarterback Kelly Stouffer, who never signed with the team. Coaches were hired and fired, but Boone stayed. The team moved to Arizona, but Boone stayed.

With the team in its new locale in 1988, coach Gene Stallings was already fuming over a lack of input in the draft. When the Cardinals drafted Stouffer over Miami defensive lineman Jerome

Brown, Stallings reportedly said, "I hope he can rush the passer." Brown fell to the Philadelphia Eagles, where he helped form a dominant defensive line. "What the hell were they doing?" Eagles coach—and future Cardinals coach—Buddy Ryan said after drafting Brown. "I'm glad they left me Brown."

Boone always disputed that coaches had no input, but he also made it clear that he was in charge of the draft. "Input? Yes," Boone said. "Doing my job? No. He was hired to coach. I was hired to scout. That's my understanding, and he said the same out of his own mouth that he was hired to coach. That's what he told me. I don't call fourth and short for him on Sunday and I don't second-guess his ass on fourth and goal line. He has to call that."

Not all of Boone's draft picks were failures. In his tenure the Cardinals did select running back O.J. Anderson, the franchise's leading rusher; left tackle Luis Sharpe, an excellent pass blocker; and tight end J.V. Cain.

Boone always felt he was unfairly labeled because of his misses in the draft. Bill Bidwill fired Boone in 1992, and, after not working for two seasons, Boone was hired by the Indianapolis Colts. In 1999 he returned to the Cardinals, serving in a lesser role in the scouting department.

But his name will forever be tied to the Cardinals organization and—fairly or unfairly—associated with poor drafts. In an interview with the *St. Louis Post-Dispatch* in 1994, Boone acknowledged he deserved part of the blame for the Cardinals' poor drafts. But he said more went on behind the scenes than people realized. For instance part of the reason the Cardinals drafted Stouffer was that Stallings supposedly was disenchanted with quarterback Neil Lomax.

"Somebody told me, 'Look at it this way, George. You had them fooled for 24 years,'" Boone told the newspaper.

91 Fitzgerald Moves to the Slot

In his first nine years in the NFL, receiver Larry Fitzgerald made seven Pro Bowls, gained more than 1,000 yards receiving six times, and delivered one of the most sensational postseason efforts in league history. So no wonder Fitzgerald felt some trepidation in 2013 when new coach Bruce Arians told the receiver more was going to be required.

Fitzgerald spent his first nine seasons playing one position: split end, otherwise known as the X receiver. Now, the plan was to move him around. Fitzgerald would play some at X but would also play the slot, or F, and eventually some flanker, the Z. The first practices were ugly as players struggled with the offense while coaches demanded more and more. "They don't like for you to come in and think, *Oh, it's just another day at the office*," Fitzgerald said of Arians and his staff at the time. "No, that's not how it is. It's like being in a cold tub every morning. They push you in there, and it's like a shock to the body."

The games weren't much prettier, but gradually things improved. At the halfway point of that first season in 2013, the offense started clicking. In 2015 the Cardinals set franchise records for points and yardage, and Fitzgerald, at 32, enjoyed one of his most productive seasons. The transition, however, was not easy, nor was it smooth. Fitzgerald cares deeply about his craft and after Arians informed him of his job change he immediately began to research it.

He called Hines Ward, the former Steelers receiver who played the position when Arians was offensive coordinator in Pittsburgh. "He was hesitant," Ward told azcentralsports.com in the fall of

2015. "But you get to the point when you reach your 30s. He's had all the accolades. He's been to Pro Bowls. He's made great money, but the one thing he and I are always talking about is him saying, 'Man, I don't care about that stuff anymore. I want a Super Bowl ring.'"

In his first nine years, Fitzgerald built a reputation by playing outside the numbers on the field. Gifted with great hands, Fitzgerald also used his 6'3", 218-pound frame to beat smaller defenders down the sideline. Playing the slot, or inside, proved to be much different. There was more contact, and more blocking was required. Receivers don't make Pro Bowls and earn big money by blocking.

But Fitzgerald accepted his role as blocker, even though it's far from his favorite thing to do. He once compared it to changing a diaper: it's dirty work no one enjoys, but it has to be done. "It wasn't something that was really high on my priority list, but for us to have great team success, it requires receivers to do some blocking," he said. "For us to have the success I know we're capable of, guys have to do some things that maybe they weren't good at before."

By mid-2015 the Cardinals were calling Fitzgerald the best blocking receiver in the NFL. More importantly to Fitzgerald, he was posting huge numbers at receiver, too, and finished with a team-record 109 receptions, 1,215 yards, and nine touchdowns. "I'm not one to ever doubt myself," Fitzgerald told azcentralsports. com. "But you play the same position and you have a lot of success for a long time, I think it would be an adjustment for anybody... but I firmly believe that Coach Arians has my best interest and this team's best interest at hand. I've embraced everything he's asked me to do."

92 Jen Welter

In March of 2015, Cardinals coach Bruce Arians pulled up a chair at the table assigned him by the NFL. He was ready to answer any and all questions from reporters gathered to interview coaches from the NFC at the annual owners' meetings. To borrow a line from songwriter John Hiatt, Arians "can talk the wings off a humming-bird." As an added bonus, most of what he says is interesting, so his table at such media affairs is a popular one.

Arians gave opinions on various topics that day, including one about the NFL hiring its first full-time female official, Sarah Thomas. His answer, however, came with a twist. "Someone asked me yesterday, 'When are we going to have female coaches?'" Arians said. "The minute they can prove they can make a player better, they'll be hired."

Arians had no plans to do it himself. But through various sources, he was put in touch with Jen Welter, who had played and coached in the Indoor Football League in Texas. That July Arians hired Welter as a coaching intern, making her the first woman to coach in the NFL.

Welter spent just six weeks with the team through the 2015 preseason, but her presence was big news. And her story became a big story.

Growing up in Florida, Welter didn't want to be a cheerleader. She wanted to play the game. She ended up doing just that, including at the professional level. One season she made $1 a game and she never cashed the $12 check given her at the end of the year. After playing, the next logical step to Welter was coaching. "The beauty of this is that, though it's a dream I never could have had, now it's a dream other girls can grow up and have," Welter said. "So I guess if that makes me a trailblazer…"

At her first news conference, Welter was as quotable as Arians, which isn't easy to pull off. She talked about being a role model for girls, who too often are viewed as "accessories" in American society, she said. Welter's hiring prompted fanfare. Initial stories of the move generated considerable Internet traffic, and most major news outlets submitted interview requests to the team. "It was going to be one of the 32 teams," team president Michael Bidwill said of Welter's hiring. "I'm glad it was us."

Arians and Welter appeared at a news conference just days before training camp started, and then Welter settled into her role as one of seven coaching interns. "[The novelty] wore off real fast," Arians said, "maybe two days. It was like, 'She's a coach, and doing a great job.' I really wish we could [hire her and] all our interns."

In addition to playing and coaching football, Welter has a PhD in psychology and quickly became known to the Cardinals as "Dr. Jen" or "Dr. J." She worked with inside linebackers and brought a different style to the coaching staff. Before the first preseason game, each inside linebacker found a handwritten note from Welter in their lockers. "It's great," linebacker Kenny Demens said. "She points out your strengths and tells you to bring them out in the game. She loves the game. She's passionate. It's just like having any coach out there. It's not anything gender-like."

Welter's internship ended near the end of training camp. In those waning days, she talked again to reporters and raved about the experience. "Everybody kept waiting for the other shoe to drop," Welter said that day. "They asked, 'What's going to happen?' And 'What's going to go horribly wrong?' It really never did. All the players were really respectful. I heard one player say it best: 'I knew Bruce and the kind of guy he was, and he wouldn't bring anyone who didn't belong.'"

At the end of Welter's internship, the Cardinals took some criticism for not hiring her for a full-time job. But it's rare for that to happen in the NFL, and none of the other six coaching interns, most of them former NFL players, were immediately hired either. Under Arians, the Cardinals have one of the NFL's largest coaching staffs, and there wasn't room for one more at the time.

Hiring Welter as an intern, however, brought the possibility of women coaching men in football to the forefront. In January of 2016, the Buffalo Bills named Kathryn Smith their special teams quality control coach, making her the NFL's first female full-time coach. Welter likely paved the way for her because of the positive treatment she received from players. "One thing I have learned from players is, 'How are you going to make me better?'" Arians said. "'If you can make me better, I don't care if you're the Green Hornet, man, I'll listen.'"

93 Take a Road Trip

In 2005 Cardinals fans Chris Goodman and two buddies started traveling at least once a season to watch their team play a road game. Back then the team had enjoyed little success in nearly two decades in the desert. It was the year before University of Phoenix Stadium opened and three years before the Cardinals made the run to the Super Bowl. They didn't see many fellow Cardinals fans on those road trips.

Opposing fans thought Goodman and friends were cute when they showed up in Cardinals gear to watch games. "People would act like they just saw Santa Claus: 'Wait. You're Cardinals fans? *Really?* That's adorable,'" said Goodman, a Phoenix lawyer. "There was one game in Washington back in 2007 where we didn't see even one other Cardinals fan...there were more people in Cowboys shirts there than Cardinals."

They didn't know it at the time, but Goodman and his buddies were trendsetters. With University of Phoenix Stadium opening in 2006 and playoff appearances in 2008 and '09, the team's fanbase grew and so did the number of Cardinals fans who make a trip or two every season. Today, it's not unusual to see people wearing Cardinals jerseys at airports in the days before and after a road game or to bump into them at hotels, restaurants, and bars.

It doesn't hurt that the team plays in the NFC West, so fans can count on a trip to Seattle and San Francisco every year. New Orleans, Chicago, Tampa Bay, and Miami are also popular destinations. In Chicago in 2015, there were thousands who made the trip to see the Cardinals. The home fans no longer think their Cardinals counterparts are so cute. "They're more worried about the game than looking at us with wonder that the Cardinals actually have fans," Goodman said. "It's great that more Cards fans are traveling now, but those of us who stuck it out years ago got to experience what it was like being an NFL outlier."

Although the game is the featured attraction, it's not the only reason to attend road games. If it was, Goodman's group would have stopped traveling long ago. From 2005 through 2014, the Cardinals went 0–12 when Goodman's group attended a road game, including Super Bowl XLIII. "It got to the point where other fans would ask us not to go on our road trips because that would guarantee a loss," Goodman said.

But memories were made in other ways. In Green Bay one year, Goodman's group went to a tailgate hosted by Brett Favre's Steakhouse. A waterfall drinking challenge between 10 Cardinals fans and 10 Packers fans was organized. "Out marched the 10 biggest, fattest Packer fans they could find, which is a high bar," Goodman said. "They were ringers. I guess they do it every week and dominate the visiting fans. We almost beat them. Packer fans seemed quite impressed; I guess that's how you win respect in Wisconsin."

Cardinals fans make memories on these trips—insane cab drivers, missed flights due to hangovers, victories, encounters with celebrities. Former major leaguer Mark Grace, a big Cardinals fan, usually makes at least one trip a year. Chicago Cubs manager Joe Maddon, also a fan, dropped by the team hotel in 2015.

For Goodman's crew most trips have ended on a positive note despite the losses—even the heartbreaker in the Super Bowl. "We sat in the stands and didn't say a word to each other for about an hour after the game," he said. "We stayed until the ushers had to ask us to leave. Outside the stadium we found a guy selling obviously unlicensed Steelers world champs T-shirts. We asked him if he had Cardinals ones in case they won. He did, so I'm the proud owner of one of the few Arizona Cardinals world champions T-shirts out there. I cherish it almost as much as my Adrian Murrell jersey."

94 Tailgate on The Great Lawn

It cost $450 million to build University of Phoenix Stadium. At that price there should be some cool stuff inside, and there is. The roof retracts, the field slides in and out on a tray, there is air conditioning and comfortable seats. But one of the best things about the stadium is a simple thing that many of us have in our homes: a grass yard. West of the stadium is something called The Great Lawn. It's 20 or so acres of pretty, green grass that fans put to great use as a tailgating area.

Pickup trucks, vans, and cars filled with supplies begin arriving hours before a Cardinals game. Soon after, canopies, grills, chairs, coolers, games, and satellite dishes are set up for hours of fun. "It's not that hard to get a spot," said Kevin Sanders, a season-ticket holder. "After that, it's like being at a lake vacation."

There is usually a live band that entertains a crowd that swells in size as the season progresses, and temperatures dip into the 70s and 80s. Kids and adults play catch with a football. Cornhole and other games are set up everywhere. Many cold beverages are consumed. It's easy to participate. Plan your own party or—better yet—join someone who does it weekly.

Afraid of missing out on NFL action earlier in the day? No worries. Plenty of people bring televisions and satellite dishes to see the early games. It's part of the fun.

You can keep your tailgate as simple as you want or try to compete for "tailgater of the game." Folks competing for that honor have been known to bring ice sculptures, hang the other team's mascot in effigy, and go to extreme lengths in building the menu. "We have a guy in our group who at the beginning of the season emails the menus for the entire year," Sanders said. "The menu has to match the team you're playing, like some kind of bird for Seattle. If Chicago is in, it's Italian beef or something like that. The food is no joke."

Here are a few tips for enjoying the tailgate even more: pick a night game or one later in the year, when the weather is cooler. Serve food by halftime of the day's first games to make sure there is time to eat, clean up, and make it inside for the Cardinals game. Take a tour of the entire area. Some people have considerable time on their hands because the setups are elaborate.

And make sure someone in the group has access to satellite TV. That way, you can keep abreast of the early games and the performances of your fantasy players.

95 Listen to Dave Pasch and Ron Wolfley

Advances in technology provide myriad ways to enjoy the NFL. We can watch any game on our phones, tablets, or computers. We can break down the same video coaches use, wield our own telestrators, and watch an entire game condensed into a 30-minute replay. But one of the best ways to enjoy a Cardinals game is to go old school and tune in the team's radio broadcast. Since 2004 Dave Pasch and Ron Wolfley have given fans a broadcast like no other.

Where else can you hear the word "dirtlicker" to describe a player who plays low to the ground? Or the unpredictability of the game described this way: "Sometimes you're the shish, and sometimes you're the kabob." Or learning a particularly vicious hit feels like this: "Stand on your kitchen counter and dive headfirst into the tile." These come from the strange, creative mind of Wolfley, whose passion for the game and for the team smacks listeners like a lead-blocking fullback with a crazed look in his eyes, which is what Wolfley was for 10 NFL seasons.

Pasch and Wolfley came from vastly different broadcasting backgrounds to form one of the most informative and entertaining game broadcasts in the country. Pasch was classically trained at Syracuse; Wolfley relies on lessons learned on football fields across America. The broadcast works because they need each other and, more importantly, like each other. "I sit there in the passenger seat and fire off some shotgun shells, metaphorically speaking," Wolfley said. "I need a person like Dave, who is so fundamentally structured and talented. He is the foundation that allows me to be as creative as I want. And you can't always do that if you're in my seat. You need someone who is really stable and fundamentally sound."

Pasch is that. He went to school at Syracuse, which has produced many play-by-play broadcasters. When he took the Cardinals job in 2001, Pasch was more buttoned-down, by-the-book. The game was the show, not him. He's still that way. But Pasch said that working with Wolfley has made him a better broadcaster. Pasch has loosened up and showed more of his personality. How could you not, when your partner is referring to the game as the "bloodsport," and constantly coming up with creative analogies and metaphors? "He made me come out of my comfort zone," said Pasch, who also broadcasts NBA games, as well as college football and basketball. "Everybody is different. I accept who he is. Some play-by-play guys only want to work with certain guys. People listen for Wolf, and I have no problem with that. Some play-by-play guys wouldn't like that."

Wolfley is the same guy on the air as he is off the air. He grew up in a football family, and his passion for the game has never waned. As a player he prepared for games by drinking copious amounts of coffee and entering a mental state in which common sense was suspended.

It worked.

Wolfley played 10 years in the NFL, including his first seven with the Cardinals, and he made the Pro Bowl four times as a special teamer. "When I'm doing the broadcast, I'm not 'Fat 53,'" Wolfley said, referring to his waistline and age. "I'm 24 with 8 percent body fat. I remember what it was like to put that helmet on, pop the mouthguard in, and just act like an unmitigated savage between those white lines."

Outside those white lines, Wolfley was always thoughtful and intelligent. And that comes through in the broadcasts, too. Writing is one of his passions, though he never shows anyone the fiction he produces. He's in love with words, and that creative process helps him create "Wolfleyisms," the unscripted analogies, metaphors, and similes that have made him somewhat of a cult figure in the broadcast world. When Wolfley says it's time to "strap on the Depends," he means it's a tense moment in the game. "Getting your back waxed" means a quarterback sack. "Time to grab your club and run downhill" means the game is about to start.

None of these are written down before the game. Some pop into Wolfley's head. Others come to him when he's writing, and he thinks, *This could work one day in a broadcast.* "I'm a melodramatic person to begin with," Wolfley said. "Words are powerful and especially in the medium of radio."

Pasch and Wolfley have common interests, including strong religious faith, and are close enough friends that they can tease each other. A few years ago, the hefty Wolfley was called upon to turn the crank of a siren during pregame festivities. He did a nice job, but his body jiggled a bit. "Next time," Pasch advised, "wear a jacket."

Neither is afraid to admit they are Cardinals fans, too, just like the people who are listening to them. "During the playoff run in 2008 after each Cardinals win, he'd do the fat lady and he'd sing until he lost his breath," Pasch said. "It was high-pitched singing. I told him I want to hear that again this year."

96 Monday Night(mares)

For some reason Cardinals fans still get excited when their team plays on Monday night. Perhaps they conveniently forget the team's awful history in those primetime games. Or maybe they are eternal optimists, believing the Cardinals' fortunes will change. From 1970 through 2014, the Cardinals were 7–15–1 on Monday nights, including losing nine of 10 from 1986 to 2012.

Not only have the Cardinals consistently lost on Monday nights, but they've also found creative ways to do it. And since moving to Arizona in 1988, a few losses on Monday night prompted sweeping changes in the organization. Let's take a look at the lowlights of the team's history in primetime.

1988

The Cardinals' first home game in Arizona came on Monday night against the Dallas Cowboys. The Cardinals lost 17–14 partly because of a disastrous decision made by coach Gene Stallings before the last play of the first half. Stallings decided to run a fake field goal rather than have Al Del Greco try a 42-yarder. Del Greco took a lateral and was stopped at the 16-yard line.

After the game Stallings admitted it wasn't a smart move on his part. "It doesn't take a Phi Beta Kappa to figure that out," he said.

1995

It was Christmas night again against the Cowboys, and it was the Cardinals' first Monday night game since 1988. It was coach and general manager Buddy Ryan's second season and his last. The Cardinals were 4–11 entering the game, and fans had turned on Ryan, who never came close to backing up his boast of bringing a winner to town.

Turmoil is not a strong enough word to describe the state of the team. Two players got into a fight in the locker room before the game as broadcaster and ex-Cardinals great Dan Dierdorf witnessed the scuffle. The Cowboys whipped the Cardinals 37–13 with the most memorable moment coming in the final seconds. Thinking the game was over, Ryan headed to the tunnel of Sun Devil Stadium, where he watched the final play of his head coaching career.

He was fired the next day.

Not-So-Happy Thanksgiving

Thanksgiving is not the only time Cardinals fans should count their blessings. They should do it every spring, too, when the NFL schedule is announced and their team is not scheduled to play on Thanksgiving. The Cardinals are awful at football on Thanksgiving. They started off just fine, beating the Chicago Bears 6–0 in 1922. But overall, the Cardinals play football on Thanksgiving like they just finished their third plate at Grandma's house. The Cardinals are 6–15–2 on Thanksgiving.

Maybe the NFL took pity, because they have played on Thanksgiving just once since 1985. They lost that night to the Eagles in Philadelphia 48–20 in 2008. "Not a whole lot of people get the NFL Network," Cardinals defensive lineman Bryan Robinson said after that game. "That's the good thing about it." That game was symbolic of all the Cardinals' futility on Thanksgiving games. Nothing went right. The Cardinals came out flat and stayed that way.

Wide receiver Anquan Boldin called it the worst game he ever played. It was hard to argue. He dropped two passes and fumbled twice. The Cardinals trailed at halftime 24–7.

Happy Thanksgiving. Seconds, anyone?

The Cardinals wouldn't say it out loud, but the NFL was partly to blame for that 2008 loss. What was the league thinking making the Cardinals play on Thanksgiving? (Never mind that they had to travel across the country to play just five days after a Sunday game.) It's not as if the Eagles were better than the Cardinals in 2008. In fact, the two teams met again for the NFC title that season with the Cardinals winning to clinch their first Super Bowl appearance.

But that game on Thanksgiving? The Cardinals stunk like two-week-old stuffing. "You win games, everything else pretty much takes care of itself," safety Antrel Rolle said that day. "That's what we got to get back to. Instead of having our eye on the big picture, we need to take care of the little picture first."

From 1950 through 2008, the Cardinals played on Thanksgiving eight times. They lost eight times. And most of the games weren't close. It was 48–20 in 2008 and 46–21 to the Dallas Cowboys in 1967. Back in the day, playing on Thanksgiving was a tradition for the Cardinals. In the 1920s they played the cross-town Bears every

Thanksgiving. In the 1970s the Cardinals even tried hosting games on Thanksgiving. In 1975 and '77, they replaced the Cowboys as hosts but lost each time. In '76 they played the Cowboys and, yep, lost that one, too. And those weren't your typical bad Cardinals teams. From 1975 through 1977, the Cardinals were 28–14.

The Thanksgiving Day games in St. Louis weren't especially popular with the locals either. According to reports at the time, St. Louis fans weren't interested because the NFL game conflicted with a traditional "Turkey Day Game" between two high schools. That claim, however, seems dubious. Both the '75 and '77 games were played in cold conditions, and good Cardinals teams were blown out each time. The Buffalo Bills beat them 32–14 in 1975, and the Miami Dolphins whipped them 55–14 in 1977.

So the Cardinals gave up hosting Thanksgiving Day games, figuring it's better to make a mess in someone else's stadium.

1999

The Cardinals lost to the San Francisco 49ers 24–10. And for once, there was nothing remarkable about them losing on Monday night. But it was a pivotal game in 49ers history. In the first half, Cardinals cornerback Aeneas Williams blitzed and hit quarterback Steve Young. As Young fell backward, he hit the back of his head on a teammate's knee, suffering a concussion.

At halftime Young lobbied to return, but coach Steve Mariucci resisted. After the game Young was lucid during interviews, joking that he was ready to fight Mariucci after the coach wouldn't let his quarterback return. But concussion symptoms continued to plague Young the rest of the year. He never played again.

2006

Coach Dennis Green overheated and melted down after the Cardinals blew a 20-point lead to lose to the Chicago Bears 24–23. His postgame tirade is legendary, and "they are who we thought they were" is now a part of the American lexicon. Coors Light even used it for a commercial. The Cardinals never recovered from the loss, finished 5–11, and Green was fired.

2008

The Arizona Cardinals won their first Monday night game, but they needed some help.

The Cardinals stopped running back Michael Robinson short of the goal line on the final play to clinch the 29–24 victory. Mike Martz, the 49ers offensive coordinator, called for a handoff to Robinson, thinking the ball was at the Cardinals 1. It was at the 2½ yard line. Worse, running back Frank Gore was lined up as a receiver. "He's their best player offensively," Cardinals safety Adrian Wilson said afterward, "and to have him out as a wideout, to me, is not a good play."

2010

The Cardinals lost to the 49ers 27–6 in embarrassing fashion. Not all the Cardinals, however, were embarrassed. Television cameras showed quarterback Derek Anderson and guard Deuce Lutui laughing in the fourth quarter. Analyst Jon Gruden was critical of the two, and Anderson lost his cool when I asked him to explain that interaction during a postgame press conference. "You think this is funny?" he asked. "I take this shit serious, real serious."

The Cardinals finished 5–11 and made sweeping changes in the offseason. Anderson left, and the club traded for Philadelphia Eagles quarterback Kevin Kolb.

97

Visit the Pat Tillman Memorial

Pat Tillman's passion and spirit have been described in newspaper articles, books, and, unfortunately, eulogies. One iconic image, however, captures the essence of Tillman as well as anything else. Fans can see it in the large white bronze sculpture on the northwest side of the University of Phoenix Stadium. The plaza surrounding the entire stadium is known as the Pat Tillman Freedom Plaza in honor of the safety who was killed in action in Afghanistan on April 22, 2004.

A nine-foot curved wall made of black concrete serves as the backdrop to the sculpture. The wall measures 42 feet across, symbolic of Tillman's jersey number at Arizona State.

To the west of the memorial is a grove of 40 oak trees in honor of Tillman's jersey number with the Cardinals. The sculpture is the featured point of the plaza, and that sculpture is approximately eight feet tall and weighs more than 500 pounds.

It's bigger than life, which is fitting for Tillman. It's free to visit it, take pictures, and reflect on how Tillman lived his life. No one lived more fully—or with more passion. It's how Tillman played football, too, which made him a favorite target of photographers covering games.

Gene Lower, a freelance photographer, was at the Cardinals game against the New Orleans Saints on December 20, 1998. The Cardinals led 13–10 in the third quarter and needed a victory to remain in the playoff hunt. The Saints were driving for a score when Tillman tackled Saints running back Lamar Smith for a loss in the third quarter and celebrated after. His helmet in one hand,

*The eight foot tall, 500-pound bronze sculpture of Pat Tillman on the
northwest side of the University of Phoenix Stadium is a must-see for any fan.*
(USA TODAY Sports Images)

mouthpiece in the other, Tillman was shouting as he ran off the field in celebration.

Lower got the perfect shot. "Pat wasn't a big player at the time, and the photo really wasn't seen by the general public," said Lower, who later became the Cardinals' team photographer. "But I always liked it. Pat was in full athletic position, meaning you could see everything—his arms, his legs, the helmet, the mouthpiece."

It was one of Lower's favorite photos, and it held a prominent spot in his portfolio. When Tillman was killed, Lower immediately thought of the photo. Lower had done some work for *Sports Illustrated* in the past and contacted the magazine to tell them about the photo. Editors loved the photo and made it the magazine's cover that week. It quickly became an iconic image of Tillman. Many Cardinals fans use it as screen savers for their phones and computers. And it was the obvious image for artists Omar Amrany and Gary Tillery to use in creating the sculpture at the memorial.

The sculptors and team officials consulted with Pat's wife, Marie, "who worked to select the image of Tillman that would be convey his character and spirit," according to the Cardinals' media guide. Lower's photo and the sculpture do that eloquently.

98 Visit Training Camp

It wasn't that long ago that most NFL training camps were quaint affairs. Between 80 and 100 men, some of them millionaires, would spend a month or so living, eating, and practicing on the campus of some small college. That's not the case now with most teams, including the Cardinals. With each passing year, more teams are conducting training camp at their home facilities, which means fewer practices are open to the public.

The Cardinals moved their training camp from Flagstaff, Arizona, to University of Phoenix Stadium in 2013, going from pine trees and mile-high elevation to saguaros and indoor practices. It was a drastic change, but the Cardinals still provide opportunities for fans that many other NFL teams don't. During the month-long camp, which begins in late July, the team practices almost daily at University of Phoenix Stadium. Admission is free. So is parking. And since there are 63,400 seats, no one is turned away.

One of the biggest concerns fans had when camp moved to Glendale was access to players. In Flagstaff, there was the opportunity to practically rub shoulder pads with the stars.

Fans lined the path from the locker room to the practice field, and it was an ideal spot to get autographs. The Cardinals were sensitive to the loss of that intimacy when they decided to move camp to Glendale. While players ride vans from their nearby hotel to the stadium, many stay after practice to sign autographs, usually on the east side of the field. Each practice day a handful of other players are assigned to sign autographs on the west concourse of the stadium.

Training camps have changed in other ways. Don't come to camp expecting to see players bludgeon each other on the field for hours. The actual practice regimen for all teams has changed drastically over the last 20 years. Coaches are fearful of losing star players to injuries in practice, so tackling ball carriers to the ground is rarely permitted. In fact coaches usually don't want to see anyone on the ground.

The collective bargaining agreement between players and the NFL also has changed the way camp is conducted. Although teams can conduct two practices a day, one is a walk-through, which is basically a practice to go over what's going to be covered in the one real practice of the day. For most teams, including the Cardinals, that happens in the afternoon, and it's the workout fans are allowed to attend.

Practices, though, can still be entertaining. Fans attending camp over the years have watched some of their favorite players go head to head, such as cornerback Patrick Peterson covering wide receiver Larry Fitzgerald. On one weekend day every camp, the team holds its annual "Red and White" practice. There are activities for kids, including a post-practice autograph session. And the actual practice is usually one of the most physical of camp.

If you're a football junkie, or just someone looking for something to do indoors during the summer in Arizona, Cardinals training camp is worth checking out.

99 Attend the *Big Red Rage*

Unless you're the neighbor of a player, a friend, or happen to bump into a guy at the grocery store, it's hard to rub shoulders with professional athletes. During the season the best chance a Cardinals fan has comes every Thursday night in Chandler, Arizona. That's where the team broadcasts its weekly *Big Red Rage* radio show on Arizona Sports 98.7 FM, its flagship station.

For the past several years, the broadcast has originated from Majerle's Sports Grill at the Chandler Fashion Center. Defensive tackle Calais Campbell has been the regular player/host for the past few seasons and he's joined by Ron Wolfley and Paul Calvisi, who are part of the team's broadcast crew. The show lasts an hour and is accessible to fans, who can eat and drink while they watch and listen to the broadcast. They can also wait in line for photos and autographs with players and other celebrities.

Cardinals fan Ganell Dunn, a season-ticket holder, has attended *Big Red Rage* broadcasts long enough to remember when only 20 to 30 fans attended. Today, there are typically around 100 people there. "Originally, it was a cool way to hang out with a hard-core group of fans and hear the show," she said. "My favorite part is watching the weekly guest interact with the host and hear some stories from the locker room and practice field. It's also interesting to see how a radio show works on the road. I don't do the photo and autograph things, but there are some nice giveaways. I've won tickets, footballs, and hats."

Every week Campbell is joined by at least one teammate, and it's often someone who has stood out in the previous games. The broadcast provides a behind-the-scenes look at players, who typically open up during the interview. The show draws good crowds, so it pays to get there early, and the bigger the game, the bigger the crowd. On the Thursday before the NFC Championship Game in the 2015 season, the *Biggest Red Rage* drew an estimated crowd of about 4,000. That broadcast featured wide receiver Larry Fitzgerald, cornerback Patrick Peterson, and team president Michael Bidwill.

The show is seasonal, running from about mid-August through the end of the football season. The broadcasts are produced by the team with broadcast and new media manager Jim Omohundro handling most of the production. Wolfley, a former Cardinals player, started that NFC Championship Game broadcast by turning the crank on the siren, which is also used to get the crowd at University of Phoenix Stadium fired up on gameday. "That is Wolf's biggest workout since he was a four-time Pro Bowler," Calvisi said.

In addition to a full menu of drinks and food, Majerle's features 27 high-definition televisions, an indoor/outdoor bar, two patios, and a place to play bocce ball and cornhole before or after the show.

100 Watch *Jerry Maguire*

Rod Tidwell appears nowhere in the Cardinals record book, but until Larry Fitzgerald came along, Tidwell was the most famous receiver in team history. Tidwell's pursuit of a new contract with the Cardinals was one of the main story lines in the 1996 movie *Jerry Maguire,* starring Tom Cruise in the title role and Cuba Gooding Jr. as Tidwell.

For Cardinals fans it's worth watching again—if only to see the scenes shot at team headquarters in Tempe and Sun Devil Stadium and to laugh at the outdated cell phones used.

In fact Maguire and Tidwell were both using landlines in their famous conversation early in the movie. Fired after writing a manifesto following a crisis of conscience, Maguire is desperate to take his clients with him. Tidwell sticks with Maguire but only after getting the agent to scream the Tidwell family's favorite phrase into the phone: "Show me the money!"

That immediately became a catchphrase and is still used today. In 2005 the American Film Institute ranked it as the 25th greatest movie quote of all time. "Show me the money!" checked in just ahead of Mae West's "Why don't you come up sometime and see me?" To a lesser extent, the idea of achieving "the Quan" became a buzz phrase as well. That's what Tidwell called securing "love, respect, community, and dollars, too."

Cameron Crowe, the writer/director of *Jerry Maguire,* claims the "Show me the money" line came from following around Cardinals safety Tim McDonald, who was a free agent in 1993 and would eventually sign with the San Francisco 49ers. "He was actually at an owners' meeting to be paraded through the lobby to get his price up because he was a free agent," Crowe told the *Toronto*

Sun in 1996. "He said, 'I've got a wife and I've got kids and I've been beaten up for five years here in Phoenix and now I'm a free agent. Show me the money.'"

Parts of the movie don't hold up well, especially if you are familiar with how business in the NFL is transacted. For instance, Maguire and Tidwell have a heated exchange in the locker room of the Cardinals facility. In reality, agents are not allowed there. And Maguire freely roams press boxes across the country. That's not allowed either.

Crowe did use the actual locker room in Tempe as the setting for the argument between Tidwell and Maguire. In it Tidwell emerges from the shower naked and listens as Maguire begs him to bury his ego. "Towel?" Maguire asks.

"No, I air dry," Tidwell said.

Their friendship deepens as the movie progresses with each character serving as the other's conscience. Maguire points out Tidwell's selfishness. Tidwell doesn't like how Maguire treats his girlfriend/new wife, played by Renee Zellweger. Their conversations often turn into arguments. One exchange ends with Maguire walking away and Tidwell shouting: "You think we're fighting, and I think we're finally talking."

Maguire is broke and needs the commission from a new contract for Tidwell, who, well, wants to be shown the money, and he thinks the Cardinals are dragging their cleats. Glenn Frey of the band the Eagles plays Cardinals general manager Dennis Wilburn, who doesn't want to show Tidwell any of the Cardinals money. "What I want is someone who is 6'3" and 220 [pounds]," Wilburn tells Maguire, "not somebody who is 5'10" and bitches in the locker room."

In the climatic game against the Dallas Cowboys, a real-life shot of Larry Centers hurdling Cowboys cornerback Larry Brown is shown. Tidwell scores the game-winning touchdown against the

Dallas Cowboys but is knocked cold in the end zone. Again, you have to suspend common sense here because an athletic trainer tries to wake him up by clapping in his face. Tidwell wakes on his own—it's a miracle!—as the *Monday Night Football* television crew broadcasts the moment to an anxious nation.

Acknowledgments

Writing a book is a daunting task, something I didn't quite realize before actually writing a book. Turns out, it requires family and friends to be patient and tactful because it's not easy to pick the right spots to ask, "How's the book coming along?" or "Aren't you done with that yet?"

My wife, Paula, was both patient and tactful. For 31 years she's been a great sounding board for me, and I can't thank her enough. Our kids—Andrew, Logan, and Chandler—were as excited about this project as I was.

I'd like to thank everyone who allowed me to write at their kitchen tables when I visited: my parents in Missouri; my mother-in-law in Salt Lake City, Utah; my friend, Gary, in Ogden, Utah; my son, Andrew, in San Antonio.

One of the great pleasures in writing this book was reading through stories about the team. Some fine writers and people have covered this team, and I'm proud to call many of them friends. That group includes but isn't limited to Lloyd Herberg, Steve Schoenfeld, Dan Bickley, Paola Boivin, Bob McManaman, Lee Rasizer, Lynn DeBruin, and Scott Bordow.

Darren Urban of azcardinals.com and I have competed for many years on the beat. More importantly, we've managed to stay friends. He was a great resource, too, because he's covered the team nearly as long as I have and he has a much better memory.

Mike Jurecki, also a friend and competitor, jogged my memory throughout this process.

Greg Schultz, a longtime Cardinals fan in Missouri, recalled with amazing detail important milestones in the team's St. Louis history.

Any Cardinals fan interested in the team's history should buy Joe Ziemba's book *When Football Was Football—The Chicago Cardinals and the Birth of the NFL*. It's meticulously researched and was a great resource for me.

I'd like to thank the many ex-players and coaches who granted me interviews. Kurt Warner's email reply to my questions was a book in and of itself. I could talk to Jake Plummer, Larry Centers, Roy Green, Jim Hart, Dan Dierdorf, and Jim Bakken all day—and I'm sure they felt like we did.

My editor at Triumph, Jeff Fedotin, was far more patient with me than he probably should have been. With a deft hand, he guided me through this process, and I can't think of a suggestion he made that wasn't spot on.

The Cardinals media relations staff, headed by Mark Dalton, also was generous with their time and patience. Matt Storey deserves special credit because he never complained about hauling newspaper clips from the bowels of the team's Tempe headquarters to the press room.

As you can tell, I had help in every step of this process. It's made me realize that the best part of covering this team for 20-plus years is the people I've met along the way.

Sources

Newspapers
The Arizona Republic
The Phoenix Gazette
East Valley Tribune
St. Louis Post-Dispatch
Chicago Tribune
The New York Times
The Washington Times
Tampa Bay Times

Websites
Azcardinals.com
Azcentralsports.com
ProFootballDaly.com
The Coffin Corner: footbalresearchers.org

Books
When Football Was Football: The Chicago Cardinals and the Birth of the NFL. Joe Ziemba, Triumph Books.
Give it to Steve! Will Bunch, Amazon Digital Services LLC.
America's Game: The Epic Story of How Pro Football Captured a Nation. Michael MacCambridge, Random House.
The Ultimate Super Bowl Book: A Complete Reference to the Stats, Stars, and Stories Behind Football's Biggest Game—and Why the Best Team Won. Bob McGinn, Quayside Publishing Group.
Don Coryell "Win With Honor." Joe Stein and Diane Clark, Joyce Press.

The St. Louis Cardinals: A Celebration of the Big Red. Greg Marecek,
Reedy Press.

Arizona Cardinals media guides

NFL Record and Fact Books

Busch Stadium Moments, St. Louis Post-Dispatch.